Political
Leadership
in
Jefferson's
Virginia

Political Leadership
in
Jefferson's Virginia

by
Daniel P. Jordan

UNIVERSITY PRESS OF VIRGINIA

Charlottesville

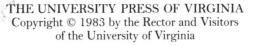

THE UNIVERSITY PRESS OF VIRGINIA
Copyright © 1983 by the Rector and Visitors
of the University of Virginia

First published 1983

Library of Congress Cataloging in Publication Data

Jordan, Daniel P.
  Political leadership in Jefferson's Virginia.

  Includes bibliographical references and index.
  1. Electioneering—Virginia—History. 2. Legislators
—Virginia—History. 3. Virginia—Politics and govern-
ment—1775–1865. 4. United States. Congress—Elections
—History. I. Title.
JK3995.J67 1983   324.7'09755   82–23867
ISBN: 0–8139–0967–8

Printed in the United States of America

To Lou
With
Love and Respect

Contents

Tables

Preface

The political history of Jeffersonian Virginia has long attracted scholarly attention. Over seventy years ago Charles H. Ambler interpreted the events of the period within the larger context of sectionalism in the Old Dominion from the Revolution to the Civil War. In recent decades Harry Ammon has investigated the Republican party, 1789–1824, and Norman K. Risjord has analyzed both the conservative Old Republicans and the minority Federalists. The latter group is also included within the scope of James H. Broussard's monograph, *The Southern Federalists*. Richard Beale Davis has reconstructed the intellectual climate of the era and has illuminated the related themes of law and politics. The 1790s have been closely examined in studies by Risjord, Lisle A. Rose, and especially Richard R. Beeman. The Dynasty presidents have all had their modern biographers, and books are available from several generations on such second-tier leaders as William Branch Giles, John George Jackson, John Randolph, Thomas Ritchie, John Taylor of Caroline, and others. Finally, numerous theses have been written on Virginia politicians who were more significant on the state than the national level.

Despite the abundance and quality of this scholarship, much remains to be said about Virginia politics in the Age of Jefferson, especially in view of the Old Dominion's preeminent national position in size and influence throughout most of the period. The leadership class per se and the political culture in general both require examination. Historians with only limited knowledge of the relationship between, for example, the candidates and voters, officeholders and constituents, and elections and society in Dynasty Virginia have assumed that the political practices of earlier times continued intact or with modest change until the advent of Jacksonian Democracy. These central but neglected topics are explored for the eventful era from 1801 to 1825 in this monograph. The point of departure is the examination of a large and powerful elective group—the ninety-eight individuals who represented the Commonwealth in the United States Congress during the administrations of Jefferson, Madison, and Monroe. The investigation of these men proceeds in three phases, each concerned with a fundamental question about the political leadership and milieu of that day.

First, who were these political leaders? Part One presents their most prominent biographical traits and the specific time and place in which they lived. It reconstructs the contemporary climate within the state and traces the major developments that shaped Virginia attitudes and events. A profile analysis of the congressmen identifies them by family background, ethnic origin, level of education, military service, occupation, property holdings, and political experience. The composite portrait is measured over time, 1801–24, as well as against that of earlier political elites in the Old Dominion.

The second fundamental question—how did these Virginians become congressmen?—is the subject of Part Two. Candidacy is analyzed from the standpoints of motive and procedure; the standard electioneering devices of campaign literature, hustings oratory, and personal courtship are treated in detail. Congressional elections are discussed in terms of voter participation, legal framework, polling practices, illegal balloting, competition for office, and sectional patterns. Interim, senatorial, and contested elections are also covered. Because these topics have never before been examined closely for Dynasty Virginia, this section should make possible a new understanding of the Old Dominion at a critical juncture in its history and should provide a basis for comparisons with other contemporary states. Elements of the Virginia style of politics are illuminated by the use of an unlikely but revealing (and fascinating) prototype in the person of John Randolph of Roanoke.

Part Three focuses on the final basic question—what did these ninety-eight individuals do once they got in office? The relationship between congressman and district is covered, as well as the important ties between the legislators, their state, and the federal government. The collective delegation is also measured against the entire Congress, and generalizations are advanced about the caliber of Virginia's representatives and senators on the national scene. Their link with the Dynasty presidents is also explored, and its impact on the Old Dominion and on national affairs is evaluated.

Preface

The concluding chapter brings the findings of this study to bear against what is likely the central question about Virginia politics in the Dynasty era—namely, the reason for the Commonwealth's decline in standing and power. Traditional explanations are discussed, and then a revisionist view is offered which connects the fall of the Old Dominion with the emergence of mass politics and the evolution of an anachronistic elite. In a larger sense, the passing of the reluctant but dutiful public servant and the clamorous appearance of the professional politician—as foreshadowed in the Virginia congressmen examined here—is a change of profound consequence for all Americans.

Having suggested what the reader is likely to discover in the following pages, I would quickly add a word of caution about what he should not expect to find. Some "arm-chair counting" has been done on occasion in this monograph, but there is no quantitative design or emphasis. The reader should also know in advance that the chronological frame of 1801–25 has not been rigidly maintained in regard to evidence of campaign practices. This is true because certain electioneering techniques of the Dynasty period can be found in the eras immediately preceding and following it; thus a broad net has been cast for examples that seem apt and representative. Except as otherwise noted, the electioneering material comes from congressional races, though of course there is similarity in the hustings style of most persons seeking office, congressional or otherwise, in the early 1800s.

The data on which these findings are based in part have been compiled in two lengthy appendixes that are available in the manuscript version of this study on deposit at the University of Virginia Library and the Virginia State Library in Richmond. Appendix I, "Biographical Profiles: Virginia Congressmen, 1801–1825," consists of a capsule description of each of the ninety-eight congressmen. A second appendix, "Virginia Congressional Returns by County, 1799–1825," represents the most comprehensive set of electoral data yet gathered for the Old Dominion in the early days of the Republic. The manuscript also contains a fifty-page bibliography and substantially fuller annotation.

It is a genuine pleasure to acknowledge a number of scholarly and personal debts that were acquired in the course of this project. Among the individuals who generously provided useful informa-

Preface

tion by mail are Professor John L. Blair, Richard Bland College, Petersburg, Virginia; Professor James C. Bradford, Texas A. & M. University, College Station; James H. Broussard, Indianapolis, Indiana; Professor Stephen W. Brown, West Virginia Institute of Technology, Montgomery; Professor Dickson D. Bruce, University of California, Irvine; Earl L. Core, Morgantown, West Virginia; Dorothy Upton Davis, Salem, West Virginia; Professor V. Dennis Golladay, Pensacola Junior College, Pensacola, Florida; Edward B. Jackson, Norfolk, Virginia; Professor Hugh B. Johnston, Jr., Atlantic Christian College, Wilson, North Carolina; Professor Charles D. Lowery, Mississippi State University, Starkville; Gertrude C. Mann, Rocky Mount, Virginia; Professor Norman K. Risjord, University of Wisconsin, Madison; Susan Bracey Sheppard, Bracey, Virginia; Kenneth D. Swope, Lewisburg, West Virginia; James Knox Trigg, Nashville, Tennessee; Professor Myron F. Wehtje, Atlantic Union College, South Lancaster, Massachusetts; and Klaus Wust, Edinburg, Virginia.

I would like to thank, especially, Philip J. Lampe of Gilbertsville, Massachusetts, for his unselfish sharing of the Virginia portion of the election data he has painstakingly gathered over the years, and Brent Tarter, for his ongoing interest and for his eagle eye in finding pertinent items for me in the world of obscure sources in which he resides and reigns supreme. M. H. Turnbull, Clerk of the Circuit Court of Brunswick County, and Gary M. Williams, Clerk of the Circuit Court of Sussex County, graciously allowed me to examine records under their legal control.

Several dozen librarians in repositories along the mid-Atlantic have been helpful. From among them, I would like to acknowledge, in particular, the aid of Katherine M. Smith and Louis H. Manarin and their respective staffs at the Virginia State Library; Howson W. Cole and Waverly K. Winfree of the Virginia Historical Society; and the staff of the Inter-Library Loan Department of Virginia Commonwealth University's Cabell Library. I cannot thank enough Dennis Robison, Librarian of the University of Richmond, for providing me with working space over a productive summer.

For permission to quote from unpublished materials, my appreciation goes to the Manuscripts Department, University of Virginia Library; Cabell Foundation, Charlottesville; Library of Congress;

Preface

Southern Historical Collection, Library of the University of North Carolina at Chapel Hill; Manuscripts Department, Duke University Library; Valentine Museum; Virginia Historical Society; Virginia State Library; and Earl Gregg Swem Library, College of William and Mary. I am also in debt to the Virginia Historical Society for permission to reprint a slightly revised version of chapter 8, which first appeared as "John Randolph of Roanoke and the Art of Winning Elections in Jeffersonian Virginia" in the *Virginia Magazine of History and Biography* 86 (1978): 389–407, and to reproduce on the dust jacket its marvelous painting, *The Convention of 1829–30*, by George Catlin.

Without holding any of them responsible for the deficiencies of this volume, I would like to acknowledge the suggestions and criticisms of Patricia P. Hickin, of Richmond; Professor James Tice Moore of Virginia Commonwealth University; the late Professor Bernard Mayo of the University of Virginia; the late William M. E. Rachal of the Virginia Historical Society; and Professor Merrill D. Peterson of the University of Virginia. The latter, my dissertation adviser and teacher, helped me more than any other person to see the meaning, dimensions, and standards of professional scholarship.

I would be remiss if I failed to mention the Thomas Jefferson Memorial Foundation's generous support of my graduate studies, the logistical aid of the Department of History at Virginia Commonwealth University, and the expert secretarial help over the years of Jeannie Roberts Lotts, Betty C. Leviner, and Wanda P. Clary. Also deserving special commendation is Peter Schulz, who shared his time and considerable talent in preparing two original maps for this volume.

Finally, I would like to recognize the encouragement, at critical points in my work, of Norman S. Fiering of the Institute of Early American History and Culture, Professor William H. Harbaugh of the University of Virginia, Professor Emeritus Joseph C. Robert of the University of Richmond, Professor Emeritus James W. Silver of the University of South Florida, and Professors Philip J. Schwarz and Melvin I. Urofsky of Virginia Commonwealth University.

As for my family, I can only state that my parents—Dr. and Mrs. Porter Jordan—have always been an inspiration to me and unqualifyingly supportive of my work and that my children—Dan, Grace, and Katherine—were a constant distraction (and I would have it no other way). My dear wife Lou—to whom this book is dedicated—joins me in bidding a hearty farewell to the ninety-eight politicians whose stay in our home has exceeded the limits of our hospitality.

Part One

The Times
and
the Men

I

Virginia in the Dynasty Era

A starting point for analyzing the Virginia congressmen of the early nineteenth century is the central fact that they were persons of a given time and place. To understand who these men were in a general sense, what they did and why, one must first define and explore the context in which they acquired and fulfilled their positions of public trust. A leaf must be taken from the various colonial historians concerned with "the present state of Virginia"—in this instance, the period 1801–25. Although scholars have characterized this era in terms of almost glacierlike stability, the Old Dominion in fact experienced both change and continuity. The old ways persevered in part but often collided with painful new realities. As a result, the fabric of Virginia was stress-ridden in Jeffersonian times, and the leadership class often found itself torn between the past and present.

The People and Their Regions

In the census of 1800 there were 514,280 white, 345,796 slave, and 20,124 free-black Virginians, divided among ninety-two counties and three separate municipal districts.[1] These statistics translated immediately into political power. As the most populous state in the Union, the Old Dominion had the largest congressional delegation—22 members at a time when the House of Representatives itself numbered only 142. Roughly one of every six congressmen represented Virginia. It also claimed the biggest electoral bloc in presidential elections, with approximately 15 percent of the total.[2] Under the federal ratio Virginia's blacks inflated the state's political strength but offered no challenge to its gentry rule. This combina-

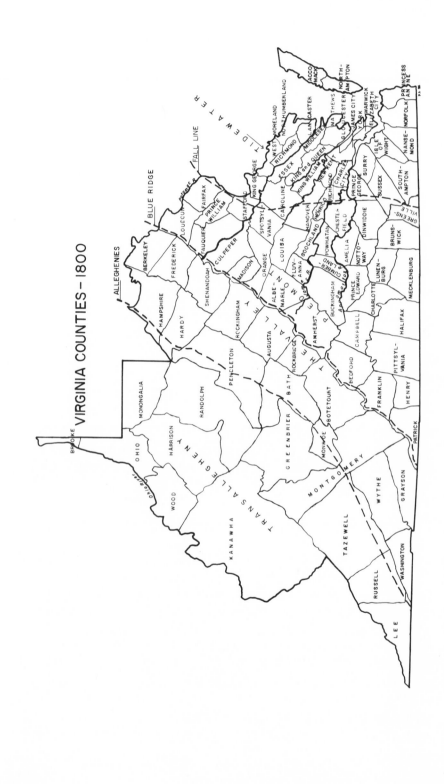

VIRGINIA COUNTIES – 1800

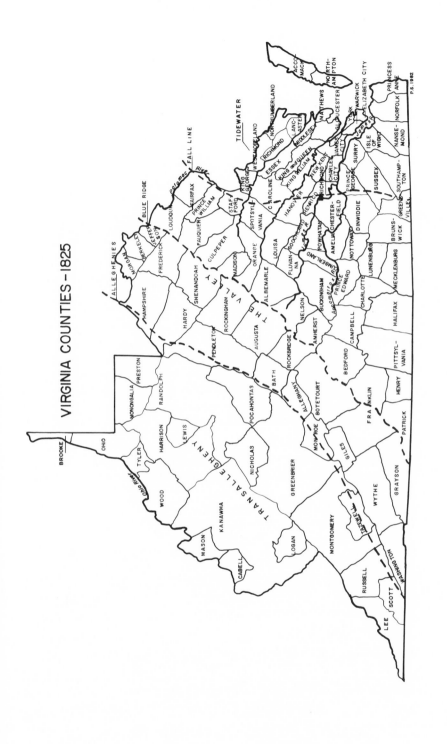

VIRGINIA COUNTIES - 1825

The Times and the Men

tion, to an English aristocrat, seemed unbeatable: "the mass of the people, who in other countries might become mobs . . . [are in Virginia] nearly altogether composed of . . . Negro slaves whose numbers are taken into the account of the votes given but who form no social check upon their master's political conduct."[3]

Although substantial, this political power was, at the same time, ephemeral. In relative terms the Old Dominion was shrinking. Its native sons were moving to the West and Southwest; few immigrants arrived to replace them. Succeeding federal censuses advertised a painful loss in people and in political weight. By 1830 Virginia ranked below two other states in population and was entitled to only 21 of the 242 congressional seats; by 1860 it had but 11 of 243.[4] This stark demographic trend both symbolized and contributed to the sad and stressful theme of declining influence, a central theme in Jeffersonian Virginia and one acknowledged and lamented by its public leaders.

The Old Dominion's population in 1800 was also significant in its dispersion and composition. So striking are the patterns that it is most proper to think not of one Virginia but of several. Contemporaries—and historians since—recognized that geographic, economic, social, and other differences divided the state into at least four natural regions (table 1).[5] Their interaction explains, as much as any one factor can, developments in the period 1801–25.

Oldest and most thoroughly settled of the regions was the Tide-

Table 1. Virginia's sections, 1800–1830

		Whites	Slaves	Total*
Tidewater	1800	152,710	167,676	333,366
	1830	167,001	185,457	381,438
Piedmont	1800	183,670	153,523	342,416
	1830	208,656	230,861	451,542
Valley	1800	106,532	18,058	125,976
	1830	134,471	34,772	174,308
Trans-Allegheny	1800	70,944	5,499	76,987
	1830	183,854	18,665	204,117

Source: *Documents, Containing Statistics of Virginia, Ordered to Be Printed by the State Convention Sitting in the City of Richmond, 1850–51* (Richmond, 1851), "Census of Virginia" table.

*Includes free blacks.

water, extending roughly from the Chesapeake Bay westward to a point where the major rivers had waterfalls and the terrain shifted from a coastal plain to a piedmont slope. Tidewater Virginia in the seventeenth century was Virginia; throughout most of the eighteenth century the section continued to set social standards, provide political leadership, and dominate an economy of agrarian capitalism. Symptomatic was the location there of Virginia's first two capitals (Jamestown and Williamsburg); the College of William and Mary, whose alumni formed the mainstream of gentry rule; and the large plantations with their ancestral mansions, whose families were indeed first in colony and state.

Political leadership in this region came from an upper class which lived according to well-defined customs, including the one of occasionally "refreshing, or finishing, their honor at the ends of their pistols."[6] The gentry naturally supported the Episcopalian church, the "established religion, in which," as was said with exaggeration, a person was "educated with strictness, if not with bigotry."[7] Living in rural isolation, they were "fond of company"; as a contemporary traveler noted, "a Virginian visit is not an afternoon merely; but they go to week it, and to month it, and to summer it." On occasion the "better sorts"—and the lesser sorts, too—were known to "keep their spirits up, by pouring spirits down."[8] It was the Tidewater population that Hugh Blair Grigsby no doubt had in mind when he reflected: "We were a *slaveholding, tobacco planting, Anglo-Saxon* people. Our character sprang from this source."[9]

Tidewater society in 1800 was settled, relatively stratified, and in a state of crisis. The region's economy was at best uncertain, at worst drifting toward disaster. For almost two centuries tobacco had been the cash crop. Grown and exported directly from the vast river network that gave "each planter," in the words of John Randolph, "a harbor at his door,"[10] it had built "a colony . . . on smoke" and established in the process great family fortunes. But the cost had been high: erratic or rigidly colonial markets, a deficient credit structure, exhausted soil, and debt-encrusted estates. Few of these problems were solved permanently when a planter shifted from small to larger holdings; from worn-out to fresh acres, usually to the west; or from tobacco to grain crops, including wheat, which had become the state's main export by 1800.[11] Severe economic adversity con-

The Times and the Men

tributed to the Tidewater's static if not declining population and its alarming loss of political influence in the state legislature as new, western counties came into being in the early 1800s. This was no mere problem of status. The General Assembly set tax rates, and increased levies on land and slaves could be disastrous to planters operating on a narrow margin between profit and indebtedness.

Fortunately for the Tidewater, many of its vested interests were shared by the Piedmont, the region between it and the Blue Ridge Mountains. The Piedmont might be considered an extension of the older section with some modifications. Its economy was more diversified, but the great "Tobacco Kingdom" in Virginia after 1800 lay almost entirely within it, in a bloc of counties that ran from the James River toward North Carolina. This Southside area, one of the state's most enduring political entities, suffered from inadequate transportation facilities and relatively poor soil, but tobacco boomed there even as it declined elsewhere. Some of the crop was produced on a plantation scale; most of it, however, was grown by smaller, largely self-sufficient farmers, with few slaves and, likely as not, other staples as well.[12]

The people of the Piedmont typically had roots in the Tidewater and were essentially English, though strains of Scotch-Irish had spilled over from the Great Valley to the west, bringing with them a staunch Presbyterianism. The Methodists and a variety of Baptist faiths also prospered, especially in the southern half of the section. Younger and more recently established, Piedmont society was less stratified. Still, the larger planters tended to provide political leadership and set social standards more or less on the Tidewater model. Some of their sons attended William and Mary, but others came to prefer such regional institutions as Hampden-Sydney (1776) and the university later established in Charlottesville that Jefferson considered central to the question of "whether we are to leave this fair inheritance to barbarians or civilized men."[13]

That the Piedmont had supplanted the Tidewater in some vital respects is less important than the bond of essential interests between them. The two sections were linked by a series of towns located at or near the falls of the state's principal rivers—Alexandria and Georgetown on the Potomac, Fredericksburg on the Rappahannock, Petersburg on the Appomatox, and the capital, Richmond, on the James. These towns, the largest being Richmond with 5,737 inhabitants in 1800, developed to meet the commercially obvious need of market centers where river transportation reached farthest into the interior. The port of Norfolk, the state's other major city, was connected to Richmond and the Piedmont by the James River but also enjoyed trade with nearby regions of North Carolina.

A young Philadelphia lawyer on tour may have been correct in observing that "Virginia is not famous for its towns,"[14] but such urban development as existed was mainly eastern. The towns, especially Richmond, served as a focal point for much of the state's surprisingly varied intellectual life, its justly famed legal establishment, its commercial activity, and, before 1816, for all three of its chartered banks (which served credit needs, east and west, and were intimately involved in Virginia politics). The major party newspapers were city-based, and, of course, the towns were favorably located for communication, by land or water, with other states and nations.[15]

The Tidewater and Piedmont shared the critical problems of population decline and economic distress, but perhaps more significant in 1800 was the presence in the east of over 90 percent of the Old Dominion's blacks and the impact of what one scholar has termed "the most sophisticated and ambitious slave conspiracy" in American history. Although abortive, Gabriel's Revolt featured brave men who were "highly assimilated, well travelled, and versatile." Governor James Monroe led an alarmed white populace against the insurrectionaries, and the combination of military power and swift justice sent thirty or more participants to their executions. Thus came to an end the "permissive, confused, and disordered state of slavery" that had characterized eighteenth-century Virginia.[16] The new direction could be seen not only in various measures adopted to prevent future rebellions but also in an antimanumission act passed in 1806. This legislation, according to Winthrop D. Jordan, was "the key step in the key state and more than any event marked the reversal of the tide which had set in strongly at the Revolution."[17] The law reflected eastern whites' great fear of losing control over black Virginians, free and slave, and the concomitant fear of revolt and intermixture. Thus a racial bond reinforced other ties between the Piedmont and Tidewater.

But in the perception of eastern Virginians, the racial issue, though critical, did not stand alone. In fact, it intermeshed with other potent concerns. Few Virginia planters could conceive of their social and economic existence, their "way of life," except on the basis of the institution of slavery, which recent scholarship suggests was prospering, not declining, in the era.[18] And one must not forget certain political and sectional realities, as well portrayed by a perceptive Yankee traveler:

As to Squire Grundy [of the eastern "Tuckahoes"] and Farmer Ashfield [of the western "Cohees"], they have certain snug matters of dispute to themselves. The Farmer insists upon it, at town-meetings and elections, that the Squire enjoys greater political privileges than he does; that the country of Tuchahoe has more representatives in the legislature than it ought to have; that all Squire Grundy's negroes go to the polls, and vote; that the seat of government ought to be removed, that the poor enslaved Cohees may not be *toted* all the way to Richmond to hear orations, and get justice; and that, finally, the Squire gives himself such airs of superiority, that there is no such thing as getting along with him. On the other hand, Squire Grundy maintains that he pays more taxes than the Farmer; that taxation and representation as naturally go together as whiskey and vagabonds; that not numbers but property ought to be represented; that his negroes are included in the number of voters because they are taxed; and that, finally, the Cohees, not being able to comprehend all this, are a set of ignorant blockheads. The Farmer says, "It is a dom lie;" and both parties are more convinced than before.[19]

This clear definition of mutual interests between the leadership of Tidewater and Piedmont Virginia helped to establish an "eastern" position on important questions before the General Assembly, especially those touching the sensitive nerve of political reform which might threaten eastern control of the state government. Even before the Constitutional Convention of 1829–30 provided an arena for debating such matters, the easterner well knew the stakes. As one such Virginian, Abel Parker Upshur, wrote another:

Should a change in the representation be effected the whole country on the seaboard must be materially injured by it. Nearly all the fund for internal improvements is expended above tide water, & when that [western] country comes to possess,—what it is now aiming at,—a decided preponderance in the legislature, there will be nothing to prevent our Western brethren from taxing us ad libitum, for the improvement of their rugged mountains. Unhappily, such is the condition of our country that a tax nominally equal, may be very unequal in its operation. Slaves are a fruitful source of revenue, & nearly all the slaves of Virginia are on the east of the Blue Ridge.[20]

As Upshur pointed out, a different set of interests was represented west of the Blue Ridge in the state's two remaining regions, the fertile Valley and the near-frontier country across the mountains to the west. Although settled about the same time as the Piedmont, the Valley was no mere extension of an earlier Virginia.[21] Much of its population had migrated down from western Pennsylvania and consisted of Scotch-Irish and Germans who settled in small, self-sufficient farming communities. Adding to this heterogenous mix, English families arrived from the east. A distinct economy quickly emerged; compared with the older sections, it depended much less on slavery and much more on interstate and interregional markets requiring river and land transportation. More diversified, it encompassed small manufacturing, cattle farming, and a variety of crops, including wheat, tobacco, and hemp.

In form, local government in the Valley resembled that of the east, after which it was patterned and by which it was authorized. The spirit, however, greatly differed, like the population itself; factions and interests were more disparate, and the system was less controlled by any one of them. Presbyterianism and the various German pietistic sects provided a variety of religious strains, and nascent academies at Staunton, Lexington, and elsewhere reflected the Scotch-Irish commitment to education.

Geographically and economically the Valley was connected to areas beyond Virginia but also to Richmond and Fredericksburg and to a handful of eastern counties, such as Loudoun and Fairfax in the upper Potomac, and to Bedford, Patrick, Henry, and others in the extreme southwestern Piedmont. With a varied and growing population, little slavery, and peculiar trade needs, the Valley also had many commonalities with the Trans-Allegheny region.

That section covered what is now West Virginia plus a few counties in the southwesternmost portion of the Commonwealth.[22] First explored in the mid-eighteenth century and settled shortly afterward, the transmontane region in 1800 retained the flavor of near-pioneer conditions. Among early congressmen from the area, George Jackson enjoyed considerable local fame as an Indian fighter; John Floyd's father had been massacred; and, as a youth of twelve, Hugh Caperton had stood guard against raiding savages.[23] All this was at a time when Tidewater natives enjoyed the fruits of almost two centuries of settlement and civilization.

The lodestone of cheap land, some of it earmarked by Revolutionary bounties, attracted a diverse population to the region. Its natural resources encouraged an equally diverse economic pattern, which included cattle, sheep, hogs, potatoes, and apples, as well as flour mills, iron furnaces, and salt mining and manufacturing, all with a minimum of slave labor. In this youthful society, material success earned social and political prominence; and the way appeared open to all.

The Trans-Allegheny region was fast growing, isolated, and faced with concrete problems, especially the need for improved banking and transportation facilities for its essentially interstate markets. It shared these needs with the Valley, along with complaints about malapportionment of the General Assembly (which assured eastern dominance) and about the property requirement for voting. On the latter point the Clarksburg *Republican Compiler* spoke for many in blasting a system that "when the taxes are levied, when the roads want working, when jurors are wanted at court, when war is declared and soldiers are wanted, then no freehold is necessary; no distinction is made—and if there is any distinction, it is universally in favor of the rich. But when the election day is here, and we approach the polls to enjoy the greatest blessings of heaven, 'tis then we hear the ridiculous and impudent question, 'Are you a freeholder?' "[24] The search for solutions to these pressing problems was a major theme of the period in the west, and the lack of success was a constant source of strain. Piecemeal gains came in 1816–17 when the senate was slightly reapportioned, a Board of Public Works was established to oversee state-funded internal improvements, and two western banks were chartered. None of these changes, however, fully met the obvious needs of an expanding region. The cry for political reform resumed in the early 1820s to be climaxed by the great—but disappointing to western interests—Constitutional Convention of 1829–30.

There is a definite relationship between Virginia's sections and its congressmen in the Jeffersonian period. In brief, different types of men represented districts in the east and west; more importantly, different interests were often represented. Most of the pertinent political questions were fought in the state legislature, but many important ones received congressional attention. Among the latter were such fundamental national issues as tariffs, banks, and internal improvements. All had sectional ramifications in the Old Dominion. Virginia's election returns also reflected an east-west pattern, Virginia's stress had a solid sectional base, and Virginia's decline, in part, would mirror the debility of a leadership class once united but increasingly divided by the great mountains of the Blue Ridge.

The Political Landscape

If a diversity in people and geography expressed itself in sectional patterns within the Old Dominion, there were concurrent commonalities for the state in its political landscape. Central to an examination of Virginia's leadership class in the Dynasty era are the shared realities of an enduring structure of government, a pervasive party system, and a changing array of political practices. In each case the pattern of the past was not fully adequate to the exigencies of the present, and the result was a stressful blend of change and continuity.

Both a symbol and a substantive part of the essential continuity in Virginia's system of government, the Constitution of 1776 remained the basic law of the state until 1830.[25] Written in the haste and urgency of Revolutionary crisis by persons long in authority and never popularly ratified, the constitution inevitably retained much of the colonial system and epitomized tradition rather than innovation. The House of Burgesses, with tremendous powers—at least in its own eyes—in the late colonial period, saw its name changed to the House of Delegates but kept and extended its primacy over taxation, legislation, and some electoral privileges. It was, on the state level, the unquestioned locus of power, and in the post-Revolutionary decades its leaders continued to be "an impressive group of wealthy, well born, well respected men."[26] The constitution provided for a senate, but its role was largely that of obstruction. Retention of apportionment and suffrage statutes assured eastern control of the legislature; omission of any provision for constitutional amendment made significant change unlikely. Reformers, largely from the west, would assail the legislative section of the constitution as fundamentally undemocratic, while conservatives, largely from the east, would in turn defend it resolutely.

Another point of contention was the "Governor or chief magistrate," who was elected annually by the General Assembly, as the senate and house together were called. He could serve no "longer than three years successively," lacked even the traditional veto power, and depended heavily on the legislature and on a constitution-authorized Privy Council which James Madison once called the "grave of all useful talents."[27] With these restrictions, and a low salary to boot, the Virginia governor seemed to carry slight political weight. One incumbent described the position as being "no more than a reading and signing clerk to the Council," "a passive instrument." The biographer of another said that "the position of chief executive of Virginia in 1827 was honorable but beautifully innocuous and impotent," and a modern-day historian stated flatly that the governor "could not buckle his shoes" without council approval.[28]

Although there is close to a scholarly consensus on this interpretation of the governorship, some caveats are needed. In the first place, the foremost men of the period held the position, which suggests the influence the office may have had merely because of the caliber of its occupants.[29] Second, the governor was commander in chief of the militia, no small role, especially in times of crisis such as 1798–1800, 1807, and 1812–15 and on any occasion of slave unrest. The governor also could shape a legislative program and influence its implementation, as biographical studies of James Monroe, John Page, and Wilson Cary Nicholas have shown.[30] And the governor had a variety of appointive powers touching even the nerve centers of local government, the county justices. Given the partisanship often associated with such appointments, the executive had critical leverage within the structure of government and party politics.[31] Of this John Taylor of Caroline wrote Jefferson in 1799:

"A decided character at the head of our [Virginia] government is of immense importance by the influence it will have upon public opinion. . . . To this influence is also attached many essential powers which occasion will bring into view, besides the important one of commanding the militia. I have therefore always thought that the republicans have been too inattentive to the consequences of having a tory first magistrate and military commander of the state."[32]

Another facet of the governor's importance is captured in the words of an incumbent who noted that "the Governor has not much power in the adoption of public measures, but their whole execution devolves upon him. . . . he is the only *executive* hand in the government. . . . strange as it may seem, destitute as he is of power, he is made on many occasions, the only responsible man in the Government."[33] Finally, the chief executive often corresponded with political and party leaders about a variety of official and partisan concerns.[34] Easterners liked the governorship as it was; westerners, however, favored a more powerful chief executive democratically chosen and more responsive to present needs.

The constitution scarcely mentioned either a state judicial system or local government. The former was provided by laws subsequently enacted, while the latter merely continued in force on the sustaining basis of two centuries of custom, practice, and accumulated legal sanction. The enormously powerful county courts consisted of almost self-perpetuating justices of the peace. "How many instances have you and I known of these monopolies of county administration!" Jefferson wrote John Taylor. "I know a county in which a particular family (a numerous one) got possession of the bench, and for a whole generation never admitted a man on it who was not of its clan or connection."[35]

The justices determined who would fill most local offices; individually and collectively, they exercised executive, judicial, and legislative authority. They were also eligible under the constitution to hold other positions, and great numbers of them were in the legislature, thus linking the most influential units of government at the state and local levels and making the JP a kingpin in the Virginia political system. Perhaps the most important and usually the most senior justice, chosen on a rotating basis, became the sheriff. By law and custom his power over election procedures was such that he could determine when, where, and by whom votes were cast. Although this manner of local government generally persisted into the nineteenth century, it was condemned by reformers as both oligarchical and inefficient, and the "gentlemen justices" gradually lost status and influence with the creation of new courts on the district and higher levels.[36]

The structure of the state's government affected Virginia's congressmen in some critical particulars. The east's control of the legislature meant, for instance, its dominant influence over laws pertaining to suffrage, congressional elections, and apportionment of congressional districts. United States senators were elected by the General Assembly, which commonly instructed those senators and "advised" representatives on a variety of national questions. The continuation of the late-colonial structure helped perpetuate a system in which the county courts were inordinately powerful and in which offices were relatively limited to members of the gentry, often with favorable family ties, who advanced after having been trained and found acceptable at the grass-roots level. The system continued to help gentlemen move up the political ladder, but unlike the colonial era when one's ambition usually stopped at leadership in the House of Burgesses, the ceiling had been elevated to include service on the national level.[37] Reform-minded Virginians felt the system had outlived its usefulness.

The presence of political parties, like the general structure of government, affected the leadership class in every section of the state.[38] In a primitive way the parties dated from regional divisions and factions in the General Assembly in the 1780s, and they further developed with Virginia's ratification struggle in 1788. The early 1790s brought new concerns — largely national and mainly over Hamilton's financial program and America's relationship with France and England—that reinforced earlier alignments and separated Virginians into two better-defined camps of political rivals: the Federalist supporters of Washington and Adams and the Republican opposition that rallied around Jefferson and Madison.[39]

Later generations have found the party spirit of the 1790s full of volcanic emotion. Perhaps this passionate climate can partially explain some otherwise bizarre developments. For example, Episcopalian, Anglo-Saxon, Revolutionary War captain, Tidewater gentleman-planter John Taylor of Caroline feared a Federalist "anglo-monarchic-aristocratic-military government," while the rustic Federalist frontiersman Daniel Morgan, a strange target for Taylor's antielitism, said the Republicans "at this time [1798] look like a parsell of Egg sucking Dogs that have been caut Breaking up Hens' Nests."[40] Professional aristocrat John Randolph signed and addressed his letters with a "Citizen" prefix, and partisan William and Mary students refused the admonitions of their college president to "wear a piece of crape as a testimony of esteem and respect" for the deceased George Washington.[41] A local party leader recommended as late as 1805, "never trust one of the federal party, with any of the most unimportant offices again"; and "the old party distinctions of 'Republican' and 'Federalist'" could still excite voter interest on occasion in the 1820s.[42]

It was an era of "black cockade Federalists" and tricolored Republicans, of irresponsible language, of partisan and personal journalism, and of public meetings and mass resolutions—all in the process helping to define party interests, build party organizations, and divide previously united Virginians.[43] High tide for this party spirit was roughly 1797–1801, when the emotional issues of the Quasi-War with France, the Alien and Sedition Acts, and the Virginia Resolutions formed the mainstream of partisan activity. The legislative debates on the famous Resolutions, the heated elections of 1799, and the presidential contest of 1800 served Federalist and Republican alike in refining party doctrine and structure to an unprecedented degree.[44] The experience, especially to the many young politicians beginning careers in the late 1790s, served as a critical prelude to the Dynasty years.

Although a minority in Virginia politics, the Federalists maintained regional power on the Eastern Shore, in the upper Potomac, and west of the Blue Ridge, with some strength in commercial centers such as Richmond and Norfolk. As a competitive party they peaked in the warmly contested elections of 1799. Even then, however, they won only about a fourth of the General Assembly races and a minority of the congressional seats.[45] The Republicans used their control of the state legislature to elect James Monroe governor and to pass a general election law giving all of Virginia's electoral votes in the presidential contest of 1800 to the candidate with the highest statewide total, as opposed to the former practice of dividing them by electoral districts. Jefferson predictably carried the Old Dominion by a wide margin and received all its electoral votes.[46]

With Republican dominance of the state government and the death of heroes George Washington and Patrick Henry in 1799, the Federalists were never again powerful, much less united or organized effectively statewide. Although the party enjoyed a slight renaissance as a rallying point against the Embargo and although it remained influential in some locales as late as the 1820s, never after 1801 did the Federalists elect more than six of twenty-three congressmen or did the combined opposition to Dynasty presidential candidates ever receive more than a fraction of the Commonwealth's popular votes.[47]

The essence of Virginia party politics after 1800 was thus one of Republican rule. Well-organized, ably led, broadly based, and fortified with doctrines suited for both a Virginia constituency and a national opposition to the Federalists, the Republicans controlled the Old Dominion to the degree that it was virtually a one-party state in the Dynasty era.

Party supremacy, however, was not synonymous with party unity or with an absence of stress. The major political questions and contests of the period often pitted rival Republican factions. These intraparty developments are best understood by dividing the era roughly at 1817. Before then most Republicans remained loyal to Jefferson and Madison and to their policies, foreign and domestic. Dissent became overt during Jefferson's second term and was divided between two groups, neither of which was ever formally structured. The more extreme and smaller one rallied around former party lieutenant John Randolph, who had broken with Jefferson for political and personal reasons and who soon came to personify a narrow, states'-rights particularism—a literal devotion to a petrified version of the Republican creed of the 1790s. One measure of Jefferson's political skill was the way he isolated—without silencing—Randolph until he had only limited influence even in Virginia.[48]

A second wing of dissident Republicans concurred with Randolph's states'-rights principles, his displeasure at administration policy, and his abhorrence of Madison, who was seen as "the evil genius of Republicanism," responsible for its aberrations. But this group rejected the eccentric Randolph's leadership, remained personally attached to Jefferson, and sought to influence policy within party circles.[49] It included John Taylor of Caroline, Littleton Waller Tazewell, and, to a degree, James Monroe, around whom the anti-Madison forces rallied without success in the election of 1808.[50]

After 1817 the minority position grew in favor until it became the majority persuasion in the Commonwealth—though with stressful dissent in the West. One reason for this neoconservativism was eastern Virginia's general distaste for the prospects of constitutional reform at home and the nationalistic program enacted by Congress in 1816; banks, tariffs, and internal improvements seemed to benefit regions other than itself. "Senex," writing in the *Richmond Enquirer*, expressed his alarm "at the spirit of political innovation that pervades my country generally, and 'my own, my native state,' particularly."[51] The conservative revival within the Old Dominion was immediately apparent in its congressional delegation. Almost half of Virginia's twenty-three representatives were new in 1817, and among the holdovers, some former nationalists modified their views. A change in political winds was clear. As Hugh Nelson wrote when the new Congress began in December 1817, "I shall be much more on the alert this session, if I have my health, than I have ever been. . . . I will do all I can to support the old republican doctrine in the construction of the Constitution."[52] Western congressmen, on the other hand, were more sympathetic to nationalistic programs that held forth the promise of aid for their region, aid which had not been forthcoming from the eastern-controlled state legislature.

The Panic of 1819 made gentry leaders, especially those east of the Blue Ridge, even more sensitive to doubtful economic policies; the Missouri Compromise called attention to the adverse political issue of slavery;[53] and a series of nationalistic decisions by John Marshall provided a convenient foil against which states'-rights rhetoric was refurbished, refined, and widely publicized. In the process, such keepers of the Old Republican faith as Randolph and Taylor rose in popular favor, and a younger generation of Virginians went into office echoing their doctrines, which, after all, had been those of Madison and Jefferson in the late 1790s. Concurrently, national party influence over Virginia politics declined sharply.

The Times and the Men

Leadership of the Virginia Republicans is one measure of the three Dynasty presidents. Jefferson unquestionably was active and effective; Madison was less so; and Monroe, for reasons personal and political, virtually forfeited the role.[54]

The fact of Republican dominance is of considerable consequence to a study of Virginia congressmen in the era. Associations with Jefferson, Madison, and Monroe meant political opportunity, influence, and prestige. Equally important was the broad definition of a "Republican interest" with which Virginians at large identified and on which political careers could be built and sustained. Republican candidates or officeholders also counted on sympathetic local justices, including sheriffs, and state legislators.[55] The community of party interest tended to minimize competition in an election; and campaigning, though normally an individual matter, on occasion reflected party organization on the local level.

Republican politicians also received the support of a wide majority of the state's electioneering newspapers, including most prominently Thomas Ritchie's highly partisan and influential *Richmond Enquirer*. The *Enquirer*, in the mind of one contemporary wag, had a particularly esteemed set of contributors: "Looking at the signatures of its numerous correspondents, one might suppose that all the sages and patriots of Greece and Rome had arisen from their tombs to enlighten the existing generation."[56] Wearing these classical pseudonyms were the party leaders of Jeffersonian Virginia. If, as James H. Broussard has written, "newspapers became the chief weapon of political warfare," then the anti-Republicans suffered from a limited arsenal.[57] The plight of an opposition candidate is suggested by James Mercer Garnett's lamentation to John Randolph that the newspaper *The Spirit of Seventy Six* "will afford the only good opportunity which was ever offered for men of your principles to be heard; altho' the editor, I fear, has scarcely talents to force his paper."[58] Federalist sheets were a distinct minority.[59]

Republican supremacy, it should be noted, was maintained by means other than rigid, pervasive organization and discipline. In the Dynasty era, the party in Virginia included disparate elements and was loosely structured. Its principal agency of control, the "Richmond Junto," operated rather cryptically and focused on presidential campaigns. Furthermore, there was often issue-oriented tension between the eastern and western wings of the party.

In short, a party system formed a portion of the political land-scape in Jeffersonian Virginia and had an important influence on the Commonwealth's leadership class. Beyond party, there was the equally significant reality of the political practices associated with seeking and holding office. Politicians in the Dynasty years func-tioned within a changing framework in which traditional practices confronted new realities. And, yet, the basic questions remained constant. How many elective and appointive offices were there in the state, and what were the prerequisites, legal and otherwise, for them? What influenced a man's decision to seek a public post? What was the nature and extent of electioneering? What determined a candidate's success? Were campaigns competitive? Who could vote? What happened on poll day?

These and related questions will be covered in several subse-quent chapters, but they suggest a larger preliminary question which illuminates the "present state of Virginia" in the period from 1801 to 1825. How unique were the political practices of the Dynasty era, when compared with those of earlier and later periods in the Old Dominion? The Jeffersonian era generally has been treated as an extension of the previous Revolutionary one. Richard R. Bee-man's overview chapter on the 1790s is entitled "The Continuity of Political Life." Charles S. Sydnor used phrases like "colonial Vir-ginia" and "revolutionary Virginia" to indicate the scope of his *Gentlemen Freeholders*, but in fact he ranged well into the nine-teenth century to demonstrate how the process operated, and he avoided the question of how it might have changed.[60] Richard P. McCormick suggested the state's second party system emerged in the 1830s basically out of the one identified by Sydnor. The Old Dominion "inherited from its colonial past," wrote McCormick, "an ordering of political relationships among socio-economic groups that persisted at least through the first half of the nineteenth century." Furthermore, he contended, Virginia was "the oldest and most stable political community in the United States."[61]

The idea of continuity from the colonial period to the second party era obscures the genuine change in political practices that took place. Although somewhat stressful, the change was evolutionary and piecemeal rather than radical or sudden, and it was caused by a variety of developments at different levels of government and at different times. A focus on the Dynasty years puts this change in sharp relief and reveals the central pattern of transition as the political process evolved from one familiar to Revolutionary fathers to one which latter-day Democrats and Whigs would recognize.[62]

In the late colonial period, the only popularly elected officials were the members of the House of Burgesses; service was often as much a chore or duty as an opportunity for self-advancement. For the General Assembly of 1758–61, with two burgesses from each of fifty-one counties and one each from four special districts, there were only 106 elective positions in the entire Commonwealth.[63] Candidates were chiefly large planters, who usually campaigned on a basis other than the few issues facing the colony. Instead, they "won or lost by appeals to local or personal interests," Lucille Griffith concluded: "Hot races did occur, apparently the result of personal rivalry"; the contests were "not so much a question of *what* as *who*" and were "almost always . . . between men of equal wealth, position, and public experience."[64]

Victory came as a result of a candidate's personal reputation and associations and his success at "treating" the freeholders and "soliciting" their ballots on or before election day. In the absence of burning issues, class conflicts, organized political parties, widespread suffrage and literacy, or the requirement to seek the votes of other than freeholder neighbors, electioneering was informal. "Campaign ballyhoo in Virginia," wrote Griffith, "is largely the invention of a later age; paid political advertisements, printed, or well-formulated, platforms, even editorials . . . were all missing until the very eve of the Revolution."[65] Hustings speeches were also rare in the late colonial period.

Misbehavior by an incumbent, either in conduct or in the failure to secure locally needed legislation, might lead to his removal at the next poll, which was held irregularly, that is, at the governor's call rather than on an annual or biennial basis. Historians disagree on the size and participation of the colonial Virginia electorate. A recent estimate, and one of the best documented, suggests that "between 55 and 60 percent" of adult white males were eligible and "more than forty percent of the potential voters" generally went to the polls.[66]

By the Dynasty era the traditional pattern had been clearly altered. In the first place there were far more public offices. The Virginia Constitution of 1776 added a senate, elected from multicounty districts, and a governor and council, selected by the General Assembly. The latter also chose delegates to the various Continental and Confederation congresses. Later, the United States Constitution called for national representatives, chosen by districts, and senators, selected by the Assembly. The federal establishment also required presidential elections and provided an opportunity for appointments to the executive and judicial branches in which the Old Dominion would be well represented. Finally, by 1780 there were over seventy counties, and despite the loss of Kentucky, by the early 1800s there were nearly a hundred, or almost twice the number of counties that had existed in 1760. If Sydnor's figure of from ten to thirty-six justices per county is correct, this increased by the hundreds the chances of service in one of the most powerful positions in Virginia politics.[67]

Such a wide variety of new political positions opened the Virginia system internally, as in the additional court and Assembly seats, and also vertically, as in the federal posts that would be filled by the kind of talented men who formerly rose no higher than leadership in the House of Burgesses. Office seekers continued to be of the upper class, but they were increasingly lawyers or lawyer-planters rather than gentlemen-planters. Moreover, they aspired to higher positions and often had to gain election by campaigning beyond home grounds and among unfamiliar voters.

Continental developments—the Revolution, the creation of governments under the Confederation and Constitution, successive domestic and foreign crises—injected external questions into Virginia elections and made them at times more issue-oriented. This shift was accelerated by developments within the state in the Dynasty era. Growing sectional rivalry and economic decline added controversial questions of political reform (suffrage and reapportionment) and economic legislation (tariffs, internal improvements, and banks). National and state issues often dovetailed in congressional campaigns.

The simultaneous emergence of political parties introduced another element into Virginia elections. The rivalry between Republicans and Federalists in the 1790s provided a competitive partisan standard for candidates; campaigns were sometimes guided or influenced by party leaders at the state or national level, and the development of parties contributed directly to the broadening of electioneering appeals and tactics. Republican dominance in the Dynasty era should not obscure Federalist strength in some locales, sectional rivalries within the Republican ranks, or the fact that even one-party races still might reflect party considerations. The Richmond Junto was chiefly concerned with presidential elections, but those national contests could affect the results of local and congressional campaigns.

With these significant changes came not only more substantive issues, a broader political ideology, and a greater competition for more offices but also a corresponding increase in the variety and scope of campaign techniques. This is seen clearly, though not exclusively, in congressional races. Hustings speeches became common, as did the use of the printed word in letters, circulars, pamphlets, and the press. The latter soared in importance with the large rise in the number of newspapers, many with editors having clearly partisan ties or opinions. An expanded and improved postal service was likewise of consequence, in part because Virginia politicians elected by freeholders in the Old Dominion were now representing them beyond the state's borders, in the national capital.

Despite such alterations, the earlier political system retained much of its character. Suffrage was slightly broadened in 1785, but voter participation in nonpresidential races seems to have remained roughly what it had been in the burgess elections of the colonial period.[68] Candidates were still essentially of the gentry, local questions and interests continued to be pertinent (and would always be so), campaigns were often uncontested, and above all, "the naked question of personal popularity"[69] still decided many elections.

The old and the new were symbolized at Charlotte Courthouse in March 1799 in a meeting between candidates representing each national party. The Federalist spokesman, making his last political race, was the aging Patrick Henry; the Republican, in his first contest, was the twenty-four-year-old John Randolph. At the urging of George Washington, Henry was running for the Virginia House of Delegates. Randolph, with the sponsorship of a district party leader, sought election to Congress. Focusing on national issues raised by the XYZ affair, the Alien-Sedition Acts, and the Virginia and Kentucky Resolutions, Henry spoke in defense of the Federalist position. Minutes later he was answered by Randolph in his first public address. Both gentlemen were well received; in fact, after various polls, both were elected.

The episode is instructive. As a young man in the 1760s Henry was an aberrant for using oratorical skills in politics. By 1799, however, a hustings speech was expected of even a novice like Randolph. The race had other features scarcely predictable only three decades earlier: multicounty campaigns, one of them for a national office; party initiative and organization behind the candidates; partisan "continental" issues; and the use of handbills and the press. Middle-class freeholders remained arbiters of gentry candidates, who still confronted them directly. Yet, though Henry and Randolph represented polar positions as to age, party, and ideology, the voters chose them both. Personality could still be the paramount factor in Virginia politics.

The changes underway at the time of Randolph's first victory in 1799 were almost complete by his last, in 1833. The Jacksonian era saw the emergence of two viable parties in Virginia and genuine competition between them. Across the state in the late 1830s both Democrats and Whigs, in the words of one authority, "elaborated their organization, increased their discipline, altered their campaign techniques, and broadened the nature of their appeal."[70] This second party system brought an increased concern for sectional questions within the Old Dominion and for national issues beyond, thus moving Virginia politics a step away from its traditional emphasis on selecting officeholders largely on the basis of personal popularity or community standing. National nominating conventions filled the void caused by the demise of the old caucus system, and rival national tickets attracted devoted followers in the state. Electioneering devices were refined and broadened to arouse mass participation. Nongentry candidates were common, and voter interest soared to record levels.[71]

The competition for votes and for statewide support benefited the populous region west of the Blue Ridge, which had grown to be a suitor worthy of courting. The long-standing western demand for genuine constitutional revision was met in the convention of 1850–51. Among its reforms were the institution of an adult white male franchise and the creation of more elective offices, including that of the governor. In the meantime more and more counties were added; by 1840 the number was 119, and by 1861 it was 149, thus providing new political space while the state's population remained relatively static. Understandably, Richard P. McCormick concluded from his survey of political practices in the various states: "In few did the change over from the old to the new style of politics represent so great a transformation as in Virginia."[72]

In summary, the Dynasty era highlighted an important transition. The period provided a bridge between nonparty and two-party systems; between local, informal, personal campaigns and those which were organized for broad appeal over frequently large geographic areas; between a constricted, deferential, at times apathetic electorate and one which was large, vocal, and demanding; between only one elective office and many; between gentry candidates and those of various classes; in short, between a simple, stable oligarchy and a complex, turbulent, contentious, emerging democracy. And through it all, Virginia leaders faced a series of largely adverse events and trends that often originated elsewhere but came to shape attitudes and the economic and political landscape of the Commonwealth during the Dynasty years.

Economic Distress, Patriotism, and Decline

Because the state's economy was geared to external trade, a variation in national or international markets could produce severe repercussions. Conditions in the Dynasty era were almost continuously adverse, placing additional pressure on an already vulnerable economy (especially east of the Blue Ridge). The outbreak of war in Europe in 1803 stirred foreign demand for American goods and stimulated trade in the Old Dominion, but from 1805 to 1815 that same war caused direct or indirect interdiction or prohibition of its foreign markets.[73] Napoleon's Continental System and England's Orders in Council made commerce uncertain; Jefferson's Embargo (1807–9) relieved the uncertainty by stopping the trade and brought to the Commonwealth "many and great privations and inconveniences."[74]

Most Virginians patriotically supported the measure, but it did shake the Old Dominion's weak economic foundation and heighten political tension. The "Dambargo" sparked voices of opposition from anti-Madison Republicans, a mildly revived Federalist party, and urban merchants like Richmond's Robert Gamble, who blasted "the Cursed Wicked Frenchified" policy.[75] Furthermore it led to other forms of economic coercion, followed by the War of 1812, which not only disrupted trade but also caused considerable physical destruction in Virginia's coastal areas. Postwar prosperity was short-lived and in a sense unfortunate because it encouraged many planters to overextend their credit in a climate of optimism soon to vanish in the Panic of 1819 and its lingering aftermath. Although the state at large felt the pressure of economic distress, for the east, in particular, it brought acute hardship. "This was the period," wrote Charles Ambler, "when Madison was unable to get a loan he wanted from the United States Bank, because of the poor security he had to offer; when Jefferson mortgaged his home to make good the financial failures of friends; and when Monroe sold his beautiful home at Oak Hill and became dependent upon friends and relatives in New York City."[76]

Without question the declining economy contributed to the great movement of Virginians during the Jeffersonian years. Often overlooked is the fact that much of this moving was internal. For example, to recoup his political and financial fortunes, George Tucker left the "gaieties and dissipations" of Richmond in 1806 for opportunities in law, land, and public service in the counties of first Frederick and then Pittsylvania, "where education and refinement had just begun to dawn." Within a decade he relocated in Lynchburg, later settled in Charlottesville, and eventually abandoned the state altogether. While Tucker left the capital and moved west, William Wirt left Albemarle County (after several earlier relocations) and moved east to Richmond, then to Williamsburg, and then, in the path of his friend Littleton Waller Tazewell, to Norfolk, before returning to Richmond in 1806. Like Tucker, Wirt in time left Virginia.[77]

So great was the movement out of the Commonwealth that Jefferson wrote William Branch Giles in 1818 that "emigration to the West and South is going on beyond anything imaginable."[78] The Old Dominion's population grew only slightly in the period, and between 1830 and 1840 it actually declined 2 percent. From 1800 to 1850 Virginia's population increased only 50 percent, a fraction of that of other older states, such as New York (600 percent), Massachusetts (300 percent), Pennsylvania (500 percent), and North Carolina (200 percent). By the year 1850, 388,000 Virginia-born whites and free blacks were residing elsewhere. Among the expatriates born before 1810 were at least 227 congressmen. This suggests that Joseph Glover Baldwin, himself an expatriate, was correct in saying "from Cape May to Puget's Sound [Virginia] has colonized the other States and the territories with her surplus talent."[79] John Randolph even predicted, in the words of his biographer, that if the situation did not change, "instead of the master advertising for the runaway slave, the slave would soon be advertising for the runaway master." The slave, however, was less a runaway than an involuntary migrant, with about 120,000 being sold or taken out of the Old Dominion in the 1830s alone.[80]

Many other Virginians bemoaned their lot but decided against leaving. In 1802 Jefferson's son-in-law Thomas Mann Randolph seriously considered taking his family to the Mississippi Territory, having been "allured by the immensely profitable culture of cotton" there; and he later thought of moving to Georgia. In 1803 Wirt noted that the most prominent Virginians were not "amassing at the bar, in this country, wealth . . . more than the most ordinary lawyer in Kentucky is able to do in five or six years."[81] Since Wirt never found in the Old Dominion the financial security he craved and since Randolph, though a serious and progressive farmer, went bankrupt, one can only speculate about the psychological toll exacted from them and those like them who rejected the lure of opportunities elsewhere. Another result of economic dislocation was the magnification of an old Virginia problem, personal indebtedness. It often became a network of indebtedness binding two or more prominent families and reflecting abrupt changes of financial status.[82]

Economic hardship also prompted a search for solutions on a variety of fronts. During the Dynasty period considerable emphasis was put on improving market conditions—by state support of such projects as the James River and Kanawha Canal, the Chesapeake and Ohio Canal, and similar ventures; by developing new crops or manufactured articles to export; and by opening new foreign markets. It was also a time for serious criticism of slavery as a principal cause of the state's economic backwardness. This condemnation underlay colonization efforts championed by Virginians and was a prominent theme in both the Constitutional Convention of 1829–30 and the "great slavery debate" in the General Assembly in 1831–32. Other Virginians experimented with better farming techniques and implements and circulated their findings. Chief among these agricultural reformers was John Taylor of Caroline, who set a personal example, published influential essays entitled *The Arator*, and was a founder and leader of the state's agricultural society.[83]

Finally, economic turmoil had important political ramifications. Eastern Virginia was in no mood to lessen the power that protected its property from increased taxation, to tax itself for projects required in the west, or to support national schemes that might benefit competitor states or make other regions more desirable to potential migrants. Conversely, western Virginia, unable to satisfy its needs for credit, commercial expansion, and improved transportation within the Commonwealth, turned more frequently to the federal government and such attractive programs as Henry Clay's American System. At the same time the west struggled more vigorously within the state for the political reforms that would give it a greater voice over economic policy in Virginia.[84]

On a personal scale, debt-ridden planters or lawyers no doubt reconsidered the burden of holding office at a time when family finances were disordered and demanded attention. On the other hand, some Virginians probably hoped the additional compensation of a public position might relieve a portion of their economic distress or open the path to other rewards.[85] Finally, Virginians inevitably and understandably resorted to the psychological device of scapegoatism. Financially impoverished, they often found it easier to blame their woes on external forces than to face conditions close at hand. In the Dynasty era, there is no doubt that new circumstances had disrupted the old economic pattern in a stressful fashion and that Virginians were sensitive to questions affecting the state's economy. Both realities were well understood by their political leaders in Richmond and in Washington.

The traumatic self-pity and pessimism of economic dislocation and political decline were partly counterbalanced by national events throughout the period, which brought gusts of patriotism and optimism to the Old Dominion. Of no small significance in these highly nationalistic outbursts was the role of Virginians who had been born too late for the Revolutionary struggle. They grew up with a desire to prove themselves as manly and worthy as their fathers had been in the 1770s. National events provided an important opportunity for a generation under stress to align itself with the reassuring principles and emotions of past moments of glory.

Such an opportunity came without warning in the *Chesapeake* affair of June 1807, when a British man-of-war halted and fired upon an American naval vessel off the Virginia capes. The Old Dominion responded immediately and with passionate bellicosity. As a contemporary recalled it:

The people held meetings, passed fiery resolutions, ate indignant dinners, drank belligerent toasts, and uttered threatening sentiments. Old armories were ransacked, old weapons of war were burnished anew, military companies were formed, regimentals were discussed, the drum and fife and martial bands of music woke the morning and evening echoes of town and country; and the whole land was filled with the din, the clamour, the glitter, the array of serried hosts. . . . Twenty-five years had rolled over the Revolution. The generation which grew to manhood in this interval, were educated in all the reminiscences of the war of Seventy-six, which, fresh in the narratives of every fireside, flamed the imagination of the young with its thousand marvels of soldierlike adventure. These were told with the amplification and the unction characteristic of the veteran, and were heard by his youthful listener, with many a secret sign, that such days of heroic hazards were not to return for him. . . . Now, in 1807, whilst these emotions still swayed the breast of the sons of those who had won the independence of the nation, the same enemy was about to confront them.

The day that many had dreamed of was about to arrive; and many a secret aspiration was breathed for a field to realize its hopes.[86]

"A vociferous demand for revenge arose" and "party animosity practically disappeared" as "a genuine grass roots movement" swept through the Commonwealth, and protest meetings, reminiscent of Revolutionary times, were held in all corners of the Old Dominion.[87]

Fortunately Jefferson reacted with less emotion and the *Chesapeake* crisis passed, though relations between the United States and Great Britain remained strained. That strain was increased by the presence of a war hawk element in the state and in its congressional delegation. In addition, other Virginia congressmen, formerly willing to negotiate or to try commercial coercion, came to believe that the choice had been reduced to war or national disgrace, and this may have been decisive in Madison's call to arms in June 1812.[88] The war itself, for all its frustrations and alarms in Virginia and the nation, provided an opportunity for patriotic service, often, as in the case of John Tyler and William Wirt, with "military laurels . . . bloodless."[89] Although there were vocal dissenters, even a die-hard opponent like John Randolph spent time as a mounted sentinel during one crisis. The Treaty of Ghent settled little in the immediate sense but was warmly celebrated across the Commonwealth.[90]

The Dynasty era ended in a fantastic extravaganza, the tour of the marquis de Lafayette in 1824 and 1825. The Revolutionary hero traveled extensively in the Old Dominion and was greeted everywhere with fanfare and elaborate receptions. The celebrations saluted Revolutionary ideals and recounted the political and personal virtues that Virginians held dear. "I have seen General La Fayette," wrote one individual, "and such a man I never before saw, and never expect to see again. In his manners there is great simplicity, they must have been formed by the manners of the Virginia gentlemen with whom he associated in our revolutionary war. I verily believe him to be the purist republican, and man, now alive."[91] The influence of such events in helping the popular mind to redefine itself was not without importance. Again, two generations experienced nationalistic emotions that carried young and old alike backward in time to a rekindling of the Spirit of '76. "Honor to the

Patriots of the Revolution," rang one of the innumerable toasts. "May the conduct of their descendants prove them heirs to their virtues."[92]

Virginians could also take native pride in the three American presidents of the era. The Dynasty's significance, however, was more than a matter of state prestige and a corresponding anti-Virginia spirit elsewhere; it directly affected politics within the Old Dominion. Jefferson, for example, relied on Virginians for congressional leadership and in other ways. The large number of state politicians in administration circles gave a certain Virginia cast to them and in turn gave a certain national cast to developments in the Old Dominion. In a similar vein, presidential recruitment of Virginians to seek public office or to serve in some appointive capacity also influenced affairs in the Commonwealth.

If Virginians took pride in their presidents and responded patriotically to certain national events, they found little to applaud in others which presaged a decline for the Commonwealth. The flood of humanity westward, the rise of a manufacturing interest in New England and of a cotton interest in the Southwest, the addition of new states—not one of which, John Randolph boasted, he had voted for—the end of the Dynasty, the demise of the presidential caucus system, the death of Jefferson on the fiftieth anniversary of the Declaration of Independence all suggested the power and glory of the Old Dominion were passing. And eastern Virginians saw this clearly. "We may struggle 'till doomsday,'" wrote Francis Walker Gilmer in 1821, "but Virginia is a barren country, and all which it inherit must be poor—adventitious circumstances have deceived us—but nature will work its way—we may boast of the Chesapeake bay, and think we are a great people; but we are from this day forth, tributary to northern shoe makers, Irish potato, pumpkin, and Rutabaga-man."[93]

A few years earlier, Gilmer's friend John Randolph had returned from a trip to Philadelphia with similar views:

My journey . . . has only inspired me with regret—we are not only some centuries behind our Northern neighbours, but at least forty years behind ourselves. It cannot be disguised that there has been something radically wrong with our policy—& that when a few of the present generation who have imbibed from their predecessors "the spirit of a gentleman," shall have died off, there will be nothing left in Virginia worth living for. The two-legged swine that inhabit Pennsylvania are at least well-fed. But we are poverty-stricken, flat-sided & long-legged, fit only to thrust our noses thro' the hedges of our friend Arator.[94]

Historian James Schouler phrased it in simple, if extreme, terms: "As a member of the Union, Virginia was not set to the meridian of a new era. Her golden age glowed in a vanishing horizon. Her illustrious men were dead or dying, and a pigmy race aspired to their vacant places."[95]

Virginians also recognized the state's internal problems—an erratic, declining economy, sectional tensions (and stakes), a static and discredited structure of government, a shifting or falling population. And, with them all, as if to emphasize and symbolize the stress and burden of change, the Revolutionary generation was rapidly dying and, with it, the Commonwealth's last sure claim to national distinction. Under the circumstances, there is little wonder at an element of "nostalgia, pessimism, and malaise" in "the doomed aristocrat[s] in late-Jeffersonian Virginia,"[96] an often stressful time for the men who rose to positions of political leadership and responsibility.

II

Collective Biography of
a Leadership Class

Throughout the Dynasty era the setting in which the Virginia leaders functioned clearly—and perhaps predictably—blended continuity and change, stability in some regards, stress in many others. The leaders themselves? Perhaps the group most easily identifiable yet significant in size and influence is the ninety-eight individuals who served in the United States Congress from 1801 to 1825. Included are scores of persons who held other major offices from the level of local government to the American presidency, with governors, cabinet members, Supreme Court justices, and ambassadors in between. The senators were chosen by the legislature, and the representatives by voters in districts throughout the Commonwealth, an elective base as broad as any in the state.

Of course, the group is not all encompassing. Missing are the Dynasty presidents; a few state leaders like Governor William H. Cabell and his brother, the influential legislator Joseph C. Cabell; such Junto stalwarts as editor Thomas Ritchie, Judge Spencer Roane, and Attorney General P. N. Nicholas; and Chief Justice Marshall (though he was relatively inactive in Virginia politics after 1801). Yet their biographical profiles are virtually identical to those of the congressmen, and the two groups are one and the same as measured by ties of blood and marriage. Also, the three presidents and Marshall each had prior service on the congressional level.[1] Thus an investigation of this large contingent of officeholders, elected from throughout the Commonwealth but serving on the national scene, should reveal much about the leadership class that dominated Virginia in the Dynasty era.

A biographical profile will be established for each of the following categories: nativity and family background, education, religion, military service, occupation (to include property holdings), and political experience. Composite patterns will then be identified and analyzed.[2]

Nativity and Family Background

Ninety-eight individuals represented the Old Dominion in one or both houses of the United States Congress between 1801 and 1825. Six served only in the Senate, eighty-six only in the House, and six at different times in both. Of the ninety-eight, at least eighty-six were native sons, fifty-eight were natives of their districts, and only two (William McKinley and Alexander Smyth) were immigrants (table 2). About a third of the congressmen were born before 1765; about two-thirds, before 1775. Over half claimed Virginia roots from earlier than 1700. Of the seventy-nine whose ethnic strains have been identified, fifty were English or Welsh, thirteen were Scotch-Irish, and twelve were Scotch.

The variable of age correlates neither with section nor party but is important for generational attitudes. As will be discussed in later chapters, the older congressmen shared the experience of the Revolution and of an earlier ideal of public service, while the younger men felt the stress of post-Revolutionary change and different motives for political careers.

Most congressmen, regardless of age, were born not only in the Old Dominion but into its most prominent families. A striking eighty-three had two or more notables within the immediate family circle; sixty-one counted at least one other congressman as a close relative; fifty-four (of the eighty-two known to have had wives) married into another distinguished family. Putting eminence in perspective is a subjective task, but one approach is to suggest categories that indicate prominence and then to measure the number of congressmen falling into each. A plausible scale might consist of the following: (1) Virginia origins before 1700, (2) two or more notables in the immediate family, (3) at least one other congressman in the immediate family, and (4) marriage ties to an eminent family. Table 3 shows that twenty-four congressmen scored in all four categories, another thirty-six in three, and another twenty-three in two. Only

Table 2. Nativity and family background

	Total	By house			By party				By section			
		Both	USS	HR	R	F	(M)*	?	TW	PM	V	TA
Aggregate no.	98	6	6	86	77	19	(5)	2	26	41	17	14
Nativity												
Virginia	86	6	0	74	69	15	(5)	2	26	39	10	11
Other Amer.	7	0	0	7	5	2	0	0	0	1	4	2
Immigrant	2†	0	0	2	2	0	0	0	0	0	1	1
Unknown	3	0	0	3	1	2	0	0	0	1	2	0
Before 1765	28	4	3	21	23	5	(1)	0	8	10	6	4
1765–1775	35	2	2	31	26	9	(4)	0	9	17	6	3
After 1775	30	0	1	29	25	4	0	1	9	12	4	5
Unknown	5	0	0	5	3	1	0	1	0	2	1	2
Same as cong. district	58‡+	5	NA	53	44	13	(4)	1	18	27	7	6
Va. origins												
Before 1650	18	2	1	15	15	3	(1)	0	6	7	5	0
1650–1699	33	3	5	25	31	1	(3)	1	13	20	0	0
1700–1749	15	1	0	14	9	6	(1)	0	3	5	3	4
1750–1775	10	0	0	10	7	2	0	1	1	0	4	5
After 1775	5	0	0	5	3	2	0	0	0	2	2	1
Unknown	17	0	0	17	12	5	0	0	3	7	3	4
Ethnic origins												
English	48	5	5	38	43	4	(4)	1	22	21	5	0
Scotch-Irish	13	1	0	12	9	4	0	0	0	3	3	7
Scotch	12	0	1	11	9	3	(1)	0	2	7	1	2
German	3	0	0	3	0	3	0	0	0	0	3	0
Welsh	2	0	0	2	2	0	0	0	0	2	0	0
Irish	1	0	0	1	1	0	0	0	0	0	1	0
Unknown	19	0	0	19	13	5	0	1	2	8	4	5

Table 2. Nativity and family background (cont.)

	Total	By house			By party				By section			
		Both	USS	HR	R	F	(M)*	?	TW	PM	V	TA
Marital status												
Bachelor	10	1	1	8	8	2	(1)	0	3	4	1	2
Married	64	3	5	56	51	12	(1)	1	14	29	13	8
Married twice or more	18	2	0	16	13	4	(3)	1	7	7	1	3
Unknown	6	0	0	6	5	1	0	0	2	1	2	1
Family notables§												
Two or more	83	6	6	71	68	14	(5)	1	25	35	11	12
One	5	0	0	5	3	1	0	1	0	3	2	0
Unknown	10	0	0	10	6	4	0	0	1	3	4	2
One or more congressmen	61	4	6	51	49	12	(4)	0	14	29	6	12
By marriage||	54	5	3	46	46	7	(3)	1	17	23	8	6

Note: USS: U.S. Senate; HR: U.S. House of Representatives; TW: Tidewater; PM: Piedmont; V: Valley; TA: Trans-Allegheny.

* The five "Minority" congressmen are former Republicans Matthew Clay, James Mercer Garnett, John Randolph, and Philip R. Thompson, and former Federalist Edwin Gray, all of whom are also listed under the columns for their regular parties and are shown in parentheses here to note their presence as a collective subgroup.

† The two immigrants are William McKinley, who came as a young man, and Alexander Smyth, who came as a child with his father. Although George Tucker was born in Bermuda, he is treated as a Virginian here because of his family's long association with and residence in the Old Dominion.

‡ Thomas Gholson, Jr, and David Holmes were born outside their districts but moved there as small children, and thus are counted as natives here.

§ A "notable" includes any local, colonial, state, or national officeholder, militia-military officer, church official, or a person regarded by contemporaries as being unusually prosperous. "Family" includes sons, brothers, fathers, nephews, uncles, first cousins, and grandfathers of the congressman or his wife.

|| "By marriage" means the family of the congressman's wife.

Table 3. Elite scale

Scale categories: (1) Virginia origins before 1700, (2) two or more notables in immediate family, (3) at least one other congressman in immediate family, and (4) marriage tie to a notable.

	Total	By house			By party				By section			
		Both	USS	HR	R	F	(M)	?	TW	PM	V	TA
Congressmen with												
All four	24	2	3	19	21	3	(1)	0	8	13	3	0
Three	36	4	3	29	33	3	(4)	0	11	16	4	5
Two	23	0	0	23	13	8	0	2	4	9	3	7
One	6	0	0	6	5	1	0	0	2	1	3	0
Unknown	9	0	0	9	5	4	0	0	1	2	4	2

Collective Leadership Biography

one congressman—Republican Joseph Johnson—clearly deserves the label of a self-made man.

Nativity and family background indicate several patterns. First, Virginia's twelve senators form a distinct bloc among the ninety-eight men. All were native sons, eleven were born before 1775 and had Virginia roots earlier than 1700, and ten were of English extraction. Each had two or more family notables, ten counted one or more other congressmen as kinsmen, and eight married prominently. The Republicans claimed the entire dozen, who missed by one (Andrew Moore of the Valley) being exclusively eastern.

Second, a sectional pattern is discernible, if one follows the traditional east-west division at the Blue Ridge Mountains. Almost all (sixty-five of sixty-seven) of the eastern congressmen were natives, against about two-thirds of the westerners. Two-thirds boasted Virginia origins before 1700, an ancestry matched by less than a fifth of the westerners. Two-thirds had been born in their districts, but only two-fifths of the westerners had. Of the known ethnic strains, eastern congressmen were overwhelmingly English, a heritage of only five of thirty-one westerners. Eastern congressmen had a higher percentage of ties to two or more notables, of kinship to other congressmen, and of prominent marriages. Most dramatically, on the elite scale shown in table 3, roughly one of every three easterners placed in the top category, a distinction enjoyed by only about one of every ten westerners. All five of the "Minority" men or party mavericks resided east of the Blue Ridge.

A third and somewhat erratic and surprising pattern is that of party lines. The seventy-seven Republicans vastly outnumbered the nineteen Federalists, but when percentages are used and the "unknowns" are eliminated, differences between the groups are minimized. The two have almost identical percentages, for example, in the category of individuals with other congressmen as kinsmen. The Republicans have a slight edge in native sons (89 to 88 percent), two or more family notables (96 to 93 percent), persons with a top rank on the elite scale (30 to 20 percent), and in pre-1775 birth dates (95 to 86 percent). The most obvious distinction is in ethnic strains: 67 percent of the Republicans were of English descent, while 71 percent of the Federalists were of non-English stock.

The Republicans also had substantially higher percentages of persons with pre-1700 origins and with prominent marriages. The five "Minority" men again form an extremely cohesive subgroup. All were Virginia natives with birth dates prior to 1775 and with two or more notables in the family; four had roots from before 1700, were English, were born within their congressional districts, and had one or more congressmen as kinsmen.

These patterns in nativity and ethnic origins are about what one might expect from the first and largest English colony and from a state which attracted few immigrants after the Revolution. The white eastern population continued to be predominately English and homogeneous, as accurately mirrored by its congressmen. In the west, where immigrants of varying nationalities had moved southward from Pennsylvania into the rich Shenandoah and contiguous valleys, settlement came later and was heterogeneous, and the western congressmen reflect that. Twelve of the fifteen Virginia congressmen with post-1750 roots in the state and a solid majority of its non-English representatives resided in the west. That the twelve senators should have been Republican and almost to the man eastern is symptomatic of eastern Republican dominance of the state legislature. Their being older, more settled, and having more notable kinsmen fits the idea that senators were supposed to be a cut above the more democratically elected representatives.

Also predictable but of critical significance are the existence of deep roots and family prominence. Virtually all the congressmen had been born in the state, and most were natives of their districts and had Virginia origins before 1700. Congressmen in the Old Dominion should have been well acquainted with their district needs; Virginia freeholders usually had a long time to evaluate the men who presumed to serve them. Deep roots might also suggest, as Paul Goodman has phrased it, "higher social status" or "more time to accumulate wealth and influence,"[3] though, of course, old families were not necessarily eminent families and prestige declined as well as rose. Family prominence—"connections," the "web of kinship"—pervaded all sections and both parties.[4] Relationship or marriage ties to a local justice or militia leader or member of the General Assembly or Congress could be a critical factor in a politician's career. A young man such as John Randolph, Wilson Cary Nicholas, or Stevens Thomson Mason might grow up surrounded by notables. The spur to ambition, the setting of a public example, and the transferal of a sense of elitism and a tradition of duty and service from one generation to the next no doubt help to explain the continuing presence of great family names in Virginia history.

Proper relations also could be an incalculable asset to getting into politics. Sons—like John Claiborne, John George and Edward Brake Jackson, Armistead Thomson Mason, and Littleton Waller Tazewell—followed fathers in office, and succession by brothers was even more common. The connections and influence of the Baylys and Parkers in the Eastern Shore, the Newtons of Norfolk, the Garnetts and Roanes of the Tidewater, the Masons and Mercers of the Northern Neck, the Breckinridges of the southern Valley, and the Jacksons and Lewises in the Trans-Allegheny region could be decisive in bringing forward a candidate or in carrying his election. This family factor gained increasing significance because of the need to serve and campaign in multicounty districts.

On a more limited scale, just being married into a prominent line (such as James Breckinridge's tie to the Prestons or Edward Colston's to the Marshalls and Brockenbroughs) or being the son of a respected local minister (as were Andrew Stevenson, John Dawson, and Philip R. Thompson, among others) or of a pioneer family (like the Jacksons, Floyds, and Lewises) transferred prestige and friendships and assured a hearing for a candidate. At least eighty-eight congressmen had one or more eminent persons as kinsmen.

Influential family ties also aided congressmen in office. Several Virginians—notably James Breckinridge and Wilson Cary Nicholas—were connected by blood or marriage to congressmen and leaders of other states, and all could benefit from political information received from kinsmen within the General Assembly, on the local county courts, or from home grounds. Certainly the Dynasty pattern suggests validity for an old saw: "It is said that when a man becomes prominent in New York, people ask: 'How much is he worth?' in Boston: 'What does he know?' . . . in Virginia . . . 'Who was his grandfather? What is his pedigree?'"[5]

The Times and the Men

Education

The birthright in a prominent family usually included what was then a rare opportunity for formal education. "Better never be born than ill bred" explained one planter in sending his son off to school.[6] The rudiments might be taught in the home by an older member of the family or perhaps by a tutor brought into the community of the wellborn for that purpose. Attendance at a private academy or at sessions directed by a local minister often came next; college sometimes followed.[7]

Of the eighty-eight Virginia congressmen whose formal education has been ascertained, well over half (forty-eight) reached the uncommon plateau of collegiate instruction (table 4).[8] Almost three-fourths (thirty-two) were alumni of William and Mary, "the place," wrote Jefferson with characteristic hyperbole, "where . . . are collected together all the young men of Virginia under preparation for public life."[9] Princeton with seven placed a poor second. Four Virginians, three of them doctors, studied abroad, all at the University of Edinburgh. Of the forty-eight who attended college, thirty-three graduated.

The college men included five of the six Virginians who served in both houses of Congress, five of the six in the Senate only, and thirty-eight of the eighty-six in the House only. By parties, the Republicans claimed forty-four, the Federalists a mere four, three of whom graduated from Princeton. Of thirty-two William and Mary alumni, thirty-one were Republicans.

All six of the doctor-congressmen went to non-Virginia schools, though two of them (James and Walter Jones) had earlier graduated from Hampden-Sydney and William and Mary, respectively. Several individuals went to more than one institution. Those who matriculated at Hampden-Sydney but graduated elsewhere included William S. Archer and William Cabell Rives (both William and Mary) and William Branch Giles and his close friend Abraham Venable (both Princeton). Unique in so many ways, John Randolph stood alone among the congressmen as an alumnus of three colleges but a graduate of none.

An analysis of higher education reveals a distinct sectional pattern. Of sixty-seven congressmen from the Tidewater and Pied-

	Total	By house			R	By party			By section			
		Both	USS	HR		F	(M)	?	TW	PM	V	TA
College												
Wm. and Mary												
Graduated	17	2	2	13	16	1	(1)	0	4	11	2	0
Attended	15	1	2	12	15	0	(1)	0	7	4	2	2
Other Virginia												
Graduated	2	1	0	1	2	0	0	0	0	2	0	0
Attended	1	0	0	1	1	0	0	0	0	1	0	0
Princeton												
Graduated	5	1	1	3	2	3	0	0	1	3	1	0
Attended	2	0	0	2	2	0	(1)	0	1	1	0	0
Other American												
Graduated	5	0	0	5	5	0	0	0	2	2	1	0
Attended	1	0	0	1	1	0	(1)	0	0	1	0	0
Abroad												
Graduated	4	0	0	4	4	0	0	0	1	3	1	0
Attended	0	0	0	0	0	0	0	0	0	0	0	0
Total	52	5	5	42	48	4	(4)	0	16	28	6	2
Lower ("academic," "classical," tutors, etc.)	38	1	1	36	25	11	(2)	2	11	13	7	7
Self-educated	2	0	0	2	2	0	0	0	0	0	0	2
Unknown	10	0	0	10	6	4	(1)	0	0	3	4	3
Total	102*	6	6	90	81	19	(7)	2	27	44	17	14

*This is in excess of the ninety-eight congressmen since Drs. James and Walter Jones graduated from two colleges and John Randolph attended three without graduating from any. Randolph's pattern also distorts the "minority" column.

mont, forty (60 percent) were known to have been college trained
— compared to only eight (26 percent) of thirty-one congressmen
west of the Blue Ridge. Educational achievement reflected family
background in the sense that a college diploma was the perquisite
of the gentry; and most congressmen were of the gentry, especially
those from east of the Blue Ridge. This helps to account for the
rigid sectional line among graduates, as does the proximity of William and Mary to easterners and the lack of a convenient western
institution in colonial Virginia. Hampden-Sydney, Piedmont-based
and Presbyterian-supported, originated as an academy in the mid-
1770s and did not grant college degrees until a decade later. The
former Liberty Hall Academy in the Valley perhaps had college
status by the early 1800s, but this came too late to affect more than
one Dynasty congressman.

Whatever the precise explanations—and those of proximity, class,
tradition, and minimal options seem clear—William and Mary became the training ground of almost a third of all Virginia congressmen in the Dynasty era. As such it merits closer examination,
especially given the institution's heavily political atmosphere.[10] A
student at William and Mary before 1780 found himself at the vor-
tex of Virginia politics, Williamsburg, the Commonwealth's capital
since the late seventeenth century. To the town came the colonial
elite as burgesses, judges, and in other public capacities, or merely
for social or economic interests. The government and the *Virginia
Gazette* were there even when the burgesses were not. Students
experienced firsthand the rhetoric, personalities, and practices of
Virginia politics; their kinship with the colonial elite often eliminated the gap between observation and participation. The legal and
judicial proceedings had a heavily political content, and even after
the capital moved to Richmond in 1779–80, a state court remained.

Progressive in many ways, the college curriculum included rhetoric, philosophy, law, and police, all with political import. An ample
library made available standard works on law and politics. Thus,
as a contemporary noted in 1803, "There is probably no college in
the United States in which political science is studied with so much
ardour and in which it is considered so pre-eminently a favourite
subject, as this."[11] Faculty and staff also had their influence. Of the

Collective Leadership Biography

latter one of the most inspirational was Bishop James Madison, who provided continuity by his long and dedicated service as president of the institution from 1779 to 1812. Like his famous cousin of the same name, the bishop espoused an ardent brand of Republicanism, so much so that he at times prayed not for the "Kingdom" but for the "Republic of Heaven." Students also felt the influence of his oratorical style from the pulpit and of his theology, an Episcopalian faith which drifted toward deism.[12] Young Virginians of several generations came under the direction of two distinguished law professors, George Wythe, politician, patriot, signer of the Declaration of Independence, and scholar, and his successor, Judge St. George Tucker. Both were devout Republicans, and Tucker became a prominent patron of states' rights and strict construction. Molding scores of future lawyers who attended their formal lectures, both men also served on a high court and supervised the training of numerous clerks and apprentices. With these men present, it is clear why William and Mary, unlike other American colleges, stood as a bastion of Republicanism. The degree of partisan enthusiasm there is suggested by the students' celebration of July 4, 1798, by burning in effigy President Adams, of Washington's death by irreverent behavior, and of Jefferson's election by "joy [which] almost bordered on madness . . . [marching], with shouts, huzzas, whirling of hats, Etc."[13]

Finally, each student at William and Mary was influenced politically by his fellow students. With enrollment only about sixty a year in the colonial period, and less than that figure afterward, close and lifelong friendships formed naturally among the sons of the gentry and leaders of one generation—those who would become the gentry and leaders of the next—in Virginia and beyond.[14]

The stress on college training should not obscure the contributions of Virginians with little formal instruction. A prime example is Senator James Barbour. Widely read and highly regarded for his legal talent, he received an honorary D.C.L. from Oxford University, championed schools for pauper children, and wrote the state's Literary Fund Act, seen by some as the forerunner of public education in the Old Dominion. In the same category is James Mercer Garnett, an educational pioneer who founded his own school in Essex County.

Religion

Of the seventy-nine men whose religious affiliations have been determined, fifty-three (67 percent) belonged to the Episcopal church or were closely associated with it (table 5). Of the remaining twenty-six, nineteen (24 percent) were Presbyterians in membership or ties. The Baptists are a distant third, with a mere five, including Congressman John Kerr, a minister. The latter circumstance suggests an observance in the breach of Virginia's constitutional provision against clergymen in office.[15]

Eight of the twelve (66 percent) senators were Episcopalians—the known denomination of slightly more than a majority of the House members. Generalizations about party lines are restricted by the unknown affiliation of nine of the nineteen Federalists. But the presence of forty-five Episcopalians among the Republican congressmen calls for revision of the view equating the Episcopalian gentry with the Federalists. Sectional patterns are, however, quite clear. Forty-six of the fifty-three Episcopalians lived east of the Blue Ridge; eleven of the nineteen Presbyterians resided west of it.

In accounting for the religious ties, the hand of the past seems decisive. The Episcopal church's former establishment, its close link with William and Mary and with local government, and its traditional Tidewater strength had made it the faith—in name if not in ardor—of the colonial gentry. Old-line Virginia families were eastern and Anglican, and so were most of the Dynasty congressmen. Some aristocrats conceded that a man could get to Heaven by different routes but felt that a gentleman would always choose the Episcopal one. Although the denomination declined sharply after the Revolution, it still claimed several converts among the congressmen.[16] In accounting for the preponderance of Episcopalians, one also must acknowledge the problem of sparse evidence for other groups and the validity of Norman K. Risjord's suggestion that the Anglicans "kept the best records."[17]

Presbyterian strength in the west reflects the association of that denomination with the Scotch-Irish who helped settle the Valley and who spilled over into the Piedmont and Trans-Allegheny regions in the mid-eighteenth century. Its imbalance of sixteen Republicans to three Federalists, however, challenges the contemporary

Table 5. Religion

	By house				By party				By section			
	Total	Both	USS	HR	R	F	(M)	?	TW	PM	V	TA
Episcopalian												
Definite	35	2	3	30	28	7	(3)	0	11	18	6	0
Probably, strong ties*	18	1	2	15	17	0	(1)	1	9	8	1	0
Total	53	3	5	45	45	7	(4)	1	20	26	7	0
Presbyterian												
Definite	5	0	0	5	4	1	0	0	0	2	0	3
Probably strong ties	14	1	1	12	12	2	0	0	2	4	3	5
Total	19	1	1	17	16	3	0	0	2	6	3	8
Other												
Baptist	5	0	0	5	5	0	0	0	0	2	0	3
Cath.-Epis. ties	1	1	0	0	1	0	0	0	1	0	0	0
Quaker ties	1	1	0	0	1	0	0	0	0	1	0	0
Total	7	2	0	5	7	0	0	0	1	3	0	3
Unknown	19	0	0	19	9	9	(1)	1	3	6	7	3

* "Probably" means a name identical to the congressman's is on a church roll in his home county or his name was mentioned in connection with a church activity; "strong ties" means this was the denomination of members of the congressman's family.

and scholarly interpretation that links the Scotch-Irish Presbyterians with the Federalist party.[18]

Perhaps the most unusual patterns are (1) the lack of definite information, quite often in sources otherwise a treasure of personal data, about the religious affiliations of nineteen of Virginia's ninety-eight congressmen and (2) the presence of only five Baptists and of no Methodists, despite their being the Commonwealth's largest denominations. Perhaps a French traveler perceived the truth when he observed that "few nations are less addicted to religious practices than the Virginians."[19] John B. Boles has concluded that "there is no solid evidence that revivalistic religion was a spur either to political philosophy or political participation" and that, "if anything, pietistic revivalism on an individual level decreased concern with politics."[20] The state's traditional leaders were Anglicans and the Dynasty era was one of Republican dominance, but it appears that religious ties determined neither a person's political views nor his success at the polls. In this vein one might note a number of lukewarm churchmen among the congressmen. These individuals could not be labeled, in the words of a Prince Edward native, "bigots to Presbytery" or to any sect.[21] That open skeptics like Thomas Mann Randolph held high office also suggests the absence of a religious yardstick in politics.

Several congressmen appear to have been influenced by the prevailing currents of deism in their youths or days at William and Mary, only to revert to a conventional faith as adults. Dr. James Jones returned from the University of Edinburgh to his native Amelia County and gained notoriety by his prominent role in the "Tom Paine Infidel Club," but he later joined the Presbyterian church and became an elder. John Randolph, George Tucker, William Cabell Rives, and Dr. Walter Jones went back to earlier religious tenets. On the other hand, Andrew Stevenson, John Wayles Eppes, and Thomas Mann Randolph apparently never lost their skepticism or belief in what William A. Burwell called a "genuine rational religion" not bound to any denomination.[22]

Military Service

Of Virginia's ninety-eight congressmen in the Dynasty era, at least fifty-nine held a state or national military position (table 6). As

Table 6. Highest military rank

	Total	By house			By party				By section			
		Both	USS	HR	R	F	(M)	?	TW	PM	V	TA
Revolutionary War												
Officers												
Lt. Col. or above	8	0	2	6	8	0	0	0	2	4	1	1
Major or below	4	0	0	4	4	0	(1)	0	2	2	0	0
Unspecified	4	1	0	3	3	1	0	0	0	1	2	1
Rank unknown	2	0	0	2	1	1	0	0	0	0	0	2
Total	18	1	2	15	16	2	(1)	0	4	7	3	4
War of 1812*												
Officers												
General	9	0	1	8	7	2	0	0	1	4	3	1
Lt. Col.-Col.	3	0	0	3	2	1	0	0	1	2	0	0
Major or below	8	0	0	8	6	1	0	1	3	1	2	2
Unspecified and general aide	8	0	0	8	7	1	0	0	3	3	1	1
Total	28	0	1	27	22	5	0	1	8	10	6	4
Nonwar militia												
General	6	1	1	4	6	0	0	0	0	1	4	1
Lt. Col.-Col.	12	1	1	10	10	2	0	0	2	5	1	4
Major or below	9	0	0	9	4	5	0	0	1	3	4	1
Unspecified	4	0	0	4	4	0	0	0	1	2	0	1
Total	31	2	2	27	24	7	0	0	4	11	9	7
Service in two or more of the above categories	18											
Unknown	39	4	1	34	30	8	(4)	1	11	20	5	3

* Not included are John Randolph, John Tyler, and George Tucker, whose service was very brief and under emergency circumstances.

measured by the highest rank held and allowing for service by some individuals in more than one category, the veterans subdivide as follows: the Revolutionary War (eighteen), the War of 1812 (twenty-eight), and the peacetime militia (thirty-one). With only a few possible exceptions, all were officers.

Seven of the twelve senators were veterans, and all served as officers, most with a colonelcy or higher. Even considering the unknown cases, a decided majority of representatives had military experience. The large number of "unknowns" renders hazardous any conclusions about party or sectional patterns, but the greatest involvement seems clearly to have been in the west. The explanation perhaps relates to the Indian wars of the recent past and to the settlement on western lands by veterans, such as General John Smith.

That most congressmen—as measured by section or party—had military careers is hardly surprising. White male Virginians participated as a matter of law in the militia, and many joined regular units, especially in the critical period between 1775 and 1815. Political, economic, and social leaders in peace often became leaders in time of war. Lower militia officers were nominated locally by the county courts and were of the same class—if not the same persons — as most justices themselves. On occasion during the War of 1812 and the Revolution, citizens raised volunteer companies, the support for which frequently came from the gentry, who also provided the officer material. Rarely, as in the case of Edward Colston, did a gentleman begin as a private in the ranks and work his way up to officer status.[23] Because lower appointments in the militia originated within the counties, neither party had a statewide monopoly on officers. The legislature chose the generals, who seldom were other than the kind of men who did the selecting, i.e., established gentry figures; partisan feelings did not prevent generalships from being awarded to Federalists like James Breckinridge and Charles Fenton Mercer.

Then as now, a military position could be politically advantageous. Service as an officer provided leadership training and brought contact with other gentlemen officers and with ordinary freeholders as well. That contact, of course, could demonstrate to militia citizens the unworthiness of a man for public trust. But, as a rule, military fame more likely carried with it political rewards. Of the eight congressmen who served as generals during the War of 1812, four were subsequently elected to Congress in the years 1816–18.[24]

Wartime associations frequently continued in peacetime. Well known is George Washington's earlier influence on such future Federalists as John Marshall, Henry Lee, and Daniel Morgan. Perhaps not as well known is the number of associates of Washington who later became Republicans. Stevens Thomson Mason was an aide to Washington at Yorktown, and Wilson Cary Nicholas commanded Washington's Life Guards. John and Abram Trigg, Samuel Jordan Cabell, and John Taylor served as officers under Washington's direction. All became Republicans. In fact, sixteen of the eighteen Virginia congressmen who attained their highest military rank during the Revolution became Republicans.

Also significant in an era of Revolutionary and post-Revolutionary patriotism is that political success did not require previous military service. John Randolph, the most consistent election winner among the congressmen, spent no more than a few days as a mounted sentinel during the War of 1812; John Tyler and George Tucker served only a few weeks in the same crisis. The fact that almost half of Virginia's senators and thirty-four of the eighty-six representatives had no known military record confirms the point. In addition, Alexander Smyth was "legislated out" of the army in 1813 amid disgrace and public ridicule yet was soon elected to the General Assembly and shortly after that to a long stay in the United States Congress. Henry St. George Tucker lacked the support of his men for a high militia position in November 1815 but had overwhelmingly won a congressional race earlier that year and won again two years later. Conversely, a candid citizen told General Daniel Morgan that the old soldier would be his choice as commander in chief in time of war, "but, sir, when I am to select a member of Congress, then I must vote for Mr. [Robert] Rutherford [Morgan's adversary]."[25]

Occupations

As shown in table 7, the vast majority of Virginia's congressmen earned their living from the soil. Of the thirty-seven with only a single occupation, twenty-one farmed, fourteen practiced law, one was a medical doctor, and one was a businessman. Of sixty with

Table 7. Occupation

	Total	By house			By party				By section			
		Both	USS	HR	R	F	(M)	?	TW	PM	V	TA
*Agriculture**												
Unspecified or under five slaves	6	0	0	6	4	2	0	0	0	3	1	2
Farmer	0	0	0	0	0	0	0	0	0	0	0	0
Small planter	4	0	0	4	3	1	(2)	0	1	2	1	0
Planter	8	0	1	7	8	0	(2)	0	3	5	0	0
Large planter	3	1	1	2	3	0	0	0	1	2	0	0
Total	21	1	1	19	18	3	(4)	0	5	12	2	2
Business	1	0	0	1	1	0	0	0	0	0	0	1
Professional												
Lawyer	14	0	0	14	12	1	0	1	5	4	3	2
Medical doctor	1	0	0	1	1	0	0	0	0	0	0	1
Total	15	0	0	15	13	1	0	1	5	4	3	3
Combination												
Ag.-lawyer												
Small farmer	3	0	0	3	2	0	0	1	2	0	1	0
Farmer	6	1	0	5	4	2	0	0	2	2	2	0
Small planter	10	2	1	7	9	1	0	0	2	6	2	0
Planter	11	1	1	9	10	1	(1)	0	5	6	0	0
Large planter	9	1	3	5	8	1	0	0	3	6	0	0
Ag.-M.D.												
Farmer	1	0	0	1	1	0	0	0	0	0	1	0
Small planter	3	0	0	3	3	0	0	0	1	2	0	0

Table 7. Occupation (cont.)

	Total	By house			By party				By section			
		Both	USS	HR	R	F	(M)	?	TW	PM	V	TA
Ag.-business												
Small farmer	3	0	0	3	0	3	0	0	0	0	1	2
Farmer	1	0	0	1	1	0	0	0	0	0	0	1
Small planter	1	0	0	1	1	0	0	0	0	1	0	0
Ag.-clergy												
Small farmer	1	0	0	1	1	0	0	0	0	1	0	0
Ag.-business-lawyer												
Farmer	2	0	0	2	1	1	0	0	1	1	0	0
Planter	1	0	0	1	0	1	0	0	0	0	1	0
Business-lawyer	8	0	0	8	3	5	0	0	0	0	3	5
Unknown	1	0	0	1	1	0	0	0	0	0	1	0

* Arbitrary categories were established on the basis of known agricultural ties and slaveholdings, as follows: small farmer (0–4 slaves), farmer (5–9), small planter (10–19), planter (20–50), and large planter (51 +).

more than one occupation, fifty-two made part of their income from farming. Altogether among the ninety-seven congressmen for whom an occupation has been determined, no less than seventy-three labored, wholly or in part, in agriculture, forty-two being lawyer-farmers. Business and medicine attracted a few, but almost always in conjunction with the law or the land. The dominant emphasis on law and farming can be seen in the dozen Virginia senators; ten labored in both fields and two in the latter only. None were doctors or businessmen as such; the handful of Virginians in those professions served in the House, along with fourteen lawyers and the lone clergyman-farmer.

Party lines reveal some occupational distinctions. The Federalists, for example, had ten of the seventeen persons with specific business interests (including five of eight businessmen-lawyers), while the Republicans claimed thirteen of fifteen individuals with a single profession. But this perhaps reflects sectional more than party lines. Most of the Federalists resided west of the Blue Ridge, a region which claimed fourteen of the seventeen men with business ties, while most of the Republicans and purely professionals lived in the east. Sectional lines indicate other important variations. Twenty-five percent of the eastern congressmen were full-time farmers, but only 13 percent of the westerners, and the latter typically operated smaller farms, with nine or fewer slaves. Of the fifty-two congressmen who combined another interest with agriculture, the east had forty-one and again a great majority of the large holdings. The five congressmen who practiced medicine full or part-time divided three in the east, two in the west.

The basic occupational pattern, then, is one of a great emphasis on law and agriculture, with more variety in employment and with more modest farms west of the Blue Ridge than east of it. Much of this only mirrors the state at large. Virginia was rural, and the vast majority of its citizens earned their way from its soil; the west had a more diverse economy with less slavery and smaller farms as a rule. The practice of law was, of course, not common to the general population, but it followed the traditional vocation of the state's public men, and persons whose income came exclusively from the law were more likely to reside in towns, most of which were in the east.

The leaders' preoccupation with the law and agriculture had many political overtones. A person raised on a farm and aspiring to ownership and profitable operation needed certain character traits that, as Sydnor argued, would aid a public career.[26] Managing a farm required business habits and an efficient use of one's time and money and gave a man both a degree of independence and a direct stake in society. It also demanded the ability to influence, if not get along with, persons of lower station (such as slaves, tenants, and small farmers) and of equal station (such as merchant-factors or fellow farmers who might be using one's mill or land). Since it involved a dawn-to-dusk direction of others, an acceptance of responsibility, and "the habit of command," success in farming both prepared one and advertised his ability for leadership elsewhere, logically in politics.

Farming could also provide an attendant system of values. "The independent planter and his cherished way of life," writes Robert McColley, "loom behind all the firm axioms of Virginia politics" in the Jeffersonian era.[27] These axioms included a belief in decentralized power and local self-government, "the peculiar institution," and the militia soldier rather than a standing army, as well as a hostility toward protective tariffs and governmental indebtedness and a sympathy toward France for purely commercial reasons. Of course, there were regional and partisan variations and even condemnations of some of the points in this essentially Republican creed.

Since gentlemen often inherited farms and increased them by marriage, they could accumulate large holdings in several counties. This brought familiarity beyond one's locale and perhaps a small constituency of renters or mill users who might also be dependent freeholders on election day. Planters often became embroiled in legal questions—marketing contracts, deeds, and debts—and in rural areas where full-time attorneys were rare, one might seek to learn a little law.

A connection with farming was only one of several reasons why a young Virginian might become acquainted with "old Coke" or Sir William Blackstone. The law offered the prospects of an immediate hard-cash income which could supplement or even sustain the uncertain returns of farming. And it might provide an escape from the land itself. The law also represented, in the words of Jefferson, "the most certain stepping stone to preferment in the political line,"[28] as was patently obvious to any ambitious young Virginian. In his immediate community, inspiration came from the county court, an assembly of powerful and often prestigious local citizens. The function of the court required at least a rough familiarity with the law and attracted a regular contingent of attorneys. Many counties had lawyer-politicians as justices, burgesses, and later delegates. At the colonial, state, or national level served generations of leaders who were also lawyers.

A man aspiring to wealth or fame might then seek to study if not to practice law. Madison did so "to deepen his understanding of public affairs."[29] Less dilettantish attorneys found more direct political benefits. Lawyers plied their profession before the county courts and became acquainted with local notables; from that connection often came political preference and appointment to office. Practicing before several courts or following a judicial circuit meant further contact with influential persons and freeholders alike, and might set the stage for a successful campaign for state senate or Congress in a multicounty district.[30]

A lawyer had an advantage among his fellow members of a county court or state legislature, since much of the business of both concerned legal questions. In times of crisis—such as the boiling conflict between England and America on the eve of the Revolution or during the great conventions of the Revolution itself—debates and decisions, arguments and policies were usually expressed in legal terms. Success in the law required a mental quickness and a verbal skill which were aids in electioneering, either on the speaker's platform or with the candidate's pen. It is little surprise that the great political orators and writers in Virginia had backgrounds in the law or that their speeches and writings were often legalistic in character. Amid controversy, lawyers advanced one particular interest against another, which is much of the dynamics of politics as well.

The training itself had a more immediate political influence. Most men learned the profession by a close association with some established attorney, perhaps in an academic context, such as the classes of George Wythe or St. George Tucker at William and Mary or the schools run by jurists like Creed Taylor or lawyers like John Wickham. But more commonly the link was an apprenticeship in which the fledgling observed and followed the instructions and guidance of the veteran. In either case, the mentor's political ideology—St. George Tucker's extreme states'-rightism or Creed Taylor's conservative Republicanism or John Wickham's tempered Federalism — was truly felt. Often the influence was parental, as in men like John Tyler, Littleton Tazewell, and Charles Fenton Mercer, who followed the profession and the politics of their distinguished fathers.

Taxable Property

Closely related to occupation and in a sense an extension of it is the category of taxable property, specifically the number of slaves, horses, and acres, owned by Virginia congressmen (table 8). County tax records make it possible to know what personal property (slaves and horses) 97 percent of the men possessed and how much land 96 percent of them held in their home counties at the time of their initial election to Congress.[31]

Slaves represented a considerable capital investment for the frequently indebted Virginians, and over half the congressmen had ten or more. About one-third of the politicians owned four or fewer slaves, three had none, but a tenth had fifty-one or more, and three had over 100. A third of the individuals declared fewer than five horses, but about a sixth had twenty-one or more. Land tax records show that five owned town lots only, forty-four had 750 acres or less, and forty-five 751 acres or more. Ten claimed less than 150 acres; six had over 4,000, with David S. Garland of Amherst County having the most at 5,453.

In general, Virginia's senators possessed more taxable property than their counterparts in the House. Eight of the twelve senators had twenty or more slaves, six had twenty-one or more horses, and eight had over a thousand acres. The thirty lowest holders of slaves and horses were all representatives, as were thirty of the thirty-one lowest landowners. The average Republican possessed more slaves, horses, and land than the average Federalist, but again sectional lines seem to be the key determinant. Republicans and Federalists were similar in the west, and westerners differed from the easterners. East of the Blue Ridge forty-nine of sixty-seven congressmen possessed ten slaves or more, and fourteen had at least twenty-one horses. In the west, only four of thirty-one individuals owned ten

Table 8. Taxable property

	Total	By house			By party				By section			
		Both	USS	HR	R	F	(M)	?	TW	PM	V	TA
Taxable property when elected												
Slaves												
0	3	0	0	3	2	0	0	1	1	1	0	1
1–4	27	0	0	27	19	7	0	1	4	5	6	12
5–9	15	1	0	14	8	7	0	0	3	4	7	1
10–19	19	2	1	16	17	2	(2)	0	5	12	2	0
20–50	19	1	2	16	17	2	(3)	0	8	10	1	0
51–99	11	2	2	7	10	1	0	0	3	8	0	0
100+	3	0	0	3	3	0	0	0	1	1	1	0
Unknown	1	0	1	0	1	0	0	0	1	0	0	0
Horses												
0	3	0	0	3	3	0	0	0	0	1	1	1
1–4	28	0	0	28	20	6	(1)	2	9	9	3	7
5–10	27	2	2	23	22	5	(1)	0	6	11	7	3
11–20	22	2	0	20	16	6	(3)	0	7	8	4	3
21+	15	2	4	9	13	2	0	0	3	11	1	0
Unknown	3	0	0	3	3	0	0	0	1	1	1	0

Table 8. Taxable property (*cont.*)

	Total	By house			By party				By section			
		Both	USS	HR	R	F	(M)	?	TW	PM	V	TA
Land												
Acres												
0–50	1	0	0	1	1	0	0	0	0	0	0	1
51–150	9	1	0	8	8	0	(1)	1	5	1	1	2
151–250	9	0	0	9	6	3	0	0	2	5	2	0
251–500	12	0	0	12	11	1	(1)	0	3	4	2	3
501–750	13	1	1	11	10	3	0	0	3	5	5	0
751–1000	6	1	0	5	5	1	(1)	0	2	4	0	0
1001–2000	22	2	4	16	19	3	(1)	0	6	13	1	2
2001–4000	11	1	0	10	7	4	0	0	2	4	1	4
4000+	6	0	1	5	4	2	(1)	0	1	3	1	1
Town lots only	5	0	0	5	3	1	0	1	1	1	2	1
Unknown	4	0	0	4	3	1	0	0	1	1	2	0
*Holdings of slaves and land upon leaving office**												
Same	9	0	1	8	5	4	0	0	2	1	2	4
Same/Loss	8	1	0	7	7	1	0	0	3	2	2	1
Same/Gain	16	1	2	13	12	4	0	0	4	9	2	1
Gain/Loss	16	2	1	13	11	5	(1)	0	3	9	2	2
Gain	33	2	1	30	29	2	(2)	2	9	14	5	5
Loss	11	0	1	10	8	3	(2)	0	4	4	2	1
Unknown	5	0	0	5	5	0	0	0	1	2	2	0

* This category measures the status of a congressman's holdings in slaves and land from his taking to his leaving office. If no change occurred, he is listed under "Same," if he gained in one form of property but lost in the other, he is listed as "Gain/Loss," etc.

or more slaves, and only one had twenty-one or more horses. Using 750 acres as a rough mean, easterners above that figure numbered thirty-five, westerners only ten; below 750 acres were twenty-eight easterners, sixteen westerners. Of the thirty-three congressmen owning in excess of a thousand acres, twenty-five resided in the east, only eight in the west.

Because of the availability of 95 percent of the property records for the respective years the ninety-eight men left office, some generalizations are possible on the status of their holdings while they served in Congress. A third of the congressmen gained both land and slaves; roughly a tenth lost in both categories. Nine individuals showed no change, sixteen stayed the same in one form of property but gained in the other, and eight remained the same in one but lost in the other. Sixteen congressmen increased in one category, decreased in the other. Overall, forty-nine had a clear gain, nineteen a clear loss. Significantly, in the area of absolute gains, identical percentages are shown for both senators and representatives, but the absolute loss column includes only one senator as against seventeen representatives.

Along party lines, only six of nineteen Federalists enjoyed an absolute increase, four registered no change, three lost in both slaves and acres, and five gained in one category but decreased in the second. The Republicans generally fared better, with gains in forty-one of seventy-two known estates. This partisan disparity might reflect the twin Republican advantages of greater initial wealth and longer tenure in office. Once more, however, the Blue Ridge might be the explanation; thirty-six of those who added property lived east of it and only thirteen to the west.

Perhaps the real significance of the property records is the depth they add to the occupation category. That most congressmen were sizable property owners reveals the scope of their agricultural ties. It also suggests established and clearly defined interests; state or national laws affecting slavery or trade, for instance, could hardly be moot questions to Virginians. The presence of sectional divisions in the holdings indicates why westerners disagreed sharply with easterners on those same issues of slavery and tariffs. Finally, the regional pattern among congressmen corresponds roughly to the pattern for the state at large. Eastern Virginia's concentration of slaves, for example, is reflected in the congressional holdings.

Political Profile

Of the ninety-eight individuals who represented Virginia in the halls of Congress from 1801 to 1825, seventy-seven stood with the Republicans, nineteen with the Federalists. The remaining two served late in the period and had no known party affiliations. Four Republican representatives—Matthew Clay, James Mercer Garnett, John Randolph, and Philip Thompson—and one Federalist—Edwin Gray—at some point in their careers deviated so sharply from party orthodoxy as to be labeled "Minority" men by contemporaries.

The seventy-seven Republicans include all twelve persons who were Virginia senators in the era. Six of the twelve served only in that capacity, but the remainder, earlier or later, were members of the House of Representatives. Sixty-five Republicans served only in the House. In terms of representatives alone, the Republicans dominated three of the state's four traditional sections (table 9). They had eighteen of twenty-two congressmen with party ties from the Tidewater, thirty of thirty-two from the Piedmont, and ten of fourteen from the Trans-Allegheny region. The fourth section—the Valley—was Federalist, but only by the narrow margin of nine to seven representatives.

A solidly minority party with no senators and less than a fourth of Virginia's representatives, the Federalists nonetheless had congressmen from all sections in addition to their slim majority in the Valley. The five "Minority" men divided between the Tidewater (two) and Piedmont (three) and were all representatives, as were the two individuals with no assignable party ties. By sections, the ninety-eight Virginians break down into twenty-six from the Tidewater, forty-one from the Piedmont, seventeen from the Valley, and fourteen from the Trans-Allegheny area.

As shown in table 10, fifty-eight of all Virginia representatives were natives of their districts, and thirty-two were at least forty years old at the time their terms began. Nineteen were forty-five or over; only thirteen were twenty-nine or younger. Virtually all had previously been in the state legislature, 50 percent had served at

Table 9. Parties and sections

Party	Tidewater			Piedmont				Valley			T-A[4]
	Total	East. Shore[1]	Other	Total	Loudoun	SS[2]	Other	Total	Upper Potomac[3]	Other	Total
Republican											
Both houses	6	1	1	4	0	2	2	1	0	0	0
Senate only	6	2	2	4	2	1	1	0	0	0	0
House only	65	18	17	30	0	13	17	7	0	7	10
Total	77	21	20	38	2	16	20	8	0	7	10
Federalist											
Both houses	0	0	0	0	0	0	0	0	0	0	0
Senate only	0	0	0	0	0	0	0	0	0	0	0
House only	19	4	2	2	2	0	0	9	6	3	4
Total	19	4	2	2	2	0	0	9	6	3	4
"Minority"											
Both houses	0	0	0	0	0	0	0	0	0	0	0
Senate only	0	0	0	0	0	0	0	0	0	0	0
House only	5	2	2	3	0	2	1	0	0	0	0
Total	5	2	2	3	0	2	1	0	0	0	0
Unknown											
Both houses	0	0	0	0	0	0	0	0	0	0	0
Senate only	0	0	0	0	0	0	0	0	0	0	0
House only	2	1	1	1	0	0	1	0	0	0	0
Total	2	1	1	1	0	0	1	0	0	0	0
Section totals (excluding "minority")	98	26		41				17			14

[1] The Eastern Shore consists of the counties of Accomack and Northampton.
[2] The Southside counties are Amelia, Brunswick, Buckingham, Campbell, Charlotte, Chesterfield, Cumberland, Dinwiddie, Greenville, Halifax, Lunenburg, Mecklenburg, Nottoway, Pittsylvania, Powhatan, and Prince Edward.
[3] The Upper Potomac counties of the northern Valley are Berkeley and Jefferson, which also had close ties to Hampshire (TA) and Loudoun (PM) counties.

least three terms (two years each), and 29 percent seven terms or more. Seventy-three had other local or state experience as well. Surprisingly, among the very few representatives who had not previously held a political office were notables John Randolph and William Branch Giles.

Once in Congress, the Virginians tended to remain. Of the ninety-eight, twenty-one stayed there thirteen or more years, and sixty at least five years. Twenty-three, however, served only one term or less. Careers were terminated by noncandidacy (forty-seven cases), resignation (seventeen), defeat (eighteen), and death (sixteen). Half the former congressmen later held a local or state political office; eighteen went on to federal positions, including that of the American presidency (John Tyler). Unfortunately, the contemporary evidence provides few clues as to the number of congressmen who declined to seek reelection for fear of a loss at the polls.

Compared to the representatives, the twelve Virginia senators tended to be older and more experienced in local, state, and federal positions. Ten of them served over five years in Congress, eight over nine, and one (Giles) over thirteen. Their most frequent method of leaving office was resignation (eight cases); six held subsequent political office at various levels of government.

In most categories, party differences are not extraordinary. For example, seventeen of the nineteen Federalists (89 percent) were veterans of the state legislature, but so were sixty-nine of the seventy-seven Republicans (90 percent). An exception was service in a national position before or after being in Congress. That category shows twenty-five Republicans and only one Federalist. The Federalists, however, held their own in state and local offices before or after a congressional career. A second exception is the relatively large number of Federalists (eleven of nineteen) who served only one term or less in Congress. Such brevity was matched by only ten of the seventy-seven Republicans. The Republicans also had most of the long careers in the period. Thirty-eight of them continued in Congress nine or more years; eighteen were there thirteen years or more. Thomas Newton, Jr., served thirty-one years altogether; John Randolph, about twenty-six; William Branch Giles, twenty-four; and William McCoy, twenty-two. Only three Feder-

Table 10. Political profile

	Total	By house			By party				By section			
		Both	USS	HR	R	F	(M)	?	TW	PM	V	TA
WHEN FIRST SEATED												
District native	58	5	NA	53	44	12	(4)	2	18	27	7	6
*Age**												
25–29	14	0	1†	13	13	1	(1)	0	3	7	2	2
30–34	23	0	1	22	16	6	(1)	1	8	10	1	4
35–39	22	0	2	20	17	5	(2)	0	9	6	5	2
40–44	16	0	3	13	13	3	(1)	0	2	10	2	2
45 or over	24	0	5	19	21	3	0	0	5	10	7	2
Unknown	5	0	0	5	3	1	0	1	0	2	1	2
Prior political service												
Terms in Va. legislature												
1–2	20	0	2	18	18	2	(1)	0	7	7	5	1
3–4	26	0	2	24	21	5	0	0	7	11	1	7
5–6	14	0	3	11	10	3	(2)	1	4	4	3	3
7 or more	27	0	4	23	20	7	0	0	7	13	5	2
Zero and Unknown	11	0	1	10	8	2	(2)	1	1	6	3	1
Other state or local‡	73	5	5	63	47	14	(3)	2	18	30	12	13
Federal	8	5	3	8	8	0	0	0	1	5	1	1

Table 10. Political profile (cont.)

	By house				By party				By section			
	Total	Both	USS	HR	R	F	(M)	?	TW	PM	V	TA
IN OFFICE												
Years served												
2 or less	23	0	1	22	10	11	0	2	5	8	4	6
3–4	15	0	1	14	13	2	(1)	0	3	7	3	2
5–8	19	1	1	17	16	3	(1)	0	4	8	4	3
9–12	20	4	3	13	20	0	0	0	6	7	5	2
13 or more	21	1	0	20	18	3	(3)	0	8	11	1	1
Career termination												
Death	16	1	2	13	15	1	(2)	0	5	8	3	0
Defeat	18	0	0	18	12	6	(2)	0	5	7	2	4
Noncandidacy	47	1	0	46	35	10	(1)	2	12	14	12	9
Resignation§	17	4	4	9	15	2	0	0	4	12	0	1
POSTCONGRESSIONAL SERVICE												
Federal	18	1	1	16	17	1	0	0	4	9	2	3
State or local	49	3	1	45	37	11	(2)	1	11	19	8	11

* "Age" totals are slightly skewed because the six Virginians who served in both houses are necessarily counted twice.

† Armistead T. Mason was under the constitutionally mandated age of thirty when he replaced William B. Giles (resigned) in 1816.

‡ Forty-nine of the ninety-eight congressmen served as county justices of the peace at some point in their careers.

§ At least nine congressmen resigned or did not seek reelection in order to accept another government post.

alists had as many as nine years, though Charles Fenton Mercer remained in office almost twenty-three, some of them as a Whig.

Among the sectional distinctions, easterners had a higher percentage of district natives (67 to 42 percent), which is understandable given the deeper roots of the eastern population. Westerners had a higher percentage of congressmen forty-five years or older when seated (29 to 22 percent), and the east had a higher percentage of congressmen under thirty-five (42 to 29 percent). The sections split the prior experience category; the east had more men who had been active on the federal level, the west more on the state and local levels.

In a general sense, three conclusions can be drawn from the political profile. First, the Virginia senators were veteran state politicians, as measured by age, experience, and service. Also, the fact that eight of the twelve senators resided in the Piedmont and only three in the Tidewater mirrors a basic shift in power within the General Assembly to the Piedmont. Second, the Federalists operated on an exceptionally narrow base. Of their nineteen congressmen, two resided on the Eastern Shore and eight in the upper Potomac counties of Loudoun, Jefferson, Berkeley, and Hampshire — all having similar economic interests and needs and a strong Federalist tradition. Eleven of the nineteen Federalists served one term or less, ten ended their careers by declining to seek reelection, and two others resigned—suggesting a rather shallow party commitment. Federalist candidates decreased in numbers throughout the period until only a handful entered the lists in the 1820s.[32]

Third, the political profile reveals fewer sectional distinctions than the social and economic categories. A possible explanation is the fact that the basic political unit in Virginia was the county. Whether located in the east or west, it had justices, militia officers, and burgesses (delegates); from that general pool of leaders came most congressmen, who were elected by districts almost always completely within a section, such as the Valley. Thus the prior and subsequent political experience of easterners and westerners would be predictably similar.

The ninety-eight Virginia congressmen who served from 1801 to 1825 have now been identified by their major social, economic, and political characteristics, with attention given to party and sectional patterns. But the collective biography itself must next be examined for important insights into the leadership class and political culture of the Old Dominion in the Dynasty era.

III

Patterns from
a Profile

The individual categories presented in chapter 2 collectively merge into a representative picture of political leadership in the Old Dominion. But what does the resulting group portrait reveal about politics in the Dynasty era? At least two general conclusions seem warranted. First, sectionalism explains as much or more about political strife than does either class or party division. Second, the congressmen formed an elite group, generally in the mold of the "great" Revolutionary generation.

The Politics of Section and Personality

The emphasis on sectionalism rather than class or party rests on two dimensions of the collective biography. First, Federalists and Republican congressmen alike were local notables with roughly similar profiles, thus minimizing the possibility of genuine conflict between "aristocrats" and "democrats" (whatever the rhetoric) or between rival classes in the social and economic structure. Second, congressmen within sections shared specific commonalities regardless of party and often differed with the congressmen of other sections, again without regard to party. This fundamental distinction can be made in most categories examined. The eastern region, for example, had a higher percentage of old-line Virginians, of natives (state and district), of English descendants, of notable families and prominent marriages, of college graduates, of Episcopalians, of large property owners, and of congressmen serving more than one term.

Within the composite biography, eastern Republicans were more like eastern Federalists than western Republicans, and what could be said about most western Federalists could be said about most

Patterns for a Profile

western Republicans. Eastern Federalists Thomas Bayly, Edwin Gray, Thomas Griffin, and John Stratton fit the old-line eastern Republican image very closely.[1] On the other hand, western Federalists Hugh Caperton, Daniel Sheffey, Jacob Swoope, and others were non-English, short-time Virginians with little formal education. They resembled western Republicans such as the three Jacksons, William McCoy, and William McKinley. Of course, there are exceptions to the rule, but, generally speaking, within sections the congressmen of both parties were more alike than different in their biographical profiles, and the real distinctions were between sections, not parties.[2]

This similarity in personal traits among congressmen within a section often manifested itself in a commonality of interests, positions, even ideologies on what typically were domestic issues. To cite only two examples: Edwin Gray (F) moved easily into the "Minority" camp of his fellow easterners, all erstwhile Republicans; westerners James Breckinridge (F) and John George Jackson (R) took similar stands on such questions as internal improvements, national defense, and—within Virginia—constitutional reform.[3] This regional-interest pattern, in minimizing conflicting issues within sections, often focused elections on competing personalities. The result was what might be called personality politics as opposed to issue or partisan politics. The concept neatly fits the traditional informality of Virginia elections and the minimal statewide party organization and discipline during this era.

The idea of personality politics explains, at least in part, the large number of uncontested congressional elections. A deemphasis on divisions by principle or party lessened the significance of contests themselves and often left the field to a sole contender of local respectability. Of 325 separate congressional races from 1799 through 1825, 46 percent appear to have been uncontested. Of the contested elections, only half pitted candidates of rival parties, another reflection of the focus on personality.[4]

To put it another way, in exactly 50 percent of the contested congressional elections, the candidates came from the same party. "Both of the candidates [for Congress] are well qualified for the station," reported one common election summary. "Both are genuine republicans and inflexible adherents to sound political principles—Victory is thus left to depend alone on the personal popularity and address of the contending candidates."[5] Two of numerous examples were races between solid Republicans John Tyler and Andrew Stevenson, which turned on "the naked question of personal popularity,"[6] and Thomas Mann Randolph's challenge to Republican stalwart Samuel Jordan Cabell in 1803. Incumbent Federalists Francis White (1815) and Edward Colston (1819) lost to Federalist rivals Magnus Tate and Thomas Van Swearingen, respectively. Occasionally the contests, as in those between John Wayles Eppes and John Randolph, involved opposing factions within a party, but generally the contestants were indistinguishable by their principles or party ties.

In the context of personality politics, a popular man once elected was difficult to defeat; 217 of the 246 incumbents who sought reelection were victorious. One might also assume some connection between this personality focus, the large number of uncontested elections, and the intraparty races on the one hand and Virginia voter apathy on the other.

The concept of sectional and personality politics also helps to explain some otherwise unusual developments. James Breckinridge emerged as a Federalist leader in the Valley, but his more famous brother John served as a Republican senator from Kentucky and briefly as Jefferson's attorney general. Daniel Sheffey, another staunch Federalist from the Valley, was succeeded in Congress by his law partner, Alexander Smyth, a Republican, and in 1817 Federalist James Pindall replaced his friend and business partner, Republican John George Jackson. Congressman John Smith had two prominent sons—one a Republican, one a Federalist. Jabez Leftwich was a Republican congressman, but his brother was a Federalist presidential elector. Of course, on occasion ideological considerations conjoined with personal ones. The Barbour brothers, James and Philip, had virtually identical profiles. They had the same parents, same youthful influences, same religion, same Orange County residences, and same occupations. To complete the picture, they married daughters of the same prominent local politician. Although both Barbours considered themselves Republicans, James grew increasingly nationalistic and favored legislation in the United States Senate which his brother Philip, a states'-righter,

Patterns for a Profile

opposed in the House. Later James supported Adams and became a Whig while Philip went with Jackson and the Democrats.[7]

The Continuance of a Leadership Class

The second main conclusion drawn from the composite profile is that the congressmen formed an elite group among their Virginia contemporaries and were in the tradition of earlier elites. The congressmen were among a select few persons of their day in social prominence, economic standing, and political rank. In this general way and in most biographical traits, they were like the previous generation of Virginia leaders, despite some differences that kept them from being identical elites.

Whether a congressman was Republican or Federalist, eastern or western, of Revolutionary vintage or after, he was set apart and above the ordinary citizens of the Old Dominion in the Dynasty era. Almost every category of the profile supports this rather predictable conclusion. Eighty-five percent of the congressmen had two or more notables as kinsmen, a majority married into other prominent families, and at least 54 percent were Episcopalians. In a period when blacks, women, and most white males received little if any formal education, over half of the congressmen were college alumni. In the militia or in wartime service, the great preponderance of Virginians served in the ranks, but the congressmen, almost without exception, were officers, and most were lieutenant colonels or above. In wealth, the average adult Virginian owned few or no slaves; perhaps a majority even lacked the minimum fifty unimproved acres necessary to vote. But at least 96 percent of the congressmen possessed slaves, and 53 percent had at least ten. Fifty-eight of the congressmen had five hundred acres or more. The Virginia system of government had relatively few local offices, yet a majority of the congressmen held or would hold positions on that level. Only two men from each county were elected to the lower house of the Virginia legislature, yet nearly nine of every ten congressmen had that distinction, and nearly a third of them served for seven or more terms.

In a sense the senators formed an elite within an elite, because they were generally better educated, wealthier, and had more family notables and political experience than their counterparts in the

House. Of course, senators and representatives alike shared with most white Virginians the pertinent traits of being largely natives of English descent, of an agricultural occupation, and of deep origins in the colony. But on the balance, in most of the politically significant categories, the congressmen stood on a social and economic level clearly distinct from and superior to their fellow citizens.

Were these leaders in a traditional mold? In some regards leadership in the Jeffersonian period departs from the pattern shown by studies of the earlier political elites.[8] The Dynasty profile reveals an increase in non-Episcopalians and non-English strains and a decrease in land speculators. There are also more full-time lawyers and fewer men with truly large holdings in land and slaves. These differences indicate the first stage of a transition which in time would greatly alter the prototypical political leader in the Old Dominion. But in the Jeffersonian era the transition was merely foreshadowed, not fulfilled. Most Virginia leaders continued to be experienced politicians; "well connected" and educated; of British stock; Episcopal; comfortably propertied, slave-owning farmer-lawyers; militarily experienced; and native sons. On the balance, the biographical profile shows more continuity than change. Jack P. Greene found that the eighteenth-century elite "were wealthy, derived part of their income from planting, were often related to the great Virginia families, were Anglicans, were of English (or at least British) origin, had attained a high educational level for the time and place, were experienced in local politics and came from areas settled for at least a generation."[9] That statement describes the Dynasty leadership to a surprising degree and suggests the extent to which an elite pattern had been perpetuated.

But was there a change in the leadership class during the Dynasty era itself? After all, a profile of the ninety-eight congressmen as a group imposes a static quality on the period and might obscure significant modifications that occurred within the quarter century. How alike were the delegations, for example, of 1801–2 (twenty-one members), 1811–12 (twenty-five); and 1823–24 (twenty-six)? On examination, the overall picture is continuity, not change, as shown in table 11.

Of course, some predictable shifts took place. As time passed, there was a sharp decline in the number of congressmen who had been born before 1765 and who had been in the Revolutionary

Patterns for a Profile

Table 11.   Congressional profile over time: personal data

	1801–2 delegation (19 HR, 2 USS)	1811–12 delegation (23 HR, 2 USS)	1823–24 delegation (23 HR, 3 USS)
Virginia natives	90%	92%	85%
District natives	68	61	56
Born before 1765	62	40	12
Pre-1700 Virginia origins	66	52	65
English ancestry	81	60	58
Two or more notable kinsmen	95	96	92
One or more notable kinsmen	67	52	62
Notable marriage	38	52	65
William and Mary alumni	33	32	50
Other college alumni	15	16	16
Episcopalians	71	60	69
Revolutionary War veterans	48	28	4
Other veterans	57	56	89
Farmers	38	32	19
Farmer-lawyers	47	48	57
Lawyers	10	4	12
Farmers-other	0	4	8
Lawyers-other	5	12	4
0–4 slaves	14	20	31
5–19 slaves	34	36	27
20–50 slaves	33	24	19
50+ slaves	19	16	23
0–150 acres	0	8	16
151–750 acres	38	29	45
751–2,000 acres	38	21	19
2,000+ acres	19	24	20

War. Also evident in this profile over time is a decrease in those with English ancestry and with experience in local government prior to a congressional career. As the decades passed, fewer individuals made their livelihood merely from agriculture; on the rise was the number of persons with smaller holdings in land and slaves.

Nevertheless, there is a general continuance of the basic profile.

The Times and the Men

The delegations of 1801–2 and 1823–24 are remarkably similar in percentage of native Virginians (90 to 85 percent) and of congressmen with pre-1700 family roots in the Old Dominion (66 to 65 percent), with ties to two or more notable individuals (95 to 92 percent), and with one or more other congressmen as relatives (67 to 62 percent). Virtually all the politicians were military veterans, a majority were of English stock, and most still were Episcopalians (71 to 69 percent).

The typical congressman in 1801–2, 1813–14, and 1823–24 was a lawyer-farmer and owned a substantial amount of personal and real property. Thirty-nine percent or more of all three delegations had at least 20 slaves and 751 acres. Experience in local government declined, but 58 percent of the delegation of 1823–24 still had so served (table 12). Furthermore, whether at the beginning of the Dynasty era or its end, virtually every congressman had prior service in the General Assembly.

In the category of "age when seated," the bracket between twenty-five and thirty-four years claimed 43 percent of the 1801–2 group and 46 percent of those in 1823–24. Once elected, the members of both delegations tended to stay in office a long time; 62 percent of the 1801–2 congressmen served nine or more years, as did 65 percent of the 1823–24 congressmen. An election defeat terminated the careers of only 14 percent of the 1801–2 group and 12 percent of the 1823–24 delegation. Finally, the number of William and Mary alumni actually increased from 33 percent in 1801–2 to 50 percent in 1823–24, and the percentage of congressmen with notable marriages rose from 38 to 65 percent.

Thus, even when changes within the Dynasty period are considered, the old elite model generally holds true. What accounts for the continued presence of this type of leader, for the lack of a successful challenge or competition from other types or other vested-interest blocs? This is a central question about Virginia politics in the Dynasty period and merits an extended treatment. In general, the explanation is found in what, for the gentry leader, proved to be a peculiar internal security. This security reflected at least seven pervasive conditions.

The first condition offering security arose from the nature of the Virginia party system. Political leaders had traditionally come from

Table 12.   Congressional profile over time: political data

	1801–2 delegation (19 HR, 2 USS)	1811–12 delegation (23 HR, 2 USS)	1823–24 delegation (23 HR, 3 USS)
Party			
Republican	90%	68%	92%
Federalist	10	20	8
Minority	0	12	0
Prior experience			
Local government	81	68	58
General Assembly			
Terms: 1–2	10	12	27
3–4	19	36	23
5–9	23	28	34
10 or more	14	16	12
Other state or federal	33	32	23
Congressional service			
Age when seated			
25–34	43	28	46
35–44	38	48	42
45 and over	19	24	12
Years served			
1–2	5	8	0
3–4	5	0	12
5–8	28	16	23
9–12	14	20	23
13 and over	48	56	42
Career termination			
Death	43	32	15
Defeat	14	16	12
Noncandidacy	33	40	54
Resignation	10	12	19

the gentry class, a pattern continued by the founders of the Federalist and Republican parties in the Commonwealth. The Republicans effectively exploited their early domination internally by the self-serving election laws they passed and externally by the many assets, not the least of which was prestige, resulting from their association with the Dynasty presidents. One-party rule minimized competition for ballots; thus, Virginia politicians, unlike those in some other states, never had to court the lower classes by offering them extended suffrage or other changes. The party structure remained informal and flexible. It absorbed "new" or "outside" men, such as those of pioneer families west of the Blue Ridge, who might otherwise have become disruptive or competitive elements. The Republicans benefited much—and their gentry rule was likewise enhanced—by keeping grass-roots supporters well informed as to party correctness. Success in this regard resulted from the presence of so many Virginians in the national political structure, the party's control of the state government, and the efficacy of such internal means of public communication as Ritchie's *Enquirer.*

A second source of security came from the continuance of certain traditions from the political culture of colonial and Revolutionary Virginia. The "gentlemen freeholder" system described by Sydnor had become ingrained through generations of practice, and it continued to fill potent social and psychological needs among nonelite classes. Gentry rule was shielded from change by the customary voter apathy and the presumption that candidates did not have to articulate specific programs or campaign on concrete issues. It was further protected by the fact that Virginia's constitution had no provision for amendment and that the process of calling and conducting a convention for that purpose was cumbersome and difficult. Finally, the gentry benefited from the inherent conservatism that Virginia shared with most rural societies, as well as from the tendency of past political institutions, symbols, and processes—in this case of the gentry mold—to be viable in the public mind beyond their viability in fact and the not uncommon deference by persons of lower status to those of a higher one.

A third condition was the result of Virginia's static qualities. The gentry leadership operated within what was by and large a stable and homogeneous society, unchallenged by any dynamic religious or social reform movements. The Second Great Awakening at the turn of the century failed to have "any appreciable effect on politics" in Virginia, "except perhaps even to lessen political participation."[10] Disestablishment had earlier deflated other religious pressures. Migration removed potentially malcontented or dissident persons of talent and influence.

The Dynasty generation looked to the past for its ideologies and values and relished most those of a conservative strain. The gentry-serving Constitution of 1776 had been little altered—and indeed was most difficult to alter—on the key points of representation and suffrage, and the dominant legal thought of the period tended to be retrospective and traditional. Economically, the gloomy eastern Virginia stagnated, and its spokesmen bemoaned the pattern of depression and decline. The absence of growth or of any substantial departures from an agrarian focus meant that few new interest blocs or classes developed to challenge the long-standing economic interests represented by gentry leaders. Furthermore, the dominant social and economic interests in Virginia registered equivalent power in government. The political elite in the state mirrored the social and economic elite.

The booming region west of the Blue Ridge was more fluid and dynamic in its social, economic, and political situation and more heterogeneous in population. The western challenge, however, was to eastern, not gentry, leadership because the leaders in the west were also upper-class, and some descended from old Virginia families or had ties to them. Also, the western leaders shared the essentially agricultural and legal occupations of their eastern counterparts. Finally, the potential political power of the west suffered somewhat by the very heterogeneous quality of western society, for clearly defined and different immigrant or ethnic blocs could be divisive and competitive. Of course, nonsocial factors such as the eastern control of the General Assembly also muted the potency of any western challenge.

Virginia's peculiar nonpartisan politics also contributed to the security of its leaders. The state's politically significant population remained limited and well defined. Within this group of eligible voters, power rested on the consent of an even smaller number, i.e., a majority of the actual voters. If only 50 percent of the adult white males had the right to vote in the era—to use Jefferson's yardstick — and only 40 percent of those eligible actually voted, then only 20 percent of the total adult white males participated, and a mere 11 percent of the total adult white males determined who was elected.[11] Of course, the adult white males constituted only a fraction of the total population. That a candidate needed only a modicum of adult white males to win an election is all the more significant given the presence of widespread family connections among the elite in politics. The single-slate, statewide canvass for presidential electors, legislative selection of United States senators, and the powerful Virginia tradition of General Assembly instruction of the congressmen all compounded the power of the ruling group. It also meant that further dominance, or dominance on higher levels of government, followed naturally from control of the lower levels.

The fifth feature promoting security for the state's leaders was personal influence from above or at the top of the political system. The presence of so many distinguished Virginians in the federal government was a unique circumstance. These men influenced state politics by a potent pull from above which strengthened gentry leadership. For example, Jefferson's recruitment of congressmen meant a continued role in government for talented but often politically reluctant members of the gentry. The effect was to make this type of leadership stronger than it would have been otherwise.

Restricted mobility also deterred challenges to leadership by the gentry. Travel in Jeffersonian Virginia required time, patience, physical endurance, and on occasion ingenuity and luck.[12] The gentry had the most resources for movement from place to place, and the costs came high in an essentially isolated, rural countryside, with stretches of near primeval timberland crisscrossed by countless streams and rivers and "roads, proverbial for badness, even in America."[13]

"I entered a woods," a traveler recalled about a horseback trip in 1813, "and for three days continued in a wilderness whose inhabitants were wolves, bears, deer, and other wild beasts. [For nearly a hundred miles] I saw not more than 10 or 15 huts. . . . The road by name, is chiefly a foot path, and is thro swamps and wet vallies and over high hills."[14] Wretched ferries and rotten bridges might be the only alternatives to a swollen river, and they were equally hazardous to the health, as some eminent Virginians could attest.[15] John Randolph waded through a stream "for nearly a mile up to the saddle-bags,"[16] and another congressman drowned trying to cross the Potomac, the last of the many rivers separating the Commonwealth from the nation's capital.[17] Directions? Groaned one visitor to the state, "if perchance you meet an inhabitant and enquire your way, his directions are, if possible, more perplexing than the roads themselves, for he tells you to keep the right hand path, then you'll

Patterns for a Profile

come to an old field, you are to cross that, and then you'll come to the fence of such a one's plantation, then keep that fence, and you'll come to a tobacco house; after you have passed that, you'll come to a road that has three forks . . . keep the right hand fork for about half a mile, and then you'll come to a creek."[18]

The time required? In 1813 a congressman lamented, "The roads . . . are worse than usual; it takes 38 hours to travel from Fredericksburg to Alexandria—the distance 50 miles." By 1820 the mail stage could traverse this same distance in a speedy sixteen hours. Going by the stage, however, could mean sharing limited space with "twelve . . . squalling children, stinking negroes, and republicans smoking cigars!"[19] Merely getting from home to Washington took Jabez Leftwich a week by stage from Bedford County, William Cabell Rives several days from Albemarle, and John Clopton about five from New Kent—all in the eastern half of the state.[20] On the campaign trail west of the mountains in 1809, John George Jackson once journeyed 50 miles to one county, 130 to another, 120 to a third, and 60 to a fourth.[21] In short, few freeholders had the wherewithal, much less the desire, to emulate the legislator from western Virginia who in 1819 "traveled horseback . . . over buffalo trails to reach Richmond."[22]

And finally, public office presented other clear and mundane burdens, especially at the highest levels; gentlemen could surmount them only with difficulty and most other Virginians not at all. An obvious requirement was time. Few men could afford to devote most of several or more weeks on the campaign trail. During election season in 1805, one distressed incumbent admitted not having "even one day to devote to my private affairs or more urgent law business."[23] Campaigning served only as a prelude to the real demands of the job. Congressional sessions usually lasted several months but occasionally took the better part of a year.

Another essential consideration was money. Campaign costs, though probably nominal in the Jeffersonian era, were prohibitive to the mass of freeholders, and victory posed other problems. For his trip to Washington one congressman had to borrow $45; another estimated $50 "to be amply sufficient for defraying expenses on our journey home."[24] As their time in office lengthened, the financial burden often increased to an intolerable level. Congressmen commonly served at an economic sacrifice,[25] and several paid dearly for it. Charles Fenton Mercer, after a long and distinguished career of almost twenty-three years, found himself badly strapped, and John Dawson died in office without funds and was buried "at the public expense."[26] Many incumbents declined reelection, in Henry St. George Tucker's phrase, due to "imperious circumstances alone."[27] Other politicians, sensing the problem, refused election to the United States Senate or support for a congressional race.[28] As William Wirt described a similar position, "This honour of being a Chancellor is a very empty thing, stomachically speaking; that is, although a man be full of honour his stomach may be empty; or, in other words, honour will not go to market and buy a peck of potatoes."[29] Unless a person had some financial independence—and few Virginians did—congressional service was economically questionable.

There was also a different but equally high cost in being away from home. In an age of uncertain and often insecure communication and transportation, separation could be a great financial or personal burden. The operation of a farm, or business, or a legal practice in absentia required able associates, overseers, or family members — and even then might not succeed. "My [legal] practice," complained George Tucker, "was fast leaving me by my going to Congress."[30] More than one statement of resignation followed the reasoning of Abraham B. Venable, who notified the governor: "the greatest length of time that I have been in the public service, has so far disabled me from attending my private affairs as to make the measure rather a matter of necessity than of choice."[31]

Being removed from loved ones could be especially grievous. "I am totally in the dark as to my family," wrote Hugh Nelson, imploring a friend to investigate, "having never heard a syllable from them since I left them."[32] One congressman's wife, at home, depressed, and pregnant, refused to write her husband for over two months; the husband had no better time of it and confessed he was "miserable here alone; never, never will I come again without you."[33]

Being far away when sickness or even death struck a wife or child or friend reflected the baleful side of public service. So did the necessity to be a father for a young but distant son, as related in this poignant letter:

I wish you, my dear son, as much as you can to attend to your studies so as to be improving. When you amuse yourself with your gun (which had best be but seldom) be careful of yourself in loading or at any other time that the muzzle may not be ever pointed towards yourself or any one else for fear she should go off at half bent, and also be careful not to go in the way of any trees falling on you when the negroes are cutting—make it known to them when you are going up to where they are cutting them. When you are at the mill be careful of not falling in the ponds or canals — and also be careful of not going near the gears of any of the wheels when the mill is at work, for fear any of the cogs or other parts should catch hold of your clothes.—Take care of yourself in all respects and pray to God to bless your dear Mamma, yourself, brother and sisters—for which blessing is the constant prayer of, my dear son,

your truly affectionate father[34]

Separation also meant the sacrifice of certain accustomed benefits. One Tidewater senator complained of the difficulty in obtaining Smithfield hams.[35] Others missed a prized horse, a circle of friends, a seat on the local court, or a favorite minister.[36] Life in the capital was tiresomely inconvenient; John Clopton wrote his son: "I want to get home before Congress will adjourn—Irksome—irksome indeed is my situation!—and what a miserable time have I spent during the greater part of a number of winters at this place in pain and helplessness, dependent upon strangers, while I have had at home so many servants that would have been at my command, had I been there!—Even to get this and other letters carried to the post office is as a favor. How long—how long have I borne such a state!"[37] Thomas Evans, who declined to seek reelection in 1801, spoke for many in stating, "I look forward with great private satisfaction at the approach of the day, which dismisses me from political life and restores me to my family and friends."[38]

Physical and social costs were extracted as well. Travel to and from Washington was uncomfortable when it was not time-consuming or dangerous. The boardinghouse existence of many congressmen seemed monotonous and disconcerting. "Life in Washington is very dull," wrote John Stratton, "We have to go to Alexandria for amusement, and something good to eat."[39] "The atmosphere of this place, physical and political," wrote John Randolph from Georgetown, "seems like the Dog Hole near Naples, to be fatal to *animation* in every place." On another occasion he advised a friend: "When you go 'a hunting' for lively and pleasant society let me recommend new or old Holland to you in preference to this 'metropolic' of darkness. The fields here are parched to desolation, and the life we lead rather resembles that of a garrison in Siberia than the Capital of a great country."[40] No doubt some Virginia congressmen echoed William Wirt, who asked, "What is there in the rough, unbuilt, hot and desolate hills of Washington, or in its winter rains, mud, turbulence and wrangling, that could compensate me for all those pure pleasures of the heart I should lose in such a vicinity?"[41]

Newcomers who arrived with high expectations about Washington society often met with dismay and disillusionment. William Cabell Rives, for one, got a preview when he visited the city as a young man. Full of anticipation, he was shocked by the dull and rude quality of life even among notable statesmen. Calhoun, for example, silently ate among distinguished company, then went to sleep, and snored, as Rives put it, "in horrible discord, without seeming to arouse any notice among the rest of the group." The artificial manners and dress of the diplomatic corps and the incoherent wanderings and flagrantly bad grammar of congressional orators also repelled the young Virginian.[42] A representative from a western district described Washington as "a cheerless, artificial world of gaiety and politeness where the true character is hid and we know little of the temper of those we meet with."[43] The same gentleman professed to be "somewhat shocked at the dress of the wife of the British minister . . . whose neck [was] bare almost to the waist."[44]

Illness commonly increased amid Washington's cold and damp winters and often brought strange doctors and desperate cures or, perhaps worse, solitude and anxiety.[45] "Alone and sick you may easily fancy my situation," wrote one senator, while a representative lamented: "Much distress of both body and mind do I suffer. To leave all the comforts of home to be here in my situation. O what a fool have I been!"[46]

Congressmen had to bear the tedium of committee work and the frustration of all public men about whether they were accomplishing anything worthwhile anyway,[47] as legislative hopes often fell prey to "the worst passions of human nature."[48] Conscientious representatives struggled against the demands on their time and attention. "Every five minutes someone's announced," wrote a congressman about the favor seekers. The same man also confessed that he kept waiting for half an hour one such person "under the pretense that I was unwell."[49] John Page hoped his constituents would understand his inability to write more often "owing entirely to my applying my whole time to their Business here." Page added he scarcely had time for "Exercise by Day and rest by Night as is necessary for Health."[50]

There were other hazards. Virginians were known to duel[51] and often found the lure of cards irresistible, and costly. George Tucker lost "nearly a thousand dollars" in a whist game with other congressmen and a "notorious swindler . . . [who] wore spectacles," Tucker thought, "to see the marks or scratches made on particular cards while he was dealing."[52]

A public man had to follow the straight and narrow path of personal rectitude since, as one put it, "the world is extremely censorious."[53] He also had to take criticism, which might make him share Andrew Stevenson's complaint: "I gave up a lucrative profession, with the prospect of increased wealth, to devote myself to the public service, and now I am to be repaid with denunciation and abuse!"[54]

In short, the glitter of public life was often tarnished by myriad mundane burdens and practical considerations, well summarized by a North Carolina congressman who acknowledged:

My dear friend, there is nothing in the service exclusive of the confidence and gratitude of my constituents, worth the sacrifice. The enhanced price of subsistance renders it at present unprofitable, and unworthy of the talents essential to the service; the business is arduous, when alone, on dry books, writing and study, when in company, in debate, counteracted in our best designs, and often on the brink of success disappointed; and far removed from domestic happiness, cut off from family and friends. For this no pecuniary equivalent is adequate; nothing but a consciousness of having discharged my duty, and of having obtained full confidence, could be to me a complete reward. Having secured this, I could freely give place to my fellow citizen, that others too might obtain the consolation due to faithful service.[55]

The Times and the Men

Other restrictions that an ordinary freeholder might be quick to recognize were the implicit requirement for literacy, the clear advantage of some legal training, and the willingness if not the talent to make a public address and to engage in other electioneering practices. Less easy to define but undoubtedly a factor was the general standard of social deportment and verbal dexterity that most gentlemen possessed but that might make a rough-hewn freeholder feel inadequate by comparison.[56]

Such varied, complex, and severe barriers to service explain why ordinary freeholders appeared so rarely at the highest levels of government. The obstacles suggest the great burden of holding office, even for the gentry, and raise the question of why men undertook it. With demands so large and with concrete financial gains so few, public service must be understood in the personal terms of prestige, patriotism, and noblesse oblige—all traditions of the Virginia gentry.[57] Finally, the barriers indicate why 46 percent of the congressional races went uncontested and why incumbents tended to remain in office until they died, resigned, or chose to retire.

And yet, despite the impediments and burdens, at least 537 candidates sought to represent their fellow Virginians in the United States Congress during the Dynasty years. For the prospective officeholder, the first step was to learn how and when to throw one's hat into the ring.

Part Two

Political Practices

in

Jeffersonian

Virginia

IV

Becoming a Candidate

There was an art to becoming a candidate for Congress in the Dynasty era, and the way a man practiced it could determine his success in an election. The announcement to stand for a poll often followed months of negotiation among influential constituents, thoughtful if not elaborate planning, and a general testing of the chances for victory. Public notice of candidacy was neither precipitate nor casual; it occurred frequently at least halfway into the campaign itself.

Prerequisites and Motivation

How did a Virginian become a candidate? In the first place he had to meet a specific legal requirement and less concrete but equally restricting social and economic prerequisites. According to the law, a candidate had to be "some discreet and proper person, . . . a freeholder . . . who shall have been a bona fide resident for twelve months within" his district.[1] The freehold qualification alone ruled out perhaps a third to a half of the adult white males. The cost in time and money of a campaign (and of leaving home to serve if elected), the implicit requirement for literacy, the clear advantages of legal training and family ties, and the political necessity of contacts in counties beyond one's residence were among the extralegal conditions that generally limited contenders to the gentry.

Eligibility was one consideration; ambition and availability were others. While motivation is always an individual matter and never completely ascertainable, it seems fair to say that—considering the burden of office—many gentlemen became candidates in response to inner needs for prestige or to inherited traditions of public service. These emotions were frequently stirred and intensified by friends who informally encouraged an individual to seek election.

"The Idea of representing this district in Congress never originated with *me*," wrote John Randolph, "[and] is one which I never should have entertained, had it not been suggested, in the first instance, by my friends." Robert Selden Garnett said his candidacy resulted from the solicitations of "numerous and respectable citizens," and Andrew Stevenson yielded to "a general wish on the part of the district that I should serve them." The race between Madison and Monroe for a seat in the First Congress was, in the words of each, largely the result of their respective friends.[2] Of course, these disavowals might be seen as self-effacing democratic rhetoric, establishing the candidate's obedience to the call of the people and suggesting his popularity and worthiness to those freeholders who did not know him. On the other hand, the gentry did in fact recruit and encourage promising individuals to seek office, and no wise candidate would consider a race without having been assured the support of his close associates.

On occasion the pressure to run originated with party leaders, at the grass roots or higher. Pull from the very top of the federal system accounted for the races of John Marshall (1799), Leven Powell (1799), John Page (1799), and Wilson Cary Nicholas (1807), among others.[3] Within a district, partisan stalwarts often sought out candidates, or at least sanctioned them. John Randolph got the blessing of Creed Taylor, a state senator; and John George Jackson wrote his brother-in-law James Madison that "the Republicans have taken me up for Congress in this district" as the party's best chance of success. Later, when a federal judge, Jackson in turn enlisted and "spent many hours . . . coaching" congressional candidate Joseph Johnson. Local Federalists formally urged James Breckinridge to run for the House of Representatives and promised him their support, and John Eyre received a letter and set of resolutions from Accomack County citizens who wanted him to seek office so that Eastern Shore Federalists would have "a representative in Congress of their own sentiments." The informal consultations of party chieftains led to the candidacy of Federalist Thomas Griffin of Yorktown in 1803.[4]

At times retiring congressmen played a key role in the process of candidacy. Western Republican John George Jackson personally recruited his brother Edward, who, on retirement, also chose a successor.[5] Numerous incumbents wrote letters recommending to their constituents specific politicians who wished to replace them in office.

One practice of the period that has been somewhat overlooked is that of formal nominations from special groups within congressional districts. James Breckinridge (1809), John Morrow (1809), James Stephenson (1809), John George Jackson (1809 and 1813), John Baker (1811), General Samuel Blackburn (1813), Francis White (1813), Armistead T. Mason (1815), Edward Colston (1817), and William H. Fitzhugh (1817), for example, all apparently ran for Congress as a result of having been chosen to do so in local or district meetings.[6] Only Jackson and Morrow were Republicans, thus suggesting that Virginia Federalists were, on occasion, organized on the grass-roots level.

In an informal version of the nomination method, "a sort of political caucus" might be held to narrow the field of candidates to the party's strongest man.[7] And, undoubtedly, local nonpartisan groups existed, like the one which incumbent George Tucker denounced as "a little clique who wished to make a vacancy for one of themselves."[8] The organizational approach often proved successful, but it failed in 1808 when employed to find an individual capable of defeating party maverick John Randolph, who viewed the abortive results with pleasure and commented sarcastically, "Caucussing . . . is not yet the vogue in *Congressional* elections."[9]

Party leaders, partisan groups, and personal friends might convince an individual to run, but other times candidates came forward on their own initiative and for their own particular reasons. A dramatic example of a "spontaneous" contender was Jefferson's son-in-law Thomas Mann Randolph. In 1803 Randolph resided in Jefferson's Albemarle County and thus within the congressional district of Samuel Jordan Cabell of Amherst, a staunch Republican whose circular letters had prompted a Federalist-tinged grand jury to declare him "a definite evil." Cabell had been in office since 1795 and had lain "two nights on his blanket" in the House of Representatives to help elect Jefferson president in the deadlocked contest of February 1801. Randolph kept his own counsel in electing to run, a decision which reflected both insecurity and ambition. It was a bold attempt to establish his own identity, to demonstrate that he was no mere "silly bird" among the swans at Monticello. As this instance demonstrates, candidacy could be entirely personal—even in the house of the party chieftain himself.[10]

Highly individualized motivation can also be seen in the candidacies of James H. Gholson, John George Jackson, and Daniel Morgan, to take three representative examples. Gholson lost overwhelmingly but had run for the purpose of advertising himself in the district since he had just moved to Petersburg and wanted to establish a legal practice there.[11] Never lacking for confidence or partisanship, Jackson ran in 1813 on the assumption that he alone could defeat the Federalist incumbent and thus be in a position to offer support to his beleaguered brother-in-law, President James Madison. As for crusty old Dan Morgan in 1795, he sought election to Congress from "No Poppular Motive" but only a "hearty contempt for the character who now serves us."[12]

Personal popularity—and informality—also led to the occasional practice of polling for an unannounced or even a decidedly unwilling candidate. John Taylor in 1803 flatly withstood entreaties to run from party leaders in Virginia and beyond, having concluded "that more good would result to the public, from my staying at home and providing for the education of my six sons, than from my going to Congress and thereby defeating that object." Even so, Taylor got 364 votes (not enough to separate him from his sons).[13] In 1817 an ill and besieged John Randolph told his constituents at Charlotte Courthouse that he was too sick to run again and that he was going to Europe to get well; undeterred, the Charlotte voters promptly gave Randolph a majority over a Republican candidate, to whom he lost districtwide.[14] In that same election season, General Henry St. George Tucker, a noncandidate then "in Philadelphia, awaiting the cure of his [war] wounds," received 719 votes in Frederick County to an opponent's mere 31 and was an easy winner in his whole district.[15] Two years earlier John Clopton had announced his retirement for reasons of health but was returned against his wishes to Washington, where he died before the term ended.[16] At other times in their political careers, two politicians of national prominence, John Breckinridge and Littleton Waller Tazewell, found themselves elected to the state legislature without their knowledge.

Similar to the noncandidate in avoiding a campaign was the last-minute one. Just before a poll opened, a new name sometimes appeared in rather spontaneous circumstances. A famous instance of this involved John Marshall in 1795. As he explained,

I attended at the polls to give my vote early & return to the court which was then in session at the other end of the town. As soon as the election commenced a gentleman came forward and demanded that a poll should be taken for me. I was a good deal surprized at this entirely unexpected proposition & declared my decided dissent. I said that if my fellow citizens wished it I would become a candidate at the next succeeding election, but that I could not consent to serve this year because my wishes & my honour were engaged for one of the candidates. I then voted for my friend & left the polls for the court which was open and waiting for me. The gentleman said that he had a right to demand a poll for whom he pleased, & persisted in his demand that one should be opened for me—I might if elected refuse to obey the voice of my constituents if I chose to do so. He then gave his vote for me.

As this was entirely unexpected—not even known to my brother who though of the same political opinions with myself was the active & leading partisan of the candidate against whom I had voted, the election was almost suspended for ten or twelve minutes, and a consultation took place among the principal freeholders. They then came in and in the evening information was brought me that I was elected. I regretted this for the sake of my friend. In other respects I was well satisfied at being again in the assembly.[17]

A few years later, John George Jackson had the same experience. "I can scarcely tell how it happened," he wrote, "I was taken by surprise yielding to the wishes of the people."[18] Likewise surprised was a certain Virginian who "had offered, and striven, purse and tongue, for three years to get elected, and the people would not elect him. This year, he declined, and really did not wish for the honour; and the voters tore off his coat in their zeal of putting him on the bench, and would elect him."[19] Of course, not every last-minute candidate won election. A certain "Mr. Braxton," for example, "got no votes," according to the *Norfolk Herald*, "the people being, like purchasers, desirous to see the commodity before they buy."[20]

On at least two occasions, the "spontaneity" of a late entry reflected a broader, well-calculated design. In 1811 the enemies of incumbent John Randolph saw no chance of success in a full-scale challenge. Instead, on election day they suddenly requested a poll for John Wayles Eppes. This allowed them to vote against Randolph in numbers that embarrassed him and at the same time provided an excuse for Eppes's predictable defeat. It also advertised the possibility of a more serious attempt by Eppes in the future.[21] The second instance of prior planning involved Colonel John B. D. Smith, a last-minute candidate and militia commander whose regiment "attended the polls in a body and every man voted for him."[22]

Setting the Stage

The idea of seeking office and the public announcement of that intention were often separated by a period of considerable activity. The satirical "Volponius," in his "Candidate's Guide," or "Way to Get Great" in Virginia politics, suggested as preliminary steps:

> Before you exhibit yourself in public . . . , practice in your chamber, before a large looking glass, the various bows and smiles which are used to express assent, complacency, respect or veneration. . . .
> Furnish yourself with a full suit of homespun. . . .
> [Decide if] you are more fitted to storm the fort by a furious display of party zeal, or to undermine your way by address and ingenuity.
> Get introduced to some man of influence, who is very fond of talking. . . .
> Be very sly of giving your opinions at first, but grow bolder as you get better acquainted. . . .
> Attend religious meetings occasionally—The profane will not think the worst of you for paying a prudent respect to popular prejudice, and the devout will ascribe your conduct to a promising sanctity.
> Become a free-mason as soon as you can, and get elected into all the jockey-clubs within fifty miles.[23]

In like vein, an overeager young candidate in Loudoun was advised to "first make the county . . . his permanent residence, settle upon his estate, marry a wife, mix with his fellow citizens, learn family duties, moral habits, experience in social affairs," etc.[24]

With these matters in hand, the enterprising office seeker proceeded with calculated practicality. George Tucker and William Cabell Rives used the interim between decision and announcement to move from locations of limited opportunity to places where the

congressional possibilities were clear.[25] A more common preliminary involved meeting the legal requirements for a campaign. "Send
me a deed speedily," wrote Littleton Waller Tazewell to his father,
"keeping in mind the necessary requisites made indispensable by
our law [for candidates], and framing your deed accordingly."[26] In
recruiting his nephew Bushrod as a Federalist candidate for Congress in 1799, George Washington advised him "to make a partial
removal . . . to satisfy the law" of residency. Hugh Nelson notified
the Virginia governor, "Having consented to make a tender of my
services to the Congressional District in which I reside, it is incumbent on me to resign" as judge of the General Court.[27]

When an incumbent was rumored to be retiring, potential candidates usually followed the political courtesy—and common sense
— of confirming the vacancy, often in terms that suggested a willingness to seek the position only if it would indeed be open. The
candidate might either contact the incumbent or raise the question
with a senior potential rival.[28] Or the incumbent himself might write
directly to a possible successor, as in the blunt words of John Floyd:
"Will you be a candidate if I decline? You can succeed—Think of it
until I see you."[29] On occasion a third party communicated with
the incumbent on behalf of a would-be contender.[30] A false step in
this procedure, or a failure to observe it, could be embarrassing.
Andrew Stevenson, for instance, believed John Clopton intended
to step down for reasons of health in 1811. Accordingly, Stevenson
announced his candidacy in an open letter published in the *Richmond Enquirer*; less than a week later the same newspaper carried
a second message, Stevenson's withdrawal in light of Clopton's decision to seek reelection.[31]

In short, in a system which almost guaranteed a willing incumbent's reelection, his intentions had to be ascertained by any astute
potential candidate. In the case of silence? The free press might
provide a solution, as in this advertisement:

WANTED IMMEDIATELY
CANDIDATE FOR CONGRESS
Not having heard whether our late member from the district composed of
the counties of —— —— —— —— will do the favor to serve the district,

for another term, apprehensions are entertained that the district will be left in the lurch.

The inducements for an early application are great, $8 per day, during the session, Mileage to and from the city. A right to frank all letters for sixty days before and after the sessions of Congress, with the prospect of a lucrative appointment under the administration "POLITICS AND TALENTS SUITING," if the candidate should be elected by the people. It is to be understood none need apply if the late incumbent can be prevailed upon to again honor the district with his services. Should no candidate offer, in a short time, for the ensuing election, it is probable measures may be adopted, by the next succeeding one, to have a candidate imported from the Shenandoah district, where it is understood candidates for Congress greatly abound.

A FREEHOLDER[32]

The sagacious candidate also used the preelection period to identify, minimize, or eliminate rivals. Competition might be controlled by getting one man to agree not to run if another did.[33] Supporters of one candidate might urge influential citizens to avert the race of another.[34] Early maneuvers often meant calculating the effect of known or potential support for an adversary or estimating the strength of a would-be contender.[35] Richmond merchant Robert Gamble wrote Congressman James Breckinridge that "General Trigg" had come to town and might be planning to seek Breckinridge's seat. "If you think any good will result," wrote Gamble, "I will try what attention and *good wine* will effect." Gamble's next communication reported Trigg's noncandidacy.[36]

Potential candidates and their supporters used several kinds of trial balloons. Mentioning a man's name in the newspaper, for example, could test popular reaction.[37] Or a candidate might imitate John Wayles Eppes, who announced over nine months before an election that "if the people wished him to serve, he would offer." Eppes's pledge was followed a few weeks later by another from the incumbent, John Randolph. His speech at a Charlotte court day mentioned a notion to retire unless his constituents desired otherwise. If they no longer wanted him as their representative, he would "anticipate their wishes" and "resign my pretensions" to another person.[38]

Becoming a Candidate

In an earlier election, Randolph had written his friend James Mercer Garnett that an opponent had been selected at the Buckingham court day, but "yesterday an electioneering barbeque was given to him (or rather against me) whereat he was present and declared off!" In another instance, Randolph saw a last-minute candidacy by Eppes as "an irresistable invitation to the proffer of his future services at a subsequent election, and . . . as a standard by which to measure the probability of his success. . . . [It] breaks the ice for Mr. Eppes, and at the same time saves the delicate feelings of that gentleman."[39] John Nicholas's abortive attempt to pass pro-Adams resolutions at a court day in Albemarle County in June 1798 seemed designed in part to prepare his candidacy against incumbent Samuel Jordan Cabell the next spring, and young John Breckinridge got a sense of his chances for a legislative seat by asking a local storekeeper to sample public opinion on the subject.[40]

Political winds might be measured by a virtual prerequisite to candidacy—an informal canvass throughout the district or at least attendance at court day. "You had better go to Caroline Court if possible," one candidate was instructed, "and where ever you go address the people in a short speech."[41] John Clopton suggested that if his son wanted to succeed him in Congress, "it will be well for you to cultivate acquaintance with people of Hanover and Henrico when ever you attend those Courts, as much as you can." Congressional aspirant Joseph C. Cabell learned it was "impolitick . . . to leave us so large a [?] of the year.—You must come and live amongst us—and you shall be our representative in Congress." Of course, a secure incumbent might be less concerned. As John Tyler wrote a friend in 1819: "Your last [letter] informed me that the people in your neighborhood wished me to visit them. It is, however, impossible for me to do so sooner than the election. . . . My course is before them, and I have served them for three years. I should hope, therefore, that a personal canvass might be dispensed with."[42]

Attendance at court might help a would-be candidate estimate the number of ballots needed to win. Given the fairly predictable level of voter participation and the relatively fixed quantity of a person's kinsmen and friends, a politician could gauge his chances with fair accuracy.[43] At least one potential contender went a step further by requesting a list of freeholders from the country clerk, who obligingly sent it with the addition of addresses, votes in the previous presidential election, and party preferences.[44]

The Announcement

After the preliminaries confirmed his decision to run, a candidate next had to announce his intentions formally. Close friends and political associates hardly needed to be told, since they usually had participated in the early maneuvering. Still, the final word would be passed, and allies throughout the district would be asked, in the language of one contender, to "make known among your neighbors my having offered my services" in the upcoming congressional race.[45] Aside from communication through one's coterie, an official announcement might be made either in print or in a public address.

Of the former, a common device was the broadside, which, if it ran over a page, became technically a circular. These could be mailed or posted throughout the district, as in the case of Francis Preston, who distributed "upwards of five hundred copies."[46] Two examples from many are those of John Clopton (1816) and Alexander Smyth (1817). In a statement of only four paragraphs, Clopton announced he was running for the vacancy caused by the death of his father and gave a short "avowal of my principles," which were likely to be acceptable to anyone calling himself an American. By contrast, Smyth's three-page announcement enumerated eight specific issues of pertinence to his district and juxtaposed his own position with that of his opponent, who replied in kind with a long circular.[47]

Incumbent congressmen often used their regular circular letters to constituents to announce an intention to seek reelection. Anthony New concluded a two-page sheet with the reminder: "The period when my fellow citizens will be again called upon to exercise the inestimable right of suffrage is not far distant. Permit me once more to make you a tender of my services, and to request you to consider me as a Candidate at the ensuing election of a member of Congress." A pamphlet by William McCoy contained the hint: "if my services in Congress are desired by you, you can command me at the next election."[48] These letters usually came in February or

March—that is, just before the April polling—and blended a broad review of congressional activity with a final appeal for reelection or, in some instances, a notification of the incumbent's decision to retire.[49]

Newspaper announcements were also common. Some consisted of a brief statement of candidacy in the form of local news. As Spencer Roane wrote his son William, "Judge Brockenbrough will have published in the *Enquirer* and *Argus of to-morrow* a simple notification that you are a candidate." Judge Roane added, "I sent also, near 200 *short* printed addresses to the Freeholders. It was written by Brockenbrough, and corrected and approved by me. No doubt it will please you."[50] A more elaborate means was to publish a circular letter in the press. Typically these began "To the Freeholders of . . . " with the district counties enumerated.[51] They might include a reference to the campaign, comments on specific issues, a broad statement of political principles, and the suggestion that some kind of crisis was at hand.[52]

A second formal way to announce candidacy was by a public statement, usually at court day. Typical was Federalist Magnus Tate's address of January 1815, which explained the reasons for his running, promised a "fair and manly" race, gave a few biographical highlights, and concluded with some general pledges.[53] An announcement speech might also be used to answer charges and to confound rumors, as in the case of Joseph C. Cabell, who told an audience in Nelson County: "It is deeply to be regretted that no sooner does a man offer himself for any public appointment in this part of Virginia, than he becomes a target for the arrows of calumny and detraction: no matter what may be the purity of his character, the force of his mind, or the extent of his public services: he must become the bleeding victim of every diabolical wretch, who from his lurking place, may chuse to level at him the poisoned dagger of falsehood."[54] The statement could be made by a proxy, but this required careful coordination. In one instance, under highly confused circumstances, James Monroe, who "sho. not have hesitated to serve, had I been elected," found himself unwittingly undermined at various courts either by having "no one appearing authorized to act for me" or by a "neighbor" who said Monroe "did not wish to be elected." This episode reemphasizes the importance of attendance at court by anyone either seeking office or willing to be chosen for it.[55]

Whether the announcement came in print or from the podium, timing was important. Two or three months prior to the election seems typical, but much earlier notices were not uncommon and in some cases were strategically required. John Mercer, for instance, issued a circular almost a year in advance of his election for the specified purpose of allowing his views to become known outside his own home county of Spotsylvania.[56] An early notice might either discourage or assure opposition. John Randolph had apparently decided to retire from office, but on learning of John Wayles Eppes's challenge, Randolph, ever a man of sensitive pride, wrote, "This circumstance enhances the awkwardness of my withdrawal." He later decided to seek reelection.[57]

In a context of anxieties over running, of decisions about contacts, trial balloons, timing, and the like, at least one candidate, though not for Congress, reduced the uncertainties and perplexities to a predictable assurance. That man was William Smith, about whom a local historian wrote:

He had an insatiable ambition to become a member of the legislature. Shortly after the creation of the County of Berkeley in 1772 he became a candidate for the House of Burgesses, and continued his candidacy, without success, for several years, from which he acquired the soubriquet of 'Burgess Billy.' After the revolutionary war was ended and the State constitution of 1776 was adopted . . . he pressed his claims for election to the House of Delegates from year to year, but still without success. When Morgan was formed into a separate county in 1820 he regularly entered the field every year for a seat in the legislature. At the April election of 1830 the aspirations and struggles of a long life were gratified by an election, but the adoption of the new constitution in the following August set aside the election and dashed and disappointed the hopes of his life. He never afterward had the heart to aspire to the place, and died a few years afterward, deeply impressed with the incapacity of the people to select competent and proper agents to serve them.[58]

The Voters' Prior Knowledge of the Candidate

Perhaps "Burgess Billy" failed to realize that a campaign required more than a willingness to be a candidate. Success in an election meant considerable electioneering, which often only added to what the freeholders already knew about a candidate. Even before a formal canvass began, the voters usually had a clear image of the contenders, especially if one or more of them resided in the county or if an incumbent was in the race. This preelectioneering image was based on a combination of personal and political factors long in forming and potent for that reason.

Family connections provided both an immediate constituency and an expanded circle of influence for a candidate. The vast majority of politicians who became congressmen belonged to prominent families; most married into others. Sixty of Virginia's ninety-eight congressmen in the Dynasty period had fathers, brothers, sons, uncles, cousins, or nephews who were United States senators or representatives. Ties with, for instance, what John Taylor called "the powerful Roane interest," could be more important in a county than complete mastery of campaign skills.[59] On occasion, "connections" and electioneering became one and the same. Thomas Mann Randolph reminded the freeholders of his "near alliance to that man [his father-in-law Jefferson]" and then neatly removed the question of subservience or riding a coattail by adding, "But I wave the advantage," in favor of standing on his own merits.[60]

Family bonds, though basic, often complemented other influential relationships, such as those formed through social or professional pursuits. A candidate's prior leadership in the local church, militia, agricultural society, county court, or other community institutions provided close contacts with the electorate. It meant that in most cases a man had already been sized up as congressional timber before the announcement of candidacy.

A more elite kind of screening might have occurred during an individual's formal education when he came to know and be known by future leaders of the Old Dominion. Or it might result from service in the state legislature where members worked with political leaders outside their own areas and where senators had to be elected from at least two counties.[61] Some occupations, such as the practice of law, provided considerable public exposure. To cite one case, George Tucker followed a monthly itinerary of 340 miles for the court sessions of four counties in a single judicial district.[62]

Advance approval and support of specific local leaders often minimized campaign difficulties or made electioneering wizardry superfluous—a reality clearly recognized by contemporary politicians. Friends of James Breckinridge, for instance, gave him the names of men of consequence, men whom he "ought by no means to neglect writing . . . and sending . . . occasionally papers and documents of a proper character."[63] Spencer Roane assured his son William that the "influential characters" would be notified of his candidacy.[64] John Clopton, among others, kept closely in touch with key citizens throughout his district.[65]

Individual leaders or influential persons were important, but specific bodies of otherwise ordinary freeholders were also significant for their precampaign biases. A candidate's religion, party, occupation, or social standing might alienate or attract groups within his district. Many politicians gained an advantage from being lawyers, but John Clopton's son was attacked for it.[66] He also lost where others such as John George and Edward Brake Jackson succeeded, namely, in attempting to follow his father in office. Marriage was usually an asset, but not for Isaac Coles, whose English wife became a campaign liability.[67] In a German-American district the bilingual Jacob Swoope enjoyed a decisive edge over an opponent who spoke only English.[68] In an interim election Thomas Mann Randolph faced a challenge by David Garland, who sought to demonstrate that a common man could be chosen and that Randolph and the retiring Wilson Cary Nicholas could not monopolize the position; an aristocratic Randolph supporter, John Hartwell Cocke, found it "astonishing to the last degree . . . that men possessing the share of talents of Mr. G.—should have the effrontery to stand forward, when our national affairs never stood with more need of abilities to conduct them thro' the perils of an awful crisis."[69] Finally, well before a poll, in Sydnor's words, "the Quakers or the Presbyterians, the men along the south side of a river or in the northern corner of a county—these and other groups might discuss the candidates and decide which of them to support."[70]

Individual freeholders, like the groups, also might have formed preconceived notions of a candidate based on his personal flaws and foibles. Early in his career John George Jackson survived a breach of promise suit, an illegitimate son, and accusations of Sabbath breaking and "swearing profane oaths."[71] Thomas Mann Randolph felt doomed as a candidate because of a public altercation with a worker; Magnus Tate had lost an ear in a youthful brawl; and Peterson Goodwyn had been charged with embezzling public funds during his tenure as deputy sheriff in Dinwiddie County.[72] Physical appearance also contributed to a candidate's precanvass image, though it does not seem to have been too influential. Several congressmen, James Breckinridge for instance, stood tall and handsome, but William Smith, in Grigsby's summation, "was an ugly man, very."[73]

On a more substantive level, voters might have a predetermined attitude based on the candidate's prior political record, whether locally, in Richmond, or in Washington. Almost all congressional contenders had earlier served in the state legislature and thus had been previously tested by the freeholders, were recorded on issues pertinent to their interests, and had established an image, favorable or not, with the electorate. In this regard, the congressional race between Alexander Smyth and Benjamin Estill in 1817 seems to have been largely fought over their respective activities in the House of Delegates.[74]

An incumbent congressman's service to his district, state, party, or nation was in the public eye and subject to preelection judgment. John Clopton's ability to secure a local post road, George Tucker's swallowing of his private scruples on the tariff, John George Jackson's close ties to President Madison, Philip R. Thompson's maverick politics, John Kerr's vote to raise his and other congressmen's salaries, Andrew Stevenson's support of the state's Revolutionary veterans, Thomas Newton's defense of the Embargo and John Randolph's disapproval of it—these suggest the variety of matters for which an incumbent might be praised or damned, but evaluated nonetheless, well before a campaign for reelection. Probably few incumbents felt as secure with their records as John Tyler did in 1819 when he dismissed campaigning entirely; and James Pleasants, who served in Congress from 1811 to 1819, was surely unique in never having canvassed for a seat.[75]

"In choosing a representative," complained the *Richmond Examiner* of March 23, 1803, "we look for qualities, often adverse to, and at best, accidentally associated with political merit. Has a candidate an easy exterior, condescending manners, and is he equally polite to all? Does he recollect your names, the names of your wives

Political Practices

and children, and greet you with the meretricious smile of continued placidity, and universal good humour?"[76] While the *Examiner* bemoaned the "too often" choice on such superficial grounds, it also made the point that a candidate's personality, character, reputation, and previous career were usually known locally and thus part of his public image even before he resorted to canvassing. The fact that a solid majority of Virginia's congressmen had been born and raised in their districts underscores the point.

The Necessity of a Canvass

Thus, for a variety of reasons, a candidate's potential as a vote getter appears rather predetermined. Other considerations, however, made it not so mechanical or predestined. In the first place, campaigns sometimes hinged not as much on the number of one's friends as on the number who would actively help or even be present to vote. Second, since candidates were more alike in biographical profiles than different, elections were fought within gentry circles or between contenders who could rally similar advantages in personality, training, public service, and support among influential individuals or groups. Third, congressional races involved from two to twelve counties (or boroughs) and often meant a given candidate might indeed be powerful in one section of the district but a virtual stranger in another. Finally, voters and candidates alike were humans and not machines and, as such, often defied predictability, especially under changing conditions and needs. Littleton Waller Tazewell was not the only candidate to discover on election day that "many of my *supposed* friends deserted,"[77] and even so powerful a local personage as John Randolph was turned out of office when national currents of wartime patriotism overcame the same constituents who otherwise elected him fourteen times to Congress.

In short, once candidacy had been decided and declared, the would-be public servant still had to "mix and mingle" with the freeholders and curry their favor (and votes) in a ritual which William Wirt once described as "this business of canvassing" and which was universally known as electioneering.[78]

V

Electioneering: The Written and Spoken Word

Despite prior conditions that might minimize its impact, electioneering was a common, if not central, part of a congressional campaign during the Dynasty period. In a fundamental sense, it meant establishing a favorable relationship between two parties, the candidate and the freeholder. The former had the initiative and might use it in any or all of three basic ways—by the written word, by formal speeches, and by direct personal appeals, though the last might make a gentleman feel uncomfortable.

Antielectioneering Sentiment

Virginia politicians might disagree on issues and parties and dislike each other intensely for petty or personal reasons. At the same time, as a group, they expressed a strong aversion to the practice of courting votes among the freeholders. In general, congressional candidates echoed the fictitious character, "Wou'dbe," in Robert Munford's colonial play: "Must I again be subject to the humours of a fickle crowd? Must I again resign my reason, and be nought but what each voter pleases? Must I cajole, fawn, and wheedle, for a place that brings so little profit?" Henry St. George Tucker thought not. In 1807 he won and then told his father: "Please . . . notice also that I am no *electioneer*" and "I have studiously avoided anything like canvassing." In 1815 he again boasted of victory without having "attended a public meeting or been at the home of a single individual, and though my adversary and his friends had ransacked the county in the old Electioneering Style." As a young man run-

Political Practices

ning for the General Assembly, James Mercer Garnett publicly denounced electioneering as "highly improper, and as degrading to the understanding, as it is to the integrity of freemen." In a similar race John Taylor of Caroline remained true to his pledge "not [to] use a single effort to be elected," and James Madison, as a candidate for the First Federal Congress, expressed distaste for electioneering on several occasions.[1]

And yet, many of the very men who most adamantly condemned the courting of votes were among the most skillful at it. In fact, condemnation became a form of the art itself. Whatever the rhetoric, few successful congressional candidates failed to use one or more of the three common devices for "courting popularity . . . and attempting to gain the affections or votes of the people."[2]

The Written Word

Soliciting support by the written word involved both public literature and private letters. The latter, obviously, could be significant, as seen in the example of James Madison. He acknowledged having "made great use of epistolary means" in his first campaign for Congress in 1789, and did so again two years later. Unable to attend any polls in 1791, Madison sent a series of letters, some addressed and some not, to his father and brothers. They were asked to distribute and in some cases to address them to what seems to have been at least "a friend in each County." In this medium, Madison reviewed the major activities of Congress, reported his views, and explained his absence from the district in plausible terms.[3]

In a similar vein, Charles Fenton Mercer realized he would miss a Loudoun poll and wrote an influential friend to look out for his interests there. John Clopton sent one constituent a three-page letter detailing congressional developments and Clopton's opinions and concluding with a subtle appeal, "As I expect this will reach you at the election—you will have an opportunity of communicating the contents to many of our fellow citizens." "Letters from great folks in Washington to little folks here," complained John Randolph, "industriously disseminated the germs of discontent against me."[4] In at least one instance, the candidate's correspondence was penned by his better-educated son.[5] On another occasion a brother added comments to the congressman-candidate's letters to key persons in the district.[6] Further variety is seen in John P. Preston's request that John Smith, who had German ties, write "four or five of the most respectable dutchmen of your county" on Preston's behalf.[7]

In an era of restricted travel and in a political system which rewarded family and other connections, well-placed private letters represented an efficient use of a candidate's time and resources. If a broader distribution was needed, printed circulars and broadsides could be employed with great profit. These devices were identical in format to the congressional circular letters, which in many instances served the dual purpose of electioneering sheets.[8] The document itself often expressed the advantage of this form of solicitation. "The impossibility of personal communications with all of you, in the short time between this [date] and the election," wrote Thomas Mann Randolph, "compels me to state, here, my pretensions to your approbation and confidence." Thomas M. Nelson stressed the obligation to make "public my opinions of the policy of our Government" in his circular, since he was admittedly "a stranger to many in the district." The device was a convenient one for conveying "sentiments to every freeholder's fire side" in different counties and was a common feature of congressional campaigns.[9]

The contents of the circulars could be tailored to meet a candidate's specific needs. A person in his first race might include both biographical detail and favorable references to better-known politicians in the area. And he usually followed a line of reasoning well expressed by Arthur Lee, whose circular began: "as a Candidate to represent you in the General Congress of the United States, I think it proper to declare the Principles, which shall govern my Conduct, if I have the Honour of being elected." Frequently such principles were escalated to the level of harmless if not ludicrous abstraction, such as John B. Clopton's firm assurance of "a holy love of republican principles" based on "the rights of man by nature" which, since they "can never be changed, I expect not to change them."[10] Occasionally, platitudes were joined or replaced by a discussion of genuine issues. The Alien and Sedition Acts and Virginia and Kentucky Resolutions, for example, aroused both advocates and critics.[11] John Clopton designed a circular for a friend to read "to as many [people] as he can" at the next county court,[12] and Jacob Swoope ordered versions of his literature printed in German.[13]

Circulars served the defensive purpose of answering or anticipating charges against a candidate. Incumbent John Page used the device to make a virtue of his failure to give any speeches, "a practice, which may, in time, expose electors to the mortifying reflection, that they had preferred an orator to a statesman, flashes of wit to sound judgment, and empty words to substantial proofs of genuine patriotism." By this means he also explained his failure to keep his constituents informed in person or by letter: "You will, as freemen I hope, think with me, that it is of more consequence to you and our country, that your Representative attend to his duty in Congress, than to his interest in his district. You will therefore I hope excuse me, if I take not up our precious time, in writing an account of the proceedings of Congress—but refer you to the papers and journals for information respecting them," especially, he added, since he did not want to confuse or bias his constituents by giving his own views on those matters. A similar case, perhaps, was the unsolicited assurance of young John B. Clopton that "I have had some leisure, and that leisure had been devoted to literary pursuits; among these pursuits, the acquirement of political knowledge presented itself to me as of primordial importance—I have studied the rights of the people." James Mercer Garnett, on the other hand, issued a circular specifically to answer the accusations of his "calumniators" and to defend his previously stated positions, including attacks on the Madison administration.[14]

In some instances a single circular triggered a series, as one candidate sought to refute the statement of another. In 1817 Alexander Smyth and Benjamin Estill fought a vigorous "circular war." Smyth struck first by announcing his candidacy with a three-page blast listing major points of difference between himself and Estill, and followed that by a later and separate *Postcript* [sic]. Estill countered with five pages that stated that his earlier intention to campaign only at court days had been changed by Smyth's misrepresentations, which he proceeded to dissect. Smyth replied with another three pages. Much of the controversy was substantive, though it also concerned the candidates' divergent records in the House of Delegates, the relevance of which Estill questioned in a congressional race.[15]

Circulars usually bore the signature of a contender, but in some instances sheets carried the names of supporters and in other instances displayed only a pseudonym, such as "Freeholder" or "Phocion," or lacked identification entirely.[16] Less important than authorship but also pertinent was the audience specified by the circulars. Spencer Roane prepared printed statements for his son William and advised him, "Being addressed to the Freeholders generally, they will be thereby gratified, while by endorsing them to influential characters, that will be a mark of attention to them which will also please."[17] After supporters of John G. Jackson issued an *Address to the Freeholders of Ohio County, Virginia*, friends of Jackson's opponent countered with a broadside entitled *To the Citizens of Ohio County* which asserted: "We do not address the Freeholders alone. We wish our conduct to be correctly understood by every member of the community, whether he be a voter or not."[18]

If the congressmen are an accurate measure, Virginia politicians outdistanced their counterparts elsewhere in a fondness for distributing printed circulars, and in fact they may have overdone it.[19] Or, at least the *Norfolk Herald* thought so, in complaining of "the hacknied manner of addressing Circular Letters to the Electors of Counties, full of egotism and false promises" and of their having become "so common, that scarcely a person read[s] them."[20]

Similar to broadsides and circulars and also common at election time were printed speeches and pamphlets, usually sent by incumbents with franking privileges and usually confined to a specific subject.[21] Printed literature in any form had obvious advantages in dissemination. As Spencer Roane indicated, "Some . . . may be stuck up in all public places . . . ; and the rest distributed in the form of letters." This might be done by committees or "through . . . zealous and tried friends."[22] The latter might formally post the material or merely communicate its contents orally, pass it from hand to hand, or read it as a speech on court day. Not uncommonly, the items also appeared in one or more of Virginia's newspapers.

Electioneering in the press was an inexpensive but effective way of distributing a printed broadside, circular, or speech; the wise candidate made sure friendly editors received this kind of election material. Newspapers also ran public letters, sometimes signed but often with only pseudonyms, praising or damning particular candidates.[23] On occasion rival candidates spoke to readers and voters

Political Practices

alike through a vigorous exchange in the press, or a partisan "Freeholder" might submit a series of loaded if open-ended questions and invite a response from a particular office seeker.[24]

The power of the press is well illustrated by examples involving John Randolph and John Marshall. In 1811 items appearing in the Richmond *Aurora* assailed Randolph so severely as to cause a supporter to urge that "some notice [must be] . . . taken of them before the people, either by yourself in addressing them, or by your friends in writing." To Randolph's alarm the *Aurora*'s attacks also circulated in his district in the form of handbills. In another race four years later, more than half the issues of the *Richmond Enquirer* from March 25 to April 16 carried a piece either condemning or endorsing Randolph's bid for election. Included were letters from Randolph, his enemies, and his friends, as well as the frequent and critical comments of editor Thomas Ritchie, an arch Randolph foe at the time.[25]

As suggested above, a newspaper could carry material supplied for and against a candidate, or as in the unusual case of John Marshall in 1799, the two might be joined. As a Federalist running for Congress, Marshall was attacked in an open letter by "Freeholder," who raised a series of somewhat overdrawn but pertinent and specific questions. Shortly afterwards, the press carried Marshall's answers, uniformly well phrased and well received. In recounting the episode, Beveridge concluded: "The questions of 'Freeholder' were, undoubtedly, written with Marshall's knowledge. Indeed a careful study of them leads one to suspect that he wrote or suggested them himself."[26]

One obvious advantage of disseminating an item by newspaper rather than separate publication was that it would gain as much or more circulation at virtually no expense to its sponsor.[27] Often such a newspaper notice was less stiff and sophisticated than formally prepared material. An example is the comic appeal for "Federal Sailors" to vote in an imminent congressional race in April 1803. It included a heavy dose of class ridicule, such as the assurance: "If you haven't clean duds ready never mind. I'd as least lend a friend a hand in a pair of tarr'd trossers as silk pantaloons."[28] Newspapers also occasionally carried letters with partisan arguments not quite as careful as the statements found in most broadsides. Republican "economy" was misleading, wrote one James Douglass in the *Alexandria Advertiser*; "repealing of taxes saves no money to the nation. Every man of common sense knows that the more money government receives, the more they [*sic*] can distribute."[29] Or, consider "Mentors'" blast at Burwell Bassett: "You, Sir, voted for this inquisition, tyrannical, illibertycidal law."[30]

"Spouting"

"The people at large," wrote Richmond Federalist William Heth, "require nothing but fair, and honest information, to act properly."[31] Of the ways of providing such information perhaps none matched the appeal of a hustings speech. The practice combined whatever logic and eloquence the written word might possess with the warmth and human electricity generated by the confrontation of candidate and freeholder, often within the convivial surroundings of a county court day. The ability to deliver an effective speech was an important campaign asset, in some cases even a decisive one. A Yankee newcomer noted in 1811 that "people in these parts get into office by 'Stump oratory' praising and electioneering for themselves," and a native observed that the "science of spouting" attacked every ambitious young Virginian who recognized that "eloquence is almost the only road to fame and influence in the state."[32]

The time to "spout" varied considerably. Rivals John Randolph and John Wayles Eppes exchanged addresses at a court day over half a year before the election in April 1813.[33] On another occasion, a rival of Randolph's hit the hustings trail long before protocol demanded it and well "before the adjournment of Congress, knowing his inability to contend with Mr. Randolph's extraordinary talents for public speaking."[34] Addresses might be made at court days prior to the actual poll, thus giving the freeholders a chance to listen "to those who are engaged in haranguing . . . for votes in the next election,"[35] but the minimum requirement was a statement just before the balloting commenced, as suggested in this representative account: "Mr. Newton followed Mr. Holt at considerable length and was replied to by Mr. Loyall, with much earnestness—Mr. Newton rejoined, and after a short replication from Mr. Loyall, the polls were opened and the election progressed."[36] Once, an election was actually halted by mutual consent of the candidates to allow a speech by a third party on behalf of one of them. This instance seems unique, however, because contenders normally spoke for themselves, though other examples of substitute orators could be cited.[37] A wise politician tried to speak at each court day in his district, but in a particularly heated race Henry A. Wise gave "as many as twenty-seven stump speeches, besides having one hundred and fifty cross-road skirmishes."[38]

Most electioneering orations were made at a court day, but militia musters, party or holiday celebrations, and other public occasions were also suitable.[39] Any large gathering could be fair game for an enterprising candidate, as the following recollection illustrates:

Old Fayette McMullen was canvassing his district for a nomination for Congress, years ago, and during the canvass a man was hung in that locality for murder. About ten thousand men collected to witness the scene, and among them, old Mac, who, by the favor of the sheriff, occupied a place on the platform in the rear of the gallows, his oratorical mouth watering at the sight of the magnificent audience in front. When everything was ready, as is usual in such cases, the sheriff asked the culprit if he had anything to say before the sentence of the law was passed upon him; to which the condemned responded that he would say nothing. Whereupon old Mac stepped forward, rubbing his hands, and remarked: "Mr. Sheriff, if the gentleman will yield his time to me, I will embrace this occasion to make a few remarks on the political situation, and announce myself a candidate for Congress."[40]

A candidate's preparation for a speech varied with the man. Young William Cabell Rives and Joseph C. Cabell seem to have drafted their comments in advance, John George Jackson and John Randolph spoke extemporaneously,[41] and John Wayles Eppes, according to one contemporary, relied on a "*cartload* of *authorities* [books and documents] . . . such as had never been seen by the natives," which prompted Randolph's quip, "The Gentleman is a very good *reader*."[42] An Eppesian approach, styled as "new and ingenious," was reported in the *Norfolk Herald*: "The Candidate met the Electors at Hampton, mounted a rostrum, and took from his pocket a manuscript of 17 folio sheets of paper!—He stated that the People ought to know the situation they were in, and that this paper was a *digest* (he had made) *of the Politics of the World!*—He was heard with patience to labour (with a few blunders in reading) through five sheets of the digest, when, owing to some of the auditors laughing and coughing, he began to be hoarse, and broke off, with promising to give them the balance at the *Cock fight* on Easter-Monday."[43] In stark contrast is the case of John Page, who refused to make a speech of any kind. Page bluntly confessed he was "not qualified by habit or education to harangue" his constituents, and even if he were qualified, he would not do so, for oratorical prowess was no prerequisite for public service.[44]

The oratorical style of those who did speak varied considerably. The manner of the lawyer and sometime politician Littleton Waller Tazewell was "said to have been singularly simple and free from artifice. His arguments were conversational and his gestures not more striking than those of animated converse. His postures were negligent. His voice was pleasant and of ample compass. He was never vociferous."[45] On the other hand, contemporaries described John Randolph's oratory as "distinguished by imagery and impetuosity with a ready flow of language" and marked by "parables . . . antitheses, jests, beautiful conceits. . . . [His] invective, which is always piquant, is frequently adorned with the beautiful metaphors of Burke, and animated by bursts of passion worthy of Chatham."[46] Washington Irving acknowledged that Randolph captivated his audiences, but he added, "they listen to him more to be delighted by eloquence and entertained by his ingenuity and eccentricity, than to be convinced by sound doctrine and close argument."[47]

Or compare the approaches of the Barbour brothers. Critics found the theatrical oratory of James Barbour too much "charged with guns, trumpets, and blunderbuss." In his imagery, a modest Orange County stream became "a rivulet meandering down the vale." One close observer said James could "clothe a beggarly idea in the robes of royalty and call down the lightening of heaven to kill a gnat." If James merited being called "The Thunderer" for his bombastic orations, his brother Philip spoke typically in a disciplined and legalistic fashion. A contemporary said Philip was "never more pleased than when splitting hairs and indulging in nice metaphysical distinctions."[48] John Randolph enlarged the metaphor by observing "that Phil could split a hair but that Jim could not hit a barn door."[49]

But if some orators pursued lavish rhetorical flourishes, others, like Dr. Walter Jones, employed simple "colloquial eloquence" and, like John Roane, used "language, never eloquent or refined . . . common, oftentimes even to vulgarity . . . [but] always clear, full of homely illustrations, which everybody could understand, and of proverbs, which all could apply."[50]

The proper length for an address was suggested by "Traveller" George Tucker in his observation on how to succeed as a lawyer in Virginia: "When you rise at the bar, only remember to speak as fast as possible, to shew your fluency. No matter about the choice of word, (tho', to be sure, the longer and rounder the better) but take the first . . . that comes to hand, and be careful you don't stop. . . . above all things be sure and speak long enough."[51] This "long enough" standard applied to some of the best stump orators such as Randolph or Andrew Stevenson, who could hold forth for hours at a time.[52] In some instances, however, the opposite approach—brevity—worked equally well. At an election in Kanawha County early in the century, two candidates for Congress and four or five for the General Assembly spoke in succession for a lengthy period. Finally the last of the candidates rose. "According to custom," he had to speak, but since the hour was late and his opinions were already known, he said only, in the words of one witness, "If you choose to elect me, I will serve you to the best of my abilities; if you don't, you may go to ——." He left the platform "amidst . . . vociferous cheers" and was "elected by a large majority."[53] An Albemarle poll featured long-winded orations until one Billy Meriwether rose and said simply that his neighbors had wanted him to run. He then sat down, having given what a contemporary regarded as "the shortest speech I ever heard on such an occasion." The speaker who had "held forth an hour or two" lost his bid for election, while the spare-tongued Billy gained a majority.[54] A similar ploy met with failure elsewhere, however. The final speaker merely stated "that if the Gentlemen would elect him, he could take care, if he done them no good, he would do them no harm!" A newspaper account added: "This pithy address was received with bursts of applause; but alas! not withstanding so much candor, the laconic orator lost his election," getting, in fact, only one of the 367 votes cast that day.[55]

Whatever the preparation, style, or even length of an address, a candidate had to keep his wits, because stump oratory often required a quick defense against aggressive opponents, hecklers, and unruly crowds. Repartee and a sense of humor offered protection from attack and attracted votes in the process, as illustrated in a race between challenger George W. Bolling and incumbent George C. Dromgoole. The latter was known to reinforce his mental alertness on the stump with a ready "quart of toddy, three fourths whiskey and one fourth water." Bolling asked the crowd if it preferred a man like himself, a faithful attendant in Congress, or a man like Dromgoole whose presence there had been irregular. Dromgoole responded, "Fellow citizens, had you rather have to represent you, me, who will often be absent, but who will support your interest by my speech and vote when I am present, or Colonel Bolling, who will always be present, but who will always speak and vote against you."[56] In a heated Tidewater race during the War of 1812, the antiwar John Taylor of Caroline matched arguments with the skillful John Roane. A witness recorded the exchange:

"But Mr. Roane, the taxes, sir, the taxes."
"Well, sir; the taxes, what of them? I do not fear taxes, nor do I the people. They want freedom: they don't want money."
"How high would you tax for this war?"
"I would tax them, sir, ten cents in the dollar."
"Suppose, sir, that should be insufficient?"
"Then, sir, I would tax them twenty cents in the dollar."
"But suppose they would not stand it?"
"Then, sir, I would not ask them. I would tax them thirty, forty, fifty, sixty, seventy, eighty, ninety, one hundred cents in the dollar. Col. Taylor, I would tax the shirts off the peoples' backs and make them free, whether they would or not. What is your next bugbear?"
The effect was electric.[57]

John Randolph faced a special kind of platform confrontation from a foe who followed him throughout the district "replying at one Court House to speeches which . . . [Randolph] had made at another."[58]

The Emergence and Power of Hustings Oratory

A variety among speakers is perhaps less significant than the presence of speakers at all and the great stress that Virginians placed on them. "Political oratory in the Old Dominion prior to the 1760's," concludes the closest student of the subject, "was of little importance."[59] Yet campaigns in the Jeffersonian era characteristically featured politicians "swaying" the people "at will, speaking to a crowd with decisive effect,"[60] and represent a wildly popular age of public speaking. As John Pendleton Kennedy noted: "The admiration of the masses for this talent, the ready plaudit with which they are often but too ready to reward that specious, fluent, superficial, glittering eloquence, with which they are most familiar, seem to have engendered the opinion that even the depths of juridicial science may be fathomed by the plummet of the gift of speech, and the highest honours of professional distinction be won by the wordy triumphs of the forum."[61]

What accounts for this fascination with oratory and its emergence as an electioneering device? Part of the answer lies with the politicians themselves. Most congressmen in the Dynasty era were gentlemen who had been born after 1765 and trained in the law. Gentry status meant the opportunity for a formal education which included an emphasis on, if not actual classes in, oratory and rhetoric and a heavily classical curriculum often focusing on notable political or theological figures whose greatness inevitably reflected a skill with words. Teachers in grammar schools were frequently ministers professionally concerned with oral communication and examples themselves of a new-style pulpit delivery more evocative and evangelistic than the rather restricted and liturgical manner of their colonial Anglican predecessors.[62] At William and Mary books on rhetoric were available, courses in it were required, and personal models were provided by the political figures in Williamsburg and by such inspirational orators as Bishop Madison. Literary societies and graduation addresses also encouraged and trained exemplary public speakers.

Being born within the Revolutionary era gave Dynasty politicians inspirational examples of political rhetoric. The men of '76 had great issues to define, articulate, and communicate to the rank-and-file Virginian, and they were equal to the task. The pens of Jefferson, Madison, and Mason and the lips of Patrick Henry and Richard Henry Lee, among others, established a high standard of eloquence and provided lofty and enduring themes worthy of it.

Electioneering: Written and Spoken Word

In the early decades of the Republic, traditions and circumstances emerged that both lent themselves to oratory and, concurrently, celebrated the talent. Holidays such as the Fourth of July, political meetings generated by the rise of the first party system, and the passing of the Revolutionary generation to the accompaniment of earnest and patriotic eulogies all provided opportunities for public speaking. And all came simultaneously with a boom in religious oratory brought about by the growth of evangelistic denominations, the advent of the Second Great Awakening, and the new popularity of camp meetings and prolonged revivals.

The legal training of most congressmen also helps explain their talent for public speaking. A successful attorney needed a command of words and a capacity for persuasion; his verbal skills were constantly tested and sharpened in court battles that now might range over a multicourt circuit. Many lawyers served in local courts and the state legislature where much of the work was legal in nature. A young Virginian aspiring to fame as a lawyer or politician would rightly seek to develop and hone his rhetorical talents. The gentleman's training and proficiency in oratory account in part for its central place in election campaigns in the Old Dominion.

Another part of the explanation is that in an era of primitive mass communication, public speeches served a multitude of political purposes. "Custom as well as reason prescribes," wrote one candidate, that an office seeker state his "political sentiments,"[63] an objective easily accomplished by a public address. In some instances more than general sentiments were expected; an incumbent, for example, might be required to explain some unpopular vote or position. "The people want your motives," wrote a friend of John Randolph. "They are at a loss to conceive how you could oppose Madison and in some measure the president [Jefferson] without swerving from your former (as they are pleased to style them) opinions."[64]

The public forum was a convenient place to protect one's personal or political reputation. In the state's first congressional election, Madison noted that he "actually visited two Counties, Culpeper & Louisa, and publicly contradicted the erroneous reports propagated agst. me," while in 1811 John Randolph said about his refutation of charges against him, "A long address of an hour was insufficient for their bare enumeration & denial."[65] A platform statement helped a candidate become known beyond his own county, a political requirement since congressional races encompassed districts from two to twelve counties. And, of course, oratory could manipulate or influence the electorate, a reality well understood by the politicians, and no doubt what James Mercer Garnett had in mind when he advised his friend Randolph that he would best his opposition "if you will only attend one or two courts in each county of your District & address the people as you have formerly done."[66]

A final explanation for the popularity of campaign oratory concerns the nature of the Virginia electorate. Most freeholders never seriously aspired to public office, but they did determine at the polls who among the gentry would fill the various elective positions. Speeches provided a way for freeholders to measure the men who presumed to represent them. It took little imagination to perceive, maybe illogically, that a man who was effective on the hustings would also be effective in Congress. Perhaps a politician's having to address the freeholders constituted a psychological deference to them in the tradition of "treating." Candidates stood socially above the average voters, but the requirement for a public appeal to them helped minimize class differences and established a proper democratic image for gentry office seekers.

And it must be remembered that rural isolation characterized Virginia in the Dynasty era. The typical citizen rarely saw the inside of a theater or a school and did not subscribe to the *National Intelligencer*, the *Richmond Enquirer*, or other newspapers of the period. Hustings speeches provided a substitute means of being educated, edified, and entertained.[67] Freeholders had a social and intellectual need to hear Eppes read the public documents of the day, or Walter Jones discuss in conversational tones the activities of Congress, or John Randolph deal with questions large and small in a manner at once instructive, inspirational, and amusing.

Certainly, by Jeffersonian times the hustings speech had become an integral part of the electoral process. Perhaps too often the oratory never went beyond platitudes, as was suggested by the advice of John Tyler, Sr., to John Tyler, Jr., that "the love of country admits very fine strokes of rhetoric."[68] But when issues were discussed or debated and candidates sat beside each other in the public eye, expressed their views, and responded to direct and open chal-

Electioneering: Written and Spoken Word

lenges, the democratic system itself was best served, regardless of the electioneering interests of the speakers themselves.

A candidate's use of the written and spoken word in a campaign, though of prime importance, represented only a portion of the weapons in his electioneering arsenal. Success might hinge less on them than on the right combination of appeals to the voter in a direct attempt at "personal solicitation."

VI

Electioneering:
Personal Courtship

The third and perhaps most effective of the basic electioneering devices was a direct appeal to the electorate or, as James Madison phrased it, the candidate's self-recommendation "to the voters . . . by personal solicitation." This usually meant a period of vigorous and varied activity, as would-be public servants sought to gain their fellow freeholders' votes if not their confidence. "Our elections are commencing," observed Edmund Pendleton, "and seem to be warmly canvassed, as if there were loaves and fishes to be distributed, and the feast to continue for seven years."[1]

Mixing with the Freeholders

"Can any man be elected who . . . refuses to go amongst, or to let the people look at him," wrote one veteran politician to a younger brother desiring to enter public life but reluctant to campaign.[2] The sagacious candidate thought not, and followed the advice of a friendly storekeeper to a potential office seeker: "the People . . . like you well Enough—But they think you ought to ride through the country & be known to them."[3] After all, the freeholders looked with disfavor on a gentleman who felt "he was too proud and ostentatious to make a personal appeal," and seasoned candidates in contested races recognized the possibility that an adversary might be "industrious and perhaps underhanded."[4] Thus, any aspiring congressmen had to be prepared for a vigorous commitment of time and resources in the effort to court favor with the voters. "Leave no stone unturned," General Daniel Morgan was advised on entering the political lists. "You are about to Engage in as difficult or worse piece of business than the engagement with Tarleton."[5]

Electioneering: Personal Courtship

A serious canvass might begin almost a year in advance, but it intensified as the poll drew near. "Two months before the Election," wrote one candidate, "were almost exclusively appropriated to electioneering. I traversed every part of the country, and became acquainted with almost the whole of the people, with whom before that time I was wholly unacquainted."[6] During a successful campaign of almost three months in 1799 Henry Lee spent "no more than five or six nights under his own roof," about the same as John George Jackson did that year.[7]

A typical canvass required attendance at a variety of public places and events, especially court days, and a willingness to curry the favor of freeholders there.[8] One congressional candidate sought votes "by jollying the men, hugging the ladies, and giving red stick candy to the children" and was said to have "kissed more babies than any other Southwestern Virginian."[9] Another contender accused his opponent of having "descended to the lowest and most disgraceful means,—riding from house to house, and attending day and night meetings in the cabins of the lowest of the people."[10] In the race between Episcopalian Randolph and skeptic Eppes in 1811, the former attended Presbyterian services while the latter accompanied a local Baptist minister on his preaching rounds.[11] One critic remarked that to gain popularity the Squire of Roanoke "has become 'as sweet as summer' . . . [and] mixes with all classes, and talks to every body."[12] In a Richmond race, "exertions are making here in favour of [John] Marshall—writing, speaking, printing, treating, in short nothing is spared to ensure his Election."[13] It was even asserted that Marshall courted votes by dancing around an electioneering bonfire.[14]

At times a candidate's frenetic actions went beyond "mixing and mingling" to the promise and deliverance of immediate and concrete rewards to pliant freeholders. John George Jackson's district contained several large counties with voters who lived as many as eighty miles from the polls. To encourage them to do their civic duty, Jackson promised accommodations at the family tavern.[15] A contender who lacked his own tavern was expected to make some of its offerings available nonetheless. One contemporary expressed his sorrow "that such is the disposition of my Countrymen, that nothing will induce them to attend elections of however great im-

Political Practices

portance without being treated."[16] The practice of providing food and "spiritous liquors" to the electorate had solid colonial antecedents and was no more legal then than in the Jeffersonian period. That it persisted is well documented: "the candidates offer drunkenness openly to anyone who is willing to give them his vote," noted a French traveler.[17] But there was likewise continuing hostility to such a "sistem of electioneering intrigue,"[18] though some critics, for their own political survival, became able practitioners themselves.[19]

The Aid of Friends

Although the candidate bore the brunt of a canvass, his friends, family, and supporters assisted in a variety of ways. On some occasions proxies represented a person's interests locally, rebutted attacks made in his absence, or explained the absence itself in convincing, inoffensive terms.[20] This aid was critical given the fact that a "man may have considerable Influence within a narrow Circle; but it will seldom extend thro' a County," much less a multicounty district.[21] Friends helped by drafting, publishing, and circulating campaign literature and by contacting specific groups on behalf of the candidate, as in John Preston's request that John Smith "strongly recommend me to your good honest German friends at Botetourt" and elsewhere.[22] In addition, supporters held campaign meetings, passed endorsing resolutions, organized committees (at times down to the equivalent of a precinct level),[23] and planned and sponsored large and diverse public gatherings to win votes en masse. During an Augusta County congressional race in 1809, "both parties had balls in Staunton, to which their adherents in the county were invited, with their wives and children. Each had also street processions, headed by its chief."[24] Four years later a supporter of John Clopton complained of the opposition's tactics: "not satisfied with court days and muster days, barbeques and fish-fries have been given to get the people together."[25] Public dinners, party celebrations, corresponding committees, bonfires, and court day meetings were common devices in a canvass.[26]

On the poll day itself, campaign workers became recruiters, as suggested in the following newspaper account of an election in April 1825: "Canvassing has been carried on by the friends of the different candidates with an ardor quite unprecedented. Parties have scoured the country in all directions; numerous voters have been induced to travel hither from very remote parts of the country, who have seldom before entered into the spirit of electioneering matters. — The aged and the young, and the rich and the poor freeholder, have been pressed into service of each favorite candidate; and no means have been left untried by the friends of the different parties to promote the election of their respective favorites."[27] Equally vivid is the example of a John Tyler supporter, "old Mr. Minge," who in a close election "took his horses and wagon, in a perfect fit of enthusiasm, and drove for three days over all the county, and collected the maimed, the halt, the blind, and those who never had voted for any one, and brought them to the polls."[28] Other election day responsibilities for friends included "keeping back as *corps de reserve*" a bloc of ballots for last-minute surges,[29] maintaining lists of yet-to-vote freeholders, assisting partisans with their accustomed "treats," and sustaining a proper degree of enthusiasm at the poll itself.[30]

"The Tongue of Malevolence, Partiality and Slander"

However valuable their public service, the friends of a candidate also used their private influence, though not always in so devious a fashion as charged by the sensitive John Randolph in 1811: "My enemies I find have been playing a deep game, and have played it too with great skill and address. An emissary . . . from 'the old man of the mountain' [Jefferson] has been slyly moving about the country, visiting Yancey, 'Judge' Johnson, etc. All the initiated have been busily at work like moles, underground, and this has been and is their plan of operation; to assail me by every species of calumny and whisper, but, Parthian-like, never to shew their faces, or give battle on fixed ground, moving about from individual to individual, and securing them man to man." This analysis perhaps best reflects Randolph's occasionally paranoid view of the world, but it also suggests a characteristic of many canvasses—the use of smears, rumors, and charges, often at the whisper level. In a candidate's mind, at least, too often it seemed that, as Thomas Mann Randolph suspected, "my adversary had fallen on the plan of depressing me instead of positively elevating himself."[31]

Rumors and smears were limited only by the contemporary imagination. "When my wish to represent the district was first made known to the people," wrote one candidate in a common lament, "the tongue of malevolence, partiality and slander, was not then inactive." "I have been grossly and most injuriously calumniated by some of my enemies," John Clopton wrote, "who have undertaken to ascribe to some of my political conduct an attachment to a foreign nation." John Marshall, Clopton's opponent in 1799, found himself accused of "a scandal," in his biographer's words, "in which . . . [he] and Pinckney were alleged to have been involved in Paris [and which in turn involved] the fate of a woman, her desperate voyage to America, her persecution, and sad ending." In Marshall's district, a Federalist sought to arouse anti-French (and anti-Republican) passions by distributing five hundred copies of a lurid pamphlet entitled *The Cannibal's Progress, or, The Dreadful Horrors of French Invasion! As Displayed by the Republican Officers and Soldiers, in the Perfidy, Rapacity, Ferociousness, and Brutality, Exercised towards the Innocent Inhabitants of Germany* (1798).[32]

Daniel Sheffey was accused of selling lead to the British during the War of 1812; Thomas Evans of "being a friend to aristocracy and the British Government" and of favoring "a general emancipation, to cause to be re[en]acted all the horrors of the West Indies"; and John Taylor of Caroline of ridiculing "the Caroline militia in comparison of regular troops" and of having "accused Genl. Washington of hard drinking!"[33] John Randolph felt himself plagued by insidious accusations. In 1798–99 he was charged with abolitionism and in 1814–15 with defending the British burning of Washington and favoring a limited monarchy in America.[34] In 1811 he complained that "previous to the election in Buckingham, the regular line of stages thro' that country, was diverted from the accustomed route to the great annoyance of the people, and the blame liberally thrown upon me," while in 1813 "ignorant people were made to believe that the British fleet had come into the Chesapeake to aid my election."[35] Other rumors suggested a candidate would contest an election if he lost, had withdrawn from the race, had been secretly of the wrong party stripe in some earlier crisis, had failed to qualify as a freeholder, had knuckled under in the face of opposition, and would be assisted at the polls by thugs to intimidate the electorate.[36]

Sometimes the blast went directly to the contender's character, as suggested in two examples from a western district. The ironically named "Fairplay" provided a devastating portrait of "David Chalmers: an obscure, chattering, conceited youngster, who a few years ago came into our state a wandering singing Master [whose election] would disgrace the Senate of Virginia."[37] Republican stalwart George Jackson of Harrison County wrote directly to the governor "complaining of the conduct of the High Sheriff of that County. In a suit for slander against himself [Jackson], this officer had caused to be carried to the jury, concealed in a tea-kettle, a quantity of ardent spirits with which they made merry over his case. The jury found a verdict in his favor, but set the damages at only seven shillings. Indisposed persons at the last elections had used this circumstance to his injury, by saying the County of Harrison was represented by a gentleman, whose character was valued at seven shillings."[38] Josiah Parker doubtlessly spoke for many in complaining of the "vile and dirty means practiced against" him,[39] while a contemporary described a common development: "Two gentlemen offers to represent this division in Congress and as one only is wanted I understand one makes very free with the other's reputation &c wch. I should not be surprised to hear of their having exchanged a few dry blows."[40]

Less personal and more public than rumors were specific, often substantive, charges against a candidate's conduct or that of his associates. Randolph and his friend James Mercer Garnett, for instance, were accused of aiding the British by opposing Madison's war measures.[41] Randolph also had to answer the accusation that he "paid no attention to the business of the House," that he had been disrespectful to its Speaker, that his absenteeism had deprived his constituents of adequate representation, and that he had been the aggressor in a near duel with Eppes.[42]

Joseph Lewis, Jr., was publicly damned for failing to support defensive measures in the War of 1812 and for being "at a mirthful festival" during "the most gloomy hour of peril" when the foe was "even at the water's edge."[43] John Clopton was scored for failing to "meet and oppose the [political] enemy" in his 1813 race, a charge which his supporters tried to turn to an advantage by claiming

Clopton was ill and his opponents knew it. "In a word, my friends," read one public letter, "I do not think it very fair to take advantage of this man's being sick to put forth malicious tales against him."[44] Countering rumors and charges required careful maneuvering, but in some cases, as above, it was possible to turn a defensive stance into an offensive one. In his first race for Congress, George Tucker had to answer an ugly accusation that as a young man he had mishandled funds in a school lottery. Tucker insisted on an immediate hearing, got the facts on the public record, and printed and circulated them throughout his district. He demanded and received a retraction of the charge. Alexander Smyth, on having his service in the War of 1812 challenged (perhaps justly), responded by getting and publishing in circular form a complimentary letter written by a well-known general.[45] The ostensive purpose of a public notice in a Richmond paper was to deny the rumor that Samuel Jordan Cabell had withdrawn; in fact, the notice became a platform for sounding his praises. Randolph used attacks on him as springboards for oratorical assaults on his opponents, and James Mercer Garnett issued a circular defending himself from a variety of charges.[46] In 1813 a three-phase broadside war between supporters of John George Jackson and his opponent gave each side the opportunity to convert vulnerable positions into more tenable, even aggressive ones.[47]

Another effective way of countering charges was to solicit certified statements that set the record straight or at least defended the candidate's position.[48] Authoritative documentary evidence might also be used, as in the following newspaper item:

A FEDERAL TRICK DETECTED
We are authorized to assert that John Morrow did NOT vote on the subject of Mr. Chittenden's resolution, as the Berkeley and Jefferson Intelligencer states he did. . . .the Journal of the House is lodged with the printers for their inspection.[49]

When all else failed, a clever contender could turn the tables on his adversaries by resorting to political satire:

MR. SNOWDEN,
Finding it impossible by any *fair* means, to turn out the hon. J. Lewis, the present member of Congress, we have found it necessary to have re-

course to lies, which we have found very useful especially at the late election in *Prince William*.

One of our stories, of his intention to tax *Flour*, you have unfortunately for us contradicted, which has made it proper to make a little variation, by reporting now, that a tax on all produce *except Flour*, was his object, in consequence of himself and friends being interested in that article.

We can assert of our own knowledge, that he was a great friend to the *Embargo*, and was one of Mr. J's principal advisers to recommend it to Congress. He is a *Royalist*, and a Mahometan, which is plain from his wearing a blue coat, the *secret* badge of all of them. He was in favour of paying tribute to England and France. He is a man of no *charity*, and little or no *religion*, and of a persecuting spirit; has an unbounded aversion to *Quakers* and *Dutchmen*, and their principles. He brought a bill into Congress to tax all their property, *real and personal*, and gave as a reason that they were more industrious and independent than any other class of citizens, of course were better able to bear it. He bro't in another bill providing that the *new raised army* should consist of *Quakers* only, from 60 to 75 years of age. They passed the lower house, but by the exertions of his political opponents, were fortunately, for many of his repectable constituents, lost in the Senate.

He is no *poor man's* friend, & an inveterate enemy to *old soldiers*: he wanted congress to agree to put them all to death, or let general W—— take them to New Orleans to sell as slaves to supply his table with segars, &c. which would prevent their future troublesome applications: his *hostility* to the interests of the citizens of Alexandria, Georgetown, and Washington, is obvious.

We shall lose no time in making these things known, and divers others too tedious to enumerate, both before and at the ensuing elections.

MANY.

N.B. It is whispered that he corresponds with *Bonaparte*, and is in *British* pay.[50]

"Positively Elevating"

In a sense the various rumors and charges reflect the negative side of a canvass and represent, to quote Thomas Mann Randolph, "the plan of depressing" an opponent, rather than "positively elevating" oneself. The latter device was also common and might be divided between personal and political appeals to the voters.

A stock form of personalizing a campaign was to link the candidate with some individual or some idea respected by the electorate.

Political Practices

Federalists John Marshall and Henry Lee both used with success a letter from Patrick Henry supporting them for Congress in 1799. According to Beveridge: "Henry's letter saved Marshall. Not only was the congressional district full of Henry's political followers, but it contained large numbers of his close friends. His letter was passed from hand to hand among these and by election day, was almost worn out by constant use." In a race to replace his late father, John B. Clopton stressed that association; in another contest Thomas Mann Randolph reminded voters that his father-in-law was Thomas Jefferson.[51] Some congressional contenders associated themselves with one or more of the persons running for other offices, such as the General Assembly, to be decided on the same polling day, but the reverse tactic was also used—remaining aloof from other races and thus not offending the friends of other candidates.[52]

Similar was the occasional appeal to class lines. David Garland's effort to demonstrate that an ordinary citizen might be elected proved successful but also aroused some support among the gentry for his upper-class opponent.[53] Using a variation of the "common man" tactic, solidly aristocratic John Dawson entered a crowded court-room in one election shouting, "Make way, gentlemen, for the poor man's friend!"—an exclamation well received by those who heard it.[54] Some candidates also expressed concern not for the electorate alone but for "every member of the community, whether he be a voter or not," and one contender, an established farmer, said he would "neither be driven from the path leading to the prosperity of our country by want or poverty, nor allured from it by avarice or am-bitions."[55] Several would-be congressmen broadcast their ties with important ethnic and religious groups in their districts.[56]

Finally, what voter could miss the personal physical appeal of William Branch Giles's first opponent, who bore "a wounded limb" from his Revolutionary War service; or of John Roane, Jr., who was always attired in "homespun of his own manufacture"; or of the Republican candidate who, in contrast to his gentry rival at the poll, "stood up with his waistcoat wide open and his shirt hanging out and deliberately began to comb his hair with a dirty horn comb"; or of the contender who wore native dress in a heavily German district?[57]

These widely diverse and direct personal appeals were of prime importance in a campaign, but congressional candidates also made appeals through the political principles they professed and the policies they stood for. Between generalized statements and concrete issues, most contenders followed the advice of a Virginia editor to a fellow Republican: "I hope, my friend, in your conversations with the people, you frequently recur to governmental expenses.—it is an awful field, and one on which the people ought to be well informed.—'tis in vain in the present temper of the United States to talk of *principle*; from that there has been considerable defection: we ought therefore to bring our arguments home to their feelings. — I am sorry to speak so ill of the *sovereign people*, but they have really become very mercenary, and of consequence opposed to war expenses. —Let *peace & economy* then be our constant theme."[58] The bipartisan nature of such an approach is seen in the recommendation given a Federalist congressman to get out a "concise statement of fiscal concerns" since "none strike so forcibly on the minds of the multitude as money matters."[59]

Candidates like William Cabell Rives who canvassed with a reasoned political philosophy stood in a minority against those who favored "peace and economy" or whose political stands were essentially a matter of party colors.[60] The three races between Eppes and John Randolph turned in great part on the question of partisan loyalty;[61] in other instances, arguments were offered against the effectiveness in office of a candidate who opposed administration policy or, conversely, that a man associated with the president, and agreeing with him, was likely to get more done for his constituents.[62] In his maiden race James Mercer Garnett developed the full potential of a party appeal by acknowledging his Republican ties while at the same time stressing his "independent" thinking and deprecating the "spirit of party" itself in favor of a commitment to the commonweal.[63]

Occasionally party labels broadened to the point of being open-ended, but this did not always bring victory. The Federalist-oriented "Friends of Peace, Commerce, and no Foreign Alliance" lost their Valley district in 1813, as did the more inclusive "Democratic, Republican, Proclamation, Protest, State Rights, Sink or Swim, Rotation in Office, '98 and '99 Principle Ticket" in Dinwiddie County several decades later.[64] Nor did the obliteration of partisan lines necessarily obliterate partisanship itself. In a Loudoun election in 1821, "Algernon Sidney" accused the Federalists of being "politicians who wish to affect moderation, and bury party distinctions, for the plausible purpose of gaining their point in the congressional election. . . . In one ear they whisper in soothing accents, let us AMALGAMATE, there are no party distinctions, we are all federalists, we are all republicans while in the other they proclaim away with your democracy."[65]

Certain political questions, such as the newly ratified Federal Constitution, Jay's Treaty, the Alien and Sedition Acts and Virginia and Kentucky Resolutions, the Embargo, the War of 1812, and the Compensation Act of 1816, produced solid differences of opinion in congressional districts and led to issue-oriented campaigning.[66] That campaign and issue could be conjoined is evident in, for example, a letter published in the *Richmond Enquirer* on April 6, 1813: "There is no reasonable expectation of putting an end to this partial, *unnecessary* and *ruinous* war except by a change in our representation to Congress; the President's personal pride and resentment, will urge him forward, so long as Congress will give the means of prosecuting the war."[67] "A Federal Voter" expressed a similar conjunction by advising his fellow party men to "keep the embargo, the *dam*-bargo, sounding in the ears of the farmers."[68] Localized issues are reflected in the opposition to Joseph Neville's stand on the excise tax (1793), Osborn Sprigg's earlier voting record in the General Assembly (1803), John George Jackson's role in the Yazoo affair (1805), Joseph Lewis's interests in roads and canals (1807), and Thomas Marshall's antislavery views (1823).[69]

When other devices failed, a candidate could always flood the electorate with an appeal to Malthusian statistics, as did Edwin Gray.

THE COST OF THE WAR
The hon. Mr. Gray, of Virginia, in his circular address to his constituents, has entered into some curious, but strictly correct calculations about the costs, &c. of the *war*. Amongst several others, we are forcibly struck with the following, which we earnestly recommend to the serious consideration of the *Virginia Farmers*.

"If (says Mr. Gray) the war should continue until the end of the year

Electioneering: Personal Courtship

1815, (of which there is every prospect) the increase of the *public debt* will amount to the enormous sum of ONE HUNDRED AND EIGHT MIL-LIONS OF DOLLARS, which being added to the public debt at the commencement of the war (45 millions) amounts in all to upwards of ONE HUNDRED AND FIFTY MILLIONS OF DOLLARS—rating seventeen dollars to a pound avoirdupois, it would make EIGHT MILLIONS, EIGHT HUNDRED AND TWENTY-THREE THOUSAND, FIVE HUNDRED AND TWENTY-NINE POUNDS weight of silver, would load FOUR THOUSAND FIVE HUNDRED WAGGONS, at 2000 pounds each, and being spread upon the surface of the earth, would cover *FIFTY-SEVEN ACRES, THIRTY-FIVE SQUARE RODS AND SEVENTY-TWO SQUARE FEET!!!!* Taking the amount of the expenses of this present year at 38 millions (a low calculation) it is—*FOR EVERY DAY, ONE HUNDRED AND FOUR THOUSAND ONE HUNDRED AND SIXTY-SIX DOLLARS, FOR EVERY HOUR, FOUR THOUSAND TWO HUNDRED AND FIFTY-TWO DOLLARS, AND FOR EVERY MINUTE OF THE YEAR, SEVENTY DOLLARS!!!*

Now let the man who is able and willing to pay his part of this enormous sum, for the accommodation of *British Runaways*, go to the poll, and vote for *War and Taxes*.[70]

At the Poll

Whatever the variety of personal and political appeals in a canvass, they were expected to be made, at a minimum, by the candidate himself on election day, despite the hardship of traversing, for example, a western district "larger than the state of New Hampshire."[71] Rivals—such as Madison and Monroe in 1789, Eppes and Randolph in three races, or John Tyler and Andrew Stevenson in several—might tour the district together, take seats in view of the poll, and react directly to a freeholder's choice. "We observe in the looks of the candidates & their active partizans," wrote one contemporary of an election in 1821, "all those alternations of hope & fear, of joy & sorrow, which the fluctuating state of the polls is calculated to produce."[72] This spirit is captured in the following account of the race between Clopton and Marshall in 1799:

> I vote for John Marshall.
> Thank you, sir, said the lank, easy-mannered Federalist candidate.
> Hurrah for Marshall! shouted the compact band of Federalists.
> And I vote for Clopton, cried another freeholder.

Political Practices

May you live a thousand years, my friend, said Marshall's competitor. Three cheers for Clopton! roared the crowd of Republican enthusiasts.[73]

On occasion, when a candidate could not be present, he arranged for a substitute fortified with a good excuse, which in some instances was not good enough for the voters.[74]

Attendance at the polls offered a direct chance to protect one's interest. "Your very presence," one candidate was told, "wou'd shrink into nonentity almost—those now aspiri[ng] Assassins who triumphing in their Calumnies of Absent characters—have belittled themselves even in the estimation of their adherents." The same candidate was further advised: "Your being here will prevent false representations of your Sentiment, and extravagant deviations on the minds of the *People*."[75] By being at the election, a contender could squarely answer false charges and immediately challenge bad votes, or in a few cases, such as the mass voting of militia units, even encourage them.[76] Attendance, however expedient, sometimes took courage. Hostile audiences could intimidate a timid speaker, and physical assault was a possibility. "I understand that I am to be insulted today if I attempt to address the people," said an irate John Randolph, "that a mob is prepared to lay their rude hands upon me and drag me from these hustings, for daring to exercise the rights of a freeman." "Then," wrote a contemporary, "fixing his keen eye on the malcontents and stretching out and slowly waving his long fore-finger towards them, he continued: 'My Bible teaches me that the fear of God is the beginning of wisdom, but that the fear of man is the consumation of folly.' He then turned to the people and went on with his discourse."[77]

As the above example suggests, a canvass often became heated and personal. "It happens too unfortunately, that the questions of Tariff & of Roads & Canals, which divide the public, on the grounds both of the Const[itution] & of justice," wrote Madison to Lafayette, "are blended with & greatly increase the flame kindled by the Electioneering zeal." On the day of the poll the flame might become so intense as to produce the kind of "noisy hustle and confusion" that led a reporter to exclaim, "God forbid that we should ever have reoccurence of the same scene!"[78]

The flame of partisanship at the polls might combine with the common "barrel of whiskey . . . with the head knocked in" to produce, if not drunken brawls during an election, then a riot in its aftermath.[79] And the aftermath itself might bring a panoply of reactions from the candidates. A loser could say with Hugh Nelson that the electorate had spoken and had determined he should "continue to enjoy the more pleasing station of a private Citizen," or a winner could say with Madison, after his victory over Monroe, that personal friendship had also triumphed.[80] At his moment of success, Daniel Morgan, "who could be arrogant and bombastic[,] exposed a very humble side in thanking the freeholders."[81] On losing in 1795 to Richard Brent, Richard Bland Lee was said to have been "so much mortified he either was or feigned to be unwell, and went to bed sooner than usual."[82] Lee's health may have also suffered from exposure to such postelection doggerel as appeared in the Philadelphia *Aurora*:

> In Loudoun district, Virginians bent
> The ship of State to free
> From dangerous steerage, took in *Brent*
> And turned out pilot *Lee*.[83]

On the other hand, the aftermath might produce the combination of sour grapes and self-pity experienced by John Randolph, when after a bitter loss to Eppes in 1813, he wrote one friend that he could not "by the help of newspaper puffs, patriotic toasts, or Congressional rhetoric, work myself up into a serious regret that I am no longer under the abject dominion of Mr. H. Clay & Co." To another correspondent he expressed confidence that he had done his duty, owed "the public nothing" because they had given him other than an honorable dismissal, and wondered only how "nearly one thousand freeholders should have persisted in refusing to withdraw their confidence from me—after I had been left alone to sustain the unequal conflict against the patronage and influence of both the governments, state and federal—without the aid of a single press in the State."[84]

Bitter disappointment could lead to more tragic consequences. The acrimonious campaign between Charles Fenton Mercer and former United States Senator Armistead T. Mason resulted in several duels. Mason himself was killed in one of them by his kinsman John Mason McCarty, who had supported Mercer. The two men had "at length terminated their disputes by a duel, they fought at the distance of 10 feet with musketts and ball," and Mason fell.[85]

Though diverse in their electioneering practices, candidates in Jeffersonian Virginia shared a prime concern about what would happen at that moment of truth at the poll. The elections combined a function of government with political traditions and social needs to form a unique institution in the Dynasty period.

VII

Congressional Elections

Spring in Jeffersonian Virginia was a season of restoration, a time for planting and calculating the rewards of future crops; for renewing social relations; and for enjoying warmth, sunshine, and green foliage. And, because elections took place in the spring, it was also a time for restoring the state's political system. In the odd years, part of the season's activity focused on choosing United States representatives.

The Legal Framework

The General Assembly established a legal framework for congressional races on November 22, 1788, when it passed "An act for the election of representatives pursuant to the constitution of government of the United States."[1] This statute drew heavily from traditional polling laws and retained some of them verbatim. Section I acknowledged a need to implement the new Federal Constitution and further stated: "And whereas, it is provided by the said constitution, that until the enumeration therein directed [the first census] shall be taken, Virginia shall be entitled to ten members of the house of representatives, and that the times, places, and manner of holding elections for the same, shall be prescribed by the legislature: Be it therefore enacted by the General Assembly, that the counties within this commonwealth, shall be divided into ten districts, in the manner following, to wit: ... [counties listed by name and district]." The next section covered the how, when, where, and by whom of electing "some discreet and proper person, being a freeholder, and ... a bona fide resident for twelve months within such district, as a member to the house of representatives for the United States." It also detailed the large responsibilities of the sheriff and his assistants in conducting the poll. Section III made voting mandatory, specified the procedure for certifying and transmitting the results through various levels to Congress itself, and gave the penalties for administrative remissness. The final three sections prohibited "any candidate or other person on his behalf" from "treating" "any elector or pretended elector," authorized compensation for sheriffs, and excluded Kentucky from portions of the law.

At times amid controversy, the General Assembly passed similar acts in 1792, 1802, 1813, and 1823—that is, in the wake of each decennial census and federal reapportionment.[2] The basic change from law to law concerned the grouping of counties into congressional districts. The number of districts shifted from ten (1788) to nineteen (1792), twenty-two (1802), twenty-three (1813), and twenty-two again (1823). In size they ranged from two counties or boroughs to twelve (in a Valley district, 1823–31), but the most common number was four. With very few exceptions, a district fell entirely within one of the four geographical sections of the state so that regardless of the number of counties in a given district, all were, for instance, Valley counties.[3] This allowed the social and economic differences of Virginia's regions to be mirrored in the state's congressional delegation. A representative of a Valley district had a more distinct constituency and was better able to understand and reflect its interests than would have been possible if the lines had been drawn without regard to sectional integrity. For the Old Dominion, at least, the *National Intelligencer* commented correctly in 1803: "The elections for representatives in Congress, it will be allowed, are those which, in general, form the best criterion of public sentiment."[4]

A second major change in the various laws moved the time of elections forward. Originally held in February, they shifted to March in 1793 and to April in 1801.[5] This lessened the chances of polls in adverse weather and allowed more time between the adjournment of a congressional session and an election. In the latter consideration Virginia deviated from common practice elsewhere. Regular sessions of Congress convened on the first Monday in December each year and adjourned for the final time in early March of odd-numbered years. Most states selected their congressmen a year or more before they took office. For example, delegations of the Sixth Congress convening in December 1799 had been chosen in some states in the spring of 1798, in most states in the fall of 1798, but

Congressional Elections

in Virginia in the spring of 1799, after the adjournment of the final session of the Fifth Congress. Many states, therefore, had lame-duck representatives for at least one annual session. But in the Old Dominion, as Thomas Ritchie noted with pride, "the representative is completely *functus officie* ['having performed his office; hence, resigned from office'] before he goes back to the bar of the people."[6]

The Physical Setting

The basic act of 1788 required that congressional elections take place in the various county courthouses, the customary site for polling. Subsequent laws modified this provision slightly to accommodate voters in cities, boroughs, and remote areas of large counties. Between 1812 and 1818 alone the legislature authorized nine such alternative sites. Typical was the allowance of a second polling place in Shenandoah County in 1818; the election there was to be held in the home of a justice of the peace and supervised by a deputy sheriff and "five intelligent freeholders resident within that part of the said county."[7]

As physical structures, the courthouses varied tremendously. The one in Hanover, an impressive red-brick building, had changed little since Patrick Henry advertised his talent for oratory there in the Parsons' Cause in 1763. On the frontier, however, a Virginian might find squat, crude boxes of log or stone, subject to frequent alterations.[8] The courthouses and environs led a Rip Van Winkle existence. Most of the time they were inactive and surrounded by a tiny cluster of equally quiet homes and perhaps a store or two. At least once a month, however, when the county court convened, the structures came alive as citizens of all ages left their farms and traveled by horse, wagon, carriage, or foot to be present for the day's many activities. George Tucker described what a person would discover on arrival:

The yard was thronged with people from the remotest parts of the county—they presented a most motley and grotesque collection. Here an old German with a long black beard, dressed in red and blue striped homespun—not far from him, a stout, hale, rawboned, ruddy farmer, evidently of Scotch-Irish origin—in one corner, an old woman with a little table spread with cakes, and early apples, and a boy or two to replenish her table when required—wagons were also near the court yard, containing different species of rude ware of country manufacture—some with hempen cloth, some with whiskey—and coarse pottery—spinning wheels—slaies [sleys] for weaving—and other household implements. They were all neat and clean in their dress, which, was of cotton cloth, manufactured by themselves, and striped yellow, red, and blue, in infinite variety, but producing in the *tout ensemble* the character of uniformity.[9]

Amid the hustle, bustle, and hoi polloi, the gentlemen justices oversaw the public welfare, lawyers pressed their claims, farmers transacted business and bought supplies, land might be auctioned, slaves sold, friends visited, and news and rumors passed freely.[10] "The traveler gets a many-sided entertainment," wrote one visitor, "and gains instruction as to where taxes are heavy, where wives had eloped or horses been stolen, and where the new doctor had settled."[11] The raucous side of court day often centered in and around the local tavern. The village of Tappahannock was "very full, though what they come for, God knows, except it's to get drunk," commented one observer, "No other business seems to be going on."[12] A disappointed peddler noted in his diary for November 23, 1807: "very Poor Court, no fighting or Gouging, very few Drunken people."[13] It is unfortunate the peddler missed being at Hanover Courthouse when a northern traveler stopped there:

The moment I alighted a wretched pug-nosed fellow assailed me to swap watches. I had hardly shaken him off, when I was attacked by a wild Irishman, who insisted on my "swapping horses" with him, and in a twinkling ran up the pedigree of his horse to the grand dam. Treating his importunity with little respect, I became near being involved in a boxing-match, the Irishman swearing that I did not "trate him like a jintleman." I had hardly escaped this dilemma when my attention was attracted by a fight between two very unwieldy, fat men, foaming and puffing like two furies, until one succeeding in twisting a forefinger in a side-lock of the other's hair, and in the act of thrusting, by this purchase, his thumb into the latter's eye, he bawled out "king's curse," equivalent, in technical language, to "enough."[14]

Election Day

Amid legal and business transactions, and assorted social behavior and misbehavior, the Virginia system of government functioned at the rudimentary level where voters selected men to represent them in office. Laws and contemporary accounts suggest a common pattern for these elections. When there was competition for an office, the poll was only the last phase of several months' activity and featured the "smiling indefatigable candidate, proud and happy to grasp the hand of the bone and sinew of the land—the horny handed sons of toil"[15] before he "mounted the rostrum and harangued the people."[16] Then the high sheriff ordered the balloting to begin. And it did, depending on the weather, either inside the courthouse or in a shady spot nearby. An eyewitness described what happened next:

two clerks were seated at tables with poll-books, and large sheets of papers ruled in perpendicular columns, wide enough to contain the names of the voters. At the head of these columns were written, severally, the names of the candidates, and underneath them, as the election progressed, the names of the electors who voted for them, as the votes were given *viva voce*. . . . The Sheriff was the judge of the election, and by him voters were admitted, one at a time. . . . The voter's name was entered on the poll-book, and he was asked by the Sheriff, in a voice audible over the whole courthouse, "For whom do you vote?" The elector, turning to the bench, and glancing along the line of candidates—each of whom, perhaps, at the moment is grinning on him a smile of expectancy—he announces audibly, looking, and perhaps pointing, at the preferred candidate as he speaks: "I vote for Mr. A. for Congress, and for Mr. B. and Mr. C. for the Legislature." "Thank you, sir," is simultaneously responded by Messrs. A., B., C., with a bow and a broad smile of complacency, and the voter's name is entered in each of the three columns headed with the names of these three candidates. Passing out at the end of the bar opposite that which he entered, he is taken by the friends of the candidates voted for into the courthouse yard, where their barrels or jugs of whiskey are placed, and if he uses the "critter," he is helped to a grog at each place by the aid of a tin cup and a pail of water.[17]

Critics believed the viva voce system exposed the electorate to intimidating pressures, but the practice dated from colonial times and would persist in Virginia until after the Civil War.[18] The Constitution of 1851 allowed only one exception: "in all elections . . . the votes shall be personally and publicly given *viva voce*, provided that dumb persons entitled to suffrage may vote by ballot."[19] The voice method did add color and help to personalize the polling system, especially in a close race when a freeholder's calling the name of his choice brought not only a "treat" and kind word but also a cheer from bystanding partisans. One witness parodied this sometimes ludicrous pattern:

> Hurray for McRae and Hurrau for McCraw!
> Hurray and Hurrau for McRae and McCraw!
> Hurrau for McCraw and Hurray for McRae!
> Hurrau and Hurray for McCraw and McRae!
> Hurrau for McRae and Hurray for McCraw!
> Hurray and Hurrau for McRae and McCraw!
> Hurray for McCraw and Hurrau for McRae!
> Hurrau and Hurray for McCraw and McRae![20]

Despite the opportunity for undue influence by the candidates and by the milieu itself, some voters maintained a marvelous independence. Richmond's famous "Two Parsons"—Episcopalian John Buchanan and his close friend, Presbyterian John D. Blair—shared a Federalist point of view but were not political activists, and they resented pressure applied on them to vote in the heated race between John Clopton and John Marshall in 1799. The ministers agreed to attend the election, where one supported Marshall as expected. The other, however, called Clopton's name "to the great surprise of everyone." The two men then departed, saying, "No one will probably trouble us about voting again."[21] Four years later in Shenandoah County, a spirited freeholder "declared in an audible voice that he was for *King George*" and had it "so entered on the poll-books."[22] Finally, a bemused historian of Hancock County reported:

When this county formed part of Brooke, in the early days, it was customary for the voters who wished to vote, to go to Wellsburg, that being the only place of voting within the county. Along in 1815, there was an election coming off, which was expected by the politicians to be very close. Under these circumstances, all the citizens entitled to a vote, were earnestly urged to the polls. There were three candidates in the field, and each one had his political tricksters out electioneering. They rode over the length and breadth of the county, hailing every one whom they might meet to go to the polls and vote for so-and-so. At this time there lived in the northern extremity of Brooke, two Germans, named respectively Neicewanger and Goddard, who never attended elections, and by the way were little acquainted with the laws of the land, and were easily made to believe anything that might be told them. The politicians called on them, and attempted to electioneer. But neither could be made interested in the affair. About all that they said was to shake their heads, and in their own tongue, uttered "Nein." One of them said, "I no don't care for some of dese bolitical matters what you speaks," and the other said, "des mox nix ouse." Finally they were made to believe that in case they failed to go and vote, a fine would be imposed upon them. With such positiveness was this told them, that they thought it must be true. At once they became frightened, and saddled their horses and off to Wellsburg they went. But when they reached the voting place, they were informed that they could vote or let it alone. No fine would subject them to perform this act. When this was ascertained, the Teutons got very angry to know that they had been deceived in that way. Stubbornness seized them at once, and all that the candidates could do to get them to vote, proved of no avail.

Voting then was conducted on the *viva voce* plan, and the polls were kept open for three successive days.

Neicewanger and his neighbor Goddard concluded, as they had traveled thirty-one miles to vote, they would vote for each other.

"Well," said the judge, "Mr. Neicewanger, who do you want to vote for?"

"Ov dese candidates I no like some, and I wotes for Jim Gottard."

He was informed by the judge that Goddard was not a candidate.

"I wotes for Jim Gottard anyhow," he replied.

The folks tried to reason with him, but it was no use; he only said:

"I wotes for Jim Gottard every dimes."

And when Goddard was asked the same question, he said:

"Me wotes for Neicewanger."[23]

On occasion the combination of an active electorate, a hot race, and a generous portion of liquid treats led directly to a combustible finale, as depicted in the following report: "A barrel of whiskey for all, with the head knocked in, and the majority took it straight. Independent of the political excitement, the liquour added fuel to the flame. Fights became common, and every now and then there would be a knock-down and drag-out affray." As the margin shifted from one candidate to the other, "there were shoutings and hurrahs perfectly deafening. Men were shaking fists at each other, rolling up their sleeves, cursing and swearing, with angry and furious denunications. Some became wild with agitation."[24] "Came to Henry Court 38 miles," recorded a young lawyer in his diary in 1791:

"great crowd of people it being Election day, when the Election was over the hill was covered with a thick and numerous crowd of people, rudeness displayed itself in every form imaginable with flying hats & shouts of joy. Some expressed themselves, others by loud and vociferous quarrelling would collect a Crowd, others would collect a crowd by dealing out Grog and proclaiming come and drink all the friends of —— this is his treat, when all on a sudden such a violent affray breaks out as to overset grog cryer and all."[25] Such accounts make one question the usually sage Edmund Pendleton when he wrote Thomas Jefferson that the exertions "of the people in their various elections . . . must, if properly directed, produce reform without convulsions; and in this consists the Superior Merit of a Representative Republican Form."[26]

The High Sheriff

Whether the poll led to a brawl or not, the sheriff supervised all parts of an election in his county—advertising the date, directing clerks, admitting voters, keeping order, and determining when it should close. On the latter point he had considerable latitude. At any time there appeared to be no further voters, he called aloud three times for freeholders to come forward and ballot; if none did, the poll ended. At his discretion, however, it could reopen. For reasons of inclement weather or of a large crowd yet to vote at sundown (after which balloting was prohibited) an election could continue up to three days. Although an eleven-day poll took place in Harrison County in 1790, the process normally lasted only into the first afternoon. In the instance of an uncontested race and voter apathy, a simple show of hands ("voting by view") might replace the more time-consuming viva voce method.[27]

The law required a sheriff to announce publicly the winner's name — hardly a mystery given the voice-vote system. Informal returns might be dispatched to Richmond by courier. The official results, however, had to await the clerks' approval and the certification of all sheriffs in the district, who met later "at the court-house of the county first named in such district" to compare polls, break any tie by drawing lots, and fill out in duplicate an official form designating the congressman-elect. One copy of the certificate went to the person concerned and the other to the governor and his council, who then notified Congress.[28]

The central role and power of the sheriff is evident. He determined who voted, as well as when, where, how, and how long the poll was conducted and how it was reported. His partiality could decide an election and became a common source of complaint from losing candidates. In an extreme case in 1801, the chief election official was absent, no poll was taken, and a congressional candidate thus lost a bloc of friendly votes and a close district election.[29] After his one-ballot defeat in a Buckingham poll, John Randolph wrote bitterly, "The returning officer was also my enemy and admitted many . . . bad votes."[30]

Suggestive of the sheriff's duties, authority, and potential for mischief is the following official report on a tight election in Chesterfield County in 1801:

Thomas Goode, sheriff of the said county of Chesterfield, deposeth, that sometime previous to said election, and at the time of the same he was in a very bad state of health; that he was applied to on the first day, by John W. Eppes to take the poll in person, but he informed said Eppes, that his state of health would not admit of it; and he solemnly avers, that he apprehended at the time, and still believes, that he could not have undergone the fatigue of crying the votes without difficulty; that having a complaint in his bowels he was obliged frequently to be out of the Courthouse; that so far as he was able to conduct the election in person, he did so, by attending generally at the clerks table, and consigning to his deputy only the labour of crying the votes; that when present himself, he decided all contested points agreeably to the dictates of his conscience, without favor or partiality to either candidate; that no vote was rejected by him or his deputy while he was present; but he was informed on the last day of the said election by his deputy who had opened the poll a short time before his arrival at the Courthouse, that several votes had been rejected by the joint consent of the Candidates; that he the deponent, resides about ten miles from the Courthouse, and attended there on each day of the election: that the badness of the morning of the first day and his expectation of the waters being high, so as to intimidate many people from coming to said election induced him to keep open the poll longer; that on that day the water courses somewhat intimidated him and had not his attendance as sheriff been necessary, he does not think that he should have gone to the election, that William Brown, demanded that the poll should be closed on the first day and John W. Eppes, that it should be kept open; that on the second day the waters he believes had considerably abated, but he conceived it to be his duty as he had kept open the poll two days to keep it open another day, and further thought a power vested in the sheriff to keep open the poll the fourth day, if required by either of the candidates, and gave notice to them to that effect, in the morning of the third day before it was opened; and Mr. Eppes moreover demanded, that it should be kept open the fourth day; that on one of the days during the election, in his return home, he called at the houses of Daniel Stone and Daniel Moore, and informed them how the poll stood; he also called at Abraham Dunnaphant's and asked him to go and vote, and on his saying that he had no horse he lent him one; that Daniel Stone's House is about 150 yards from the road leading from the courthouse to that of the deponent and that by Daniel Moore's house, is the nearest way for him to go home; that it is about one mile from his house to Abraham Dunnaphant's; that he expected said Dunnaphant would vote for John W. Eppes, otherwise he should not have lent him his horse; that he the deponent was applied to at said election by Archer Bolling for his opinion in regard to his right to vote and gave it as his opinion, that he the said Bolling had a right but did not ask him for whom he intended to vote; that the said opinion was required some time before the said Bolling voted, but he the deponent was not present when he did vote.[31]

A consideration less obvious but also serious was the sequence of the district polls. They were conducted in each county but generally on different court days. In 1811, for instance, Randolph attended elections on April 1 (Charlotte), April 8 (Buckingham), April 15 (Prince Edward), and April 22 (Cumberland).[32] In close contests, the situation inevitably developed as it did in Berkeley in 1803: "This being the last election in the . . . district, every effort was made to get the voters out."[33] The candidates knew precisely what votes the others had and roughly the amount needed for victory; so it boiled down to one final canvass. Having the last poll in one's home ground could work wonders. A spectacular example is that of Jabez Leftwich of Bedford, in three races, 1821, 1823, and 1825. Although from a prominent and politically active local family, Leftwich had a slow start in his first congressional contest. On April 24, 1821, the *Richmond Enquirer* reported that he was trailing by the substantial margin of 226 votes, with only one county to go, Bedford, his own. On May 1 the *Enquirer* published the

Congressional Elections

Bedford results—Leftwich 857, Callaway 60. Two years later, on April 29, 1823, the *Enquirer* announced that Leftwich was behind a new opponent, N. H. Claiborne, by 814 votes—with only Bedford remaining. But on May 6 and 9 it stated an illegal poll of four or more days had given Leftwich a 1,180–47 victory in that county and thus reelection in the district, although it was "rumored that the election will be contested." In 1825, however, the Bedford magic failed Leftwich. Claiborne entered that last county leading by 1,003 votes, too much for Leftwich to overcome, even though the Bedford polls were kept open several days on his behalf.[34]

The Sovereign Freeholder

The object of Leftwich's or any candidate's exertions was, of course, the man with a vote. As a visiting British diplomat observed, "It is indeed in every country a difficult thing to decide who and where the *People* are, and it is not seldom that the term is made to apply to a minimum of the real population, its constituents." That group, argued the essayist "Phocion," bore responsibility for all society; a vote cast on any consideration but the public good was a crime against the community itself. "In a government like ours," he wrote, "in which almost all the public functionaries are chosen either mediately or immediately by the people, everything depends upon the proper exercise of the right of suffrage."[35]

The franchise in congressional races could be exercised by "persons qualified by law to vote for members to the house of delegates," which meant, in general terms, Virginians who owned a minimum of fifty acres or twenty-five acres and a house or similar improvements, with more liberal provisions for city dwellers.[36] The Old Dominion had a more restricted electorate than many states, but its exact dimensions are difficult to judge. In the 1780s Jefferson felt a "majority" of Virginia's adult white males lacked the vote, an estimate fully supported by Jackson Turner Main's analysis of landholdings in the state during the Confederation era. Charles S. Sydnor's sampling of various polls and property lists in that period led him to suggest that from half to two-thirds of the adult white males were disqualified in 1790.[37]

On the other hand, Sydnor acknowledged that "land was relatively cheap" and the property qualification not difficult to attain.[38]

Developing this idea, Robert E. and B. Katherine Brown concluded: "If possession of the right to vote by most men is democratic rather than aristocratic, Virginia must be considered democratic as far as the electorate was concerned. Most adult white men either had or soon acquired enough property to meet the voting requirements." The Browns added the indirect evidence that "in a colony where every known grievance found its way to the legislature by way of petitions, grievances about the franchise are conspicuous by their absence."[39] For a slightly later period, however, J. R. Pole located just such petitions, but he suggests the real question of political reform was apportionment, not suffrage, an argument also advanced by Chilton Williamson.[40] For the Federal period, Richard R. Beeman accepts the contention of the Browns that virtually all the adult white males could vote. Having examined a sampling of extant polls, he stresses not eligibility but the pattern of low participation: roughly 10 to 25 percent of the adult white males turned out for the ratification campaign of 1788; for 1789–92 the average was "less than 20 percent"; in the mid-1790s, it averaged about "25 percent of the eligible voters," "occasionally dipping below 15 percent"; and in two counties late in the decade, participation rose only to 35 and 45 percent of the adult white male population.[41] For the same era, however, Norman K. Risjord has analyzed fifteen polls in nine counties and has reported a turnout of roughly 50 percent.[42]

To date there is no comprehensive, systematic study of voting patterns in the Jeffersonian era, perhaps due to the dearth of collected returns. Still, generalizations have been offered, more in the Sydnor vein than in the camp of the Browns. Richard P. McCormick hypothesizes that "at least half of the adult white males were disfranchised," a conclusion in line with an opinion offered by Jefferson in 1824 and generally accepted by scholar Chilton Williamson, but modest in contrast with Julian Chandler's estimate that "as many as three fourths or two-thirds" lacked the vote.[43]

Although narrow in scope, Pole's analysis of presidential returns is the most systematic use of election statistics covering the full sweep of Jeffersonian Virginia. His findings for the period indicate the following turnouts of adult white males: 25 percent in 1800, 11 percent in 1804, 17 percent in 1808, 18 percent in 1812, 6 percent in 1816, 3 percent in 1820, and 12 percent in 1824.[44] This pattern can be partially tested because of the availability of congressional returns for 1819–21 and a complete, county-by-county census for 1820 providing specific data on the normally elusive category of "free adult white males." Sample counties used to compile table 13 include two or more from each of the four geographical regions, at least one from each of the major subregions, and two Federalist strongholds (Jefferson and Northampton counties). The elections include contested and uncontested races, as well as intraparty and interparty campaigns.

This sampling does not take into account such matters as weather conditions on a given poll day, the number of illegal voters, or the accuracy of the census takers.[45] Yet table 13 covers all geographic areas and a variety of partisan situations, and it provides the basis for a few tentative conclusions. First, the presidential returns clearly are not an accurate measure of voter participation.[46] The first party system had faded by 1819–21 and the second had not begun, and the campaigns lacked the burning issues of 1799, 1809, or 1813. Still, in all sixteen returns, the turnout far surpassed the level of the Monroe canvass of 1820, and seven of the sixteen equaled or exceeded the percentage for 1800, the highest of any presidential race in the era. Second, the returns bring into question the almost automatic association of uncontested elections with low turnouts. Participation in the three single-candidate contests was 21, 24, and 47 percent. Third, the five intraparty races seemed to engage voter interest, with three high percentages, 35, 36, 49, and only two low, 15, 19. Finally, in six of the sixteen returns, more than a third of the adult white males voted, and the overall average was above a fourth—suggesting that some historians might have slightly underestimated both the number of eligible voters and their participation in the political process.

It should be mentioned that voting was not a matter of privilege but was mandatory for all who qualified. Those failing to comply faced legal penalties. Like so much else in Virginia's election code, this provision appears to have been observed essentially in the breach, although a few freeholders were fined for violations. A citizen could also vote in each of the counties where he met the property requirement. These and most other polling provisions fell within the traditional pattern for nonpresidential elections held in the state.[47]

Table 13. Virginia adult white males and voters, 1819–21

Section and County	AWMs 1820	Cong. elec. Votes 1819	Cong. elec. % of AWMs	Pres. elec. Votes 1820	Pres. elec. % of AWMs	Cong. elec. Votes 1821	Cong. elec. % of AWMs
Tidewater							
Isle of Wight (below James)	965	453[u]	47	87	9	476[s]	49
Northampton (East. Shore)	697	?	—	13	2	130	19
Northumberland (N. Neck)	744	264[s]	35	36	5	159[u]	21
Piedmont							
Buckingham (Southside)	1532	231[s]	15	41	3	550[s]	36
Culpeper (N. Piedmont)	2400	526	22	55	2	542[?]	23
Valley							
Botetourt (S. Valley)	2131	?	—	24	1	502[u]	24
Jefferson (Upper Potomac)	2028	395[s]	19	21	1	352[?]	17
Trans-Allegheny							
Harrison	2121	712	34	70	3	826	39
Ohio	1840	275	15	121	7	454	25

Sources: Adult white males were calculated according to the method outlined in J. R. Pole, "Representation and Authority in Virginia from the Revolution to Reform," *Journal of Southern History* 24 (1958): 49, from the population figures in the *Census of Virginia for 1820*, published as an addendum to the Virginia House of Delegates, *Journal, 1822–1823* (Richmond, 1823); presidential returns are from the manuscript tabulations in the Virginia State Library.

Note: AWMs: adult white males; *s:* same party for both candidates; *u:* uncontested candidates; *?:* unknown party tie for one candidate. All other races were between candidates of different parties.

Political Practices

"Bad Votes"

An interesting and relevant aspect of Virginia election statistics is the matter of the illegal voter—the man who lacked the franchise but for one reason or another exercised it anyway. The evidence of "bad votes" is fragmentary and frequently suspect in the context of a disgruntled loser's complaint or legal proceedings. Still, the figures in table 14 are impressive and suggestive.[48]

Ample subjective evidence—largely contemporary opinion—also indicates the commonplace quality of illegal balloting. Thomas Mann Randolph, for instance, said about his race with incumbent Samuel Jordan Cabell in 1803, "My belief at this moment is that he has more bad votes—than myself," while Robert Rutherford in 1795 charged one "Sharper" with voting under eight different names for opponent Henry Lee. Rutherford felt that only two of every five of

Table 14. Illegal voting in Virginia congressional elections, 1795–1832

Election		Total votes	Claimed bad	Declared bad	% bad
1795	Bassett	422		33	8
	Clopton	432		37	9
1803	Lewis	1,004		355	35
	Moore	832		124	15
1811	Hungerford	769		271	35
	Taliaferro	763		143	19
1813	Bassett	1,015		63	6
	Bayly	1,072		64	6
1815	McCoy	1,213	355	149	12
	Porterfield	1,165	390	171	15
	Eppes	910	172	107	12
	Randolph	972	129	50	5
1830	Loyall	935	184	113	12
	Newton	948	384	42	4
1832	Draper	2,671		421	16
	Johnston	2,749		376	14

Sources: John Randolph to Harmanus Bleecker, Oct. 7, 1815, Randolph-Bleecker Letter Book, University of Virginia; M. St. Clair Clarke and David A. Hall, comp. *Cases of Contested Elections in Congress from the Year 1789 to 1834, Inclusive* (Washington, D.C., 1834), cases XI, XX, XXXI, XXXIII, LVII, and LX.

Lee's ballots were valid but maintained his own were "neare mostly legal."[49] "Col. Claiborne got a majority of voices," according to a Richmond newspaper in 1803, "but not of *legal* votes."[50] In the spring of 1817 the *National Intelligencer* predicted Armistead T. Mason would contest his loss in a congressional race on the grounds that "nearly a hundred bad votes were given in Loudoun county" to his opponent, Charles Fenton Mercer.[51] One prominent politician wrote of an election in 1798, "Upon that occasion by the consent of all parties concerned, every free white man was permitted to vote."[52]

Under the circumstances, the *Alexandria Advertiser* must have identified a common sentiment when it reported a congressional loser who "scruples the purity of the polls and designs purging them."[53] Bad votes may have been as inevitable as they were frequent. In the first place, legal technicalities usually gave way to decades of polling practices. There is, for example, the rather simple manner of how clerks kept their poll books. Specific statutes had been passed on the subject, but a check of the rolls in four counties in a district in 1813 revealed four slightly different ways of doing it, none meeting the letter of the law and most being "justified by general practice" or "long usage."[54]

The lack of any voter registration system and records contributed to the problem of illegal ballots. A nonfreeholder who voted might be challenged at the poll itself, but this was rare and probably risky for a candidate not wishing to offend a potential supporter or his friends.[55] Even when issued, a challenge could end by the person's taking an oath. Or it might reveal that property records were not available or in order, thus making it impossible to compile a list of qualified electors.[56] Suffrage laws could be interpreted in various ways on court day, the sheriff had great personal discretion over who could vote, and informality usually characterized the entire process. Finally, "bad votes" became important only in a close election—an atypical occurrence in the Dynasty era.

Under the circumstances, the most unusual aspect of illegal voting is that there was not more of it. Nonfreeholders cast ballots with impunity, but statistics clearly indicate that most adult white non-freeholders abstained at the polls. Perhaps they did so from a respect for the law or in deference to the more wealthy citizens whose holdings entitled them to the franchise. Or perhaps nonfreeholders, with few legal or business matters to transact, were less likely to be at a court (election) day and, even when they wanted to go, were less able to get there. Perhaps men who lacked an economic stake in society did not themselves recognize any political stake or role in it. It might also be argued that the traditional Virginia apathy toward elections reached the potentially illegal voter as well as the legal one. A major reason for this indifference—even in the face of laws making voting mandatory for those eligible—is the lack of competitiveness in many of the state's elections.

Only about half of the congressional races were seriously contested; and half of those were intraparty affairs turning more on personality rather than issue or partisan questions. Voter participation, legal or otherwise, thus reflected other political realities in the Old Dominion.

Voting Patterns

Only a few poll books have survived for Virginia's congressional elections from 1799 to 1825, and the contemporary press gave the races only sporadic coverage. The most thorough compilation to date, based on a great variety of extant primary sources, is found in the supporting data gathered for this study. For the fourteen election years in the period, the confirmed data range from a low of 50 percent of the possible county results for 1807 to a high of 95 percent for 1823 (table 15). In the absence of any tabulation of contests for the state legislature, these congressional statistics represent the most comprehensive set of election returns available for Jeffersonian Virginia.[57]

This compilation, though statistically incomplete, is large enough for some tentative conclusions. First, the relative absence of competitive polling is clear from an analysis of the returns over time. In eight of the fourteen election years, a majority of the congressional districts had uncontested races. Of these eight noncompetitive years, four—1817, 1819, 1821, and 1823—came during the "era of good feelings," when party lines and rivalry tended to blur if not disappear. On the other hand, the most competitive years—1799, 1809,

Table 15. Virginia congressional elections, 1799–1825

		Contested*		Winners				Incumbents		
Year	Total	No.	Between parties	R	F	M	?	Running	Reelected	Total candidates
Regular elections										
1799	19	16	14	11	8	0	0	14	10	37
1801	19	9	5	17	2	0	0	11	10	28
1803	22	13	8	18	4	0	0	15	13	38
1805	22	9	4	20	2	0	0	20	18	31
1807	22	8	2	17	2	3	0	21	20	31
1809	22	15	11	14	6	2	0	19	17	38
1811	22	10	6	14	5	3	0	16	15	33
1813	23	16	11	17	6	0	0	21	15	41
1815	23	14	9	17	4	2	0	19	16	40
1817	23	10	2	20	3	0	0	15	13	38
1819	23	9	2	19	3	0	1	19	16	34
1821	23	10	2	21	2	0	1	22	21	34
1823	22	9	5	20	2	0	0	19	19	35
1825	22	13	2	15	1	0	6	15	14	41
Total	307	161	83	240	50	10	8	246	217	499
% of regular elections		52	27	78	16	3	3	80	71	
Special elections										
1800–1824	18	13	4	16	1	0	1	NA	NA	38
Regular and special election totals										
1799–1825	325	174	87	256	51	10	9	246	217	537
% of total elections		54	27	79	16	3	3	NA	NA	NA

* Excluded are persons who received less than ten votes or who had announced they were not candidates.

1813, and 1815—featured races in at least 70 percent of Virginia's districts and are easily associated with great national crises, such as the Alien and Sedition Acts, commercial warfare with Great Britain and France, and the War of 1812.

The returns also indicate a sectional pattern. Far more competition for office existed west of the Blue Ridge than east of it. For the entire period, a majority of western districts had competitive elections, and the Trans-Allegheny region featured three of every four races having two or more candidates. Conversely, a majority of eastern districts had uncontested campaigns, and the Piedmont had about 60 percent in that category. Phrased another way, the Piedmont section had a majority of the competitive districts in only two of the fourteen election years, the Tidewater in six, the Valley in eight, and the Trans-Allegheny in eleven of the fourteen years.

This pattern is accounted for in part by the persistence of Federalist strength, and thus party rivalry, west of the Blue Ridge and within the Tidewater counties of the Northern Neck and Eastern Shore. One might also speculate that the vitality of western politics reflected the vitality of a heterogeneous and dynamic social and economic structure, while that of the east was more settled, even static and declining. If one accepts the assumption that competition for office is an indication of democracy in a region, then Virginia mirrors a Turnerian pattern, with more democracy beyond the Blue Ridge than east of it. On the other hand, the Tidewater's competitiveness suggests a lingering party rivalry could be the crucial factor.

Special Elections

Aside from the regular biennial campaigns, competitive or otherwise, three other kinds of elections merit comment: those for United States senators, those to fill sudden vacancies in Congress, and those regular races whose final results were determined not within the district but by the House of Representatives.

Seldom did competition mark the selection of Virginia's United States senators by the General Assembly, partly because of Republican and eastern dominance of the legislature[58] and partly because the office itself loomed as a six-year burden to its holders. Of twelve Virginians who served one or more instances in the Senate from 1801 to 1825, eleven failed to complete regular terms.[59] Three died in office, but eight resigned, largely for reasons of personal convenience. Typical was William Branch Giles, whose letter of resignation to the governor in 1815 expressed a desire for the "scenes of domestic life" and stated: "In consequence of an absence from home for a portion of each year during a period of nearly five and twenty years, in which I have been engaged in serving the people in the representative character, my private concerns have become materially deranged, and in my judgment a strong obligation is therefore imposed upon me to give my personal attention to their reestablishment."[60] No incumbent senator lost a bid for reelection in the Dynasty era.

Elections for regular Senate terms or to fill vacancies occurring while the legislature was in session followed a simple pattern. Votes were taken in both houses, counted by a joint committee and announced to the governor, who notified the winner.[61] Senators-elect usually responded with letters marked by humility and a promise of dutiful service. Congressman Andrew Moore, however, added another twist when he accepted in September 1804, after having "delayed an answer for the purpose of ascertaining the wishes of the District on the subject, and also the probability of a Republican successor in the District."[62]

Several vacancies developed while the General Assembly was not meeting, and the executive made interim appointments. Governor John Page in 1804 had the unusual opportunity to fill both Senate seats by this procedure and had his choices confirmed later by the legislature.[63] Considering Republican and eastern influence in the Assembly, it is hardly surprising that of the twelve Virginians who at one time or another served in the United States Senate from 1801 to 1825, all were Republicans and all but one resided east of the Blue Ridge.[64]

A less frequent election required the filling of a sudden congressional vacancy. The governor usually received word from a resigning member or, especially in the case of an incumbent's death, from the Speaker of the House.[65] After notification—if the resignation of Christopher Clarke in 1806 can be cited as typical—the executive issued writs to the district sheriffs "directing them to hold elections in their several counties" and specifying when. In this instance the notice was ordered published "for three weeks successively" in area

Table 16. Interim elections, 1799–1825[*]

Congress	Person elected	Date took seat	Person replaced
6th	Littleton W. Tazewell (R)	Nov. 26, 1800	John Marshall (F), resigned
7th	None		
8th	Christopher Clark (R) Alexander Wilson (R)	Nov. 5, 1804 Dec. 4, 1804	John J. Trigg (R), deceased Andrew Moore (R), resigned
9th	William A. Burwell (R)	Dec. 1, 1806	Christopher Clark (R), resigned
10th	Thomas Gholson (R)	Nov. 7, 1808	John Claiborne (R), deceased
11th	William McKinley (R) David S. Garland (R)	Dec. 21, 1810 Jan. 17, 1810	John G. Jackson (R) resigned Wilson C. Nicholas (R), resigned
12th	None		
13th	Philip P. Barbour (R)	Sept. 19, 1814	John Dawson (R), deceased
14th	John Kerr (R) Thomas M. Nelson (R) John Tyler (R)	Dec. 5, 1815 Dec. 4, 1816 Dec. 17, 1816	Matthew Clay (R), deceased Thomas Gholson (R), deceased John Clopton (R), deceased
15th	John Pegram (R)	Nov. 16, 1818	Peterson Goodwyn (R), deceased
16th	William S. Archer (R) John C. Gray (R) Edward B. Jackson (R) Thomas L. Moore (?)	Jan. 18, 1820 Nov. 13, 1820 Nov. 13, 1820 Nov. 13, 1820	James Pleasants (R), resigned James Johnson (R), resigned James Pindall (F), resigned George F. Strother (R), resigned
17th	James Stephenson (F)	Dec. 2, 1822	T. V. Swearingen (F), deceased
18th	John Taliaferro (R)	April 4, 1824	William L. Ball (R), deceased

Source: Biographical Directory of the American Congress.

Table 17. Contested elections, 1789–1825

Congress	Person elected	Person contesting	Result
1st–2d	None		
3d	Francis Preston (R)	Abraham Trigg (R)	Denied
4th	John Clopton (R)	Burwell Bassett	Denied
5th	Daniel Morgan (F)	Robert Rutherford (R)	Denied
6th–7th	None		
8th	Thomas Lewis (F)	Andrew Moore (R)	Moore seated
9th–11th	None		
12th	John P. Hungerford (R)	John Taliaferro (R)	Taliaferro seated
13th	Thomas M. Bayly (F)	Burwell Bassett (R)	Denied
	John P. Hungerford (R)	John Taliaferro (R)	Denied
14th	William McCoy (R)	Robert Porterfield (F)	Denied
15th–17th	None		
18th	Jared Williams (R)	Alfred H. Powell (F)	Denied

Source: *Biographical Directory of the American Congress*; Clarke and Hall, *Cases of Contested Elections in Congress*.

newspapers. The election followed the usual procedure.[66] In the period from 1799 to 1825, eighteen interim elections took place, nine occasioned by the resignation of an incumbent and the remainder by a death (table 16). Twice Republicans replaced Federalists, once a Federalist succeeded a fellow Federalist, but the common pattern was for a Republican to take the place of another Republican. The first change in the era came in 1800, the last in 1824, but the Fourteenth Congress alone had three and the Sixteenth four.

A third kind of special election occurred when a losing candidate's complaint led to an investigation by a congressional committee and to the selection of the congressman, in the end, not by the votes of his constituents, but by those of the House of Representatives. In the period 1789–1825, forty-five such cases were recorded from various states, including nine from Virginia (table 17). In the same era the Senate also decided several cases, but none from the Old Dominion.[67]

The nine Virginia cases reveal much about the state's electoral system. They show, for example, the nebulous procedure for determining suffrage eligibility and the number of "bad votes" that a scrupulous look at the polls could uncover. The cases indicate the sheriff's central role and responsibility; several of the protests, in fact, hinged on partisan or negligent action by that officer, especially in his saying who could vote and how long the poll would be open. The investigations suggest the informality of the entire polling process and how local custom generally triumphed over the letter of the law. But also interesting is how closely congressional committees sought out and stuck to the pertinent Virginia statutes, which raises an intriguing federal-state question.[68]

Some flagrant election abuses appear in the committee reports. One of the most extreme came in the race between Abraham Trigg and Francis Preston in Montgomery County in 1793. Congressional investigators, after sifting through "evidence . . . very voluminous, and in some respects contradictory," reported the following information as being "well established":

That Capt. William Preston, brother, and agent at the election, of the sitting member [Francis Preston], was quartered near Montgomery courthouse with about 60 or 70 federal troops, of which he had the command. That, on the day of election, the said troops were marched, in a body, twice or three times round the court-house, and paraded in front of and close to the door thereof. That, toward the close of the election, the said troops were polled generally in favor of the sitting member; but their votes were put down on a separate paper, and, after the election, at the comparison of the polls of the respective counties, were rejected by the returning officers. That some of them threatened to beat any person who should vote in favor of the petitioner [Trigg]. That three soldiers stood at the door of the court-house, and refused to admit a voter because he declared he would vote for the petitioner. That many of the country people were dissatisfied with the conduct of the soldiers, which produced altercations at the election between the soldiers and the country people, the former being generally for the sitting member, and the latter for the petitioner, and terminated in a violent affray between them after the poll was closed. That some of the soldiers being afterwards interrogated why they said they would beat any man who voted for Trigg, replied, "they who are bound must obey." That, though it is doubtful whether any of the soldiers were armed at the time of the affray, after the election, Capt. Preston had a sword and dagger; and that, when the soldiers, being overpowered by the country people, retreated to their barracks, some guns were fired by the soldiers towards the country people.[69]

In several cases both protest and investigation appear to have been perfunctory. In *Samuel J. Cabell* v. *Thomas M. Randolph*, for example, the latter was finally seated a year after the session began because Cabell, the defeated incumbent and plaintiff, delayed substantiating his charges and in the end apparently never came forth to support them.[70] Of the nine Virginia cases, only two were decided for the plaintiff; incumbents were involved in six cases, five of which they lost. Two Federalists unsuccessfully challenged Republicans, and two Republicans unsuccessfully challenged Federalists. One Republican (Andrew Moore) turned out a Federalist (Thomas Lewis). Burwell Bassett was a two-time loser; John Taliaferro won one appeal and lost another, both cases involving John P. Hungerford.

In Jeffersonian Virginia the political leaders displayed considerable individuality in their approaches to becoming a candidate for office, campaigning for it, and participating in the electoral process. Yet there were common patterns among the diverse political practices, as well typified in an unlikely prototype, the Squire of Roanoke, the honorable John Randolph.

VIII

An Unlikely Prototype:
John Randolph of Roanoke

O n the first Monday in March 1799, Virginians by the hundreds
poured into the confines of a small cluster of unpretentious
buildings known collectively as Charlotte Courthouse. It was election season, and among those seeking office was the venerable Patrick Henry, who, at the urging of George Washington, had left the
tranquillity of retirement to become a Federalist candidate for the
House of Delegates. Believing it might be the last opportunity to
hear and see the great orator, two generations of Virginians formed
the audience that day. They were not disappointed with the aging
patriot's performance and roundly cheered as he fervently praised
his party's principles while denouncing with equal emotion those
of Madison and Jefferson.[1]

After roaring approval of "the great Patrick," the throng looked
in disbelief at the skinny, boyish-faced freeholder who moved forward to present the Republican case. The presumptuous gentleman seeking election to the United States House of Representatives
was John Randolph, or "Jack Randle" in the slurred pronunciation
of those who knew him then. It was his first public speech; his
throat was hoarse from a cold; the audience was jeering; and he was
following Virginia's most-famed platform figure, a man who had
always been one of his own heroes. Randolph's performance that
day is subject to dispute in its details. The consensus is perhaps
best captured in the rustic phrases of an old-timer who, after the
speaker had finished, turned to a neighbor and said, "I tell you
what, the young man is no bug-eater neither."[2]

Both Henry and Randolph were subsequently elected. For the
elder statesman, who died a few months later and never took office,

Political Practices

March Court was the last leg in a long and honorable journey. For his youthful challenger, it was merely the first audacious step. Without knowing it, the crowd at Charlotte had witnessed a dramatic event in Virginia history. The torch of eloquence passed from the preeminent orator of one generation to a worthy successor in the next.

Randolph, who had not yet added "of Roanoke" to his name, also acquired Henry's knack of getting himself elected and went on from his auspicious debut to compile an extraordinary string of campaign victories. He lost only one of fifteen races for a seat in the House of Representatives. To understand his phenomenal success is to understand much about the political culture of an elite class in Jeffersonian Virginia. Although Randolph was an original in many respects, the fact remains that from his first campaign in 1799 to his last in 1833, few Virginians better mastered or mirrored the electioneering practices of the era.[3]

The Family Name

Like many other candidates in the period, John Randolph first sought office at the urging of friends and with the sponsorship and prior approval of a key local Republican leader, in his case State Senator Creed Taylor.[4] Randolph also had the common, although not indispensable, political asset of a distinguished name. He had been born at Cawsons, Prince George County, on June 2, 1773, into one of Virginia's most illustrious, prolific, and powerful families, the descendants of William Randolph of Turkey Island.[5] The Randolphs were socially prominent and politically active. The name itself had become a calling card requiring neither introduction nor apology.

Being of a notable line also meant that Jack, whether he liked it or not, would at least be exposed to a formal education with its advantages political and otherwise. This schooling was expected of such a family and had been expressly desired in the will of his father, who died in 1775.[6] The widow Randolph, an intelligent, amiable person, first taught Jack to read and, in addition, as he later phrased it, "to aspire to be something better than a mere Country Squire."[7] Her second husband, St. George Tucker, provided him and his brothers Richard and Theodorick with an unusual opportunity to learn. Among them they attended one-teacher schools in Virginia, grammar school and college at Princeton, and Columbia College and William and Mary. Good books were always available, and in 1790 young John went to Philadelphia to read law under his kinsman, Attorney General Edmund Randolph. Less than a serious student, he disliked most of his teachers, in later life regarded his education as having been "superficial and defective," and once wrote a friend, "Except the Latin and Greek grammar I never learnt anything in school, or college, whatever."[8] But during this time he acquired voracious reading habits, an ability to express his ideas with clarity and precision, and considerable ambition to be a public figure and speaker. Finally, who could doubt the educational value of his diverse experiences, traveling around the country and even to Bermuda and learning to stand on his own two feet.[9]

Being a Randolph put Jack in close contact with many of the men dominating public affairs in his day, both locally and on the national scene. He was related to or personally acquainted with numerous political leaders in the Old Dominion and some in South Carolina through his Tucker connections and enjoyed the advantages of their friendship while a student at Columbia in New York at the beginning of Washington's first administration. His frequent attendance at congressional debates and associations with important persons there and in Philadelphia, where he and the federal government moved in 1790, whetted his appetite for politics, shaped his views, and provided an insight and perspective available to few youths of his time and of great significance to his later career.[10]

A Favorable Reputation

In Jeffersonian Virginia certain family names carried political prestige based either on the past service of their members or on their concrete and immediate advantages in wealth, education, and social standing. But the successful candidate also needed a favorable image in his own right. In Randolph's case, that was not easily accomplished and, in fact, required basic changes in his attitude and conduct. As an adolescent he had done chiefly as he wished, and his wishes had run more to sports—hunting and fishing, attending horse races, and riding about the Virginia countryside—than to study, work, or accountability to anybody but himself. His was a wild spirit, but a harsh series of personal ordeals took the lives of his mother and two brothers, shattered his engagement to the beautiful Maria Ward, carried him to the brink of death, swept loved ones into public scandal, and left him chastised, emotionally bankrupt, near physical exhaustion, responsible for his brother Richard's family, and deeply in debt for the consolidated paternal inheritance now solely in his hands.[11]

At this point, around 1797, he caught hold of himself and conscientiously worked to save the Randolph estate and to provide for those in his charge. He experimented with new farming techniques, added more land, and adopted business principles. And he got results, as his plantations Roanoke and Bizarre prospered in unprecedented style. He learned much about farm problems from his neighbors, who were beginning to see him not only as thin-skinned and sharp-tongued but also as an honest, self-reliant, serious-minded, hardworking fellow freeholder worthy of their respect.[12]

Randolph maintained his congenital interest in politics and became increasingly outspoken against what he saw as centralizing tendencies in the national government. An "Anti-Federalist," he said, "when hardly breeched," Randolph followed family and friends who had opposed ratification of the Constitution in 1788 and had remained alert to infringements on state sovereignty in the nineties. Like others of this persuasion, he rallied behind Thomas Jefferson and "republican" principles, whether in America or France.[13]

Thus it was natural for Senator Creed Taylor to see in young Randolph the essential qualities of an attractive candidate in the Jeffersonian era—that is, a person who enjoyed among the freeholders two good reputations: his family's and his own. And it was natural that Randolph, after observing the protocol of confirming that his friend the incumbent congressman would not seek reelection, would yield to the pleas of neighbors, accept Taylor's patronage, and enter the race wearing Republican colors.[14]

An Uncommon Orator

Creed Taylor's candidate left his mark that day at March Court not because he was a Randolph or John Randolph—as important as those facts were in getting him there—but because he could make a speech. Oratory was a central electioneering device in the era and was frequently at the heart of a successful political career. Randolph's talent for it served him uncommonly well. His reputation in parliamentary debate is clearly established by the testimony of those who served with him in Congress, but contemporaries thought his speeches were even better on the hustings.[15]

Randolph cut a distinctive platform figure, in part because of certain physical characteristics and in part because of peculiarities of style. Among the former, the most widely acclaimed were his small, dark, hazel eyes, which flashed rapidly and ubiquitously about the audience and seemed to penetrate the soul of every man there; his lean, bony forefinger, like an officer's saber, used infrequently, a threat when sheathed and a terror when employed; his singular voice, high-pitched but not harsh, with a melodic quality; his "long, thin legs, about as thick as a stout walking cane, and of much such a shape"; and his face, handsome enough but beardless and surprisingly, bizarrely youthful, even when prematurely covered with wrinkles and the signs of advancing age.[16]

His delivery was equally striking. In relaxed fashion, seldom raising his voice and saving his gestures only for special purposes, Randolph appeared to be carrying on an intimate conversation with each man present. Until late in his career when physical infirmities forced him to speak from a seated position, he paced slowly about the platform, talking very deliberately with a flawless diction which carried his words across the crowd and seldom strained the hearing of anyone. He frequently started at a slow tempo, increased his speed as he went along, and spoke for hours.[17]

His effectiveness was greatly enhanced by an exceptionally keen memory and by the great store of knowledge he could call into action at will. In the well-stocked arsenal of his mind were not only apt quotations and historical and literary allusions but also intimate details about the people in his hearing and a canny understanding of their collective mood.[18] To get his point across Randolph drew from a wide variety of oratorical devices—wit, invective, audience dialogue, sarcasm, rustic analogies, fanciful metaphors, epithets, appeals to recognized authority, rhetorical questions, pathos, classical references—all used easily, almost artlessly, and with clear purpose. As a rule, he "was more efficient in putting down than in building up."[19]

In an era of rough-and-tumble politics, the audience often threw jeers and slurs at the platform speaker. Randolph thrived on this give-and-take and used his repartee as both shield and sword. It protected him from serious challengers and often provided the opportunity to accent a point with incisive results. His rapierlike replies usually brought outbursts of approval from the crowd.[20] One of the best substantiated of many examples of his adroitness at repartee occurred during the election of 1813. Randolph compared his opponent John Wayles Eppes, who had moved into the district, to a racehorse imported to run against him. This was unnecessary, he added, because there were able contenders among the home-grown stock.

"Where are your Daniels, your Bouldins and your Carringtons?" [he asked.]

"And your Spencers," interrupted Col. Gideon Spencer.

"Yes, and your Spencers," rejoined Randolph, "always excepting you, Colonel."

The colonel nearly exploded in anger, but Randolph snapped, "Let him alone, Fellow-Citizens, a barking dog never bites." For that date, Randolph's diary reads: "Court. Meet Eppes. Episode of Gideon Spencer. 'The sword of Gideon not the sword of the Lord.' "[21]

On the hustings Randolph seldom prepared a text. Such an extemporaneous approach often led to verbosity, aimless rambling, and needless repetition.[22] A critic noted that his "remarks followed one another on no other principle governing them than that of involuntary suggestion. They seemed to run riot, without any act of the will to control the selection, the order, or the limits."[23] But even in his most discursive addresses, Randolph could be a fascinating, captivating speaker. The audience usually preferred his nonsense, as a contemporary put it, to "any body else's sense."[24] That he could attract a throng and cast a verbal spell over it is well recorded. People came from all directions and from far away to be edified, informed, or entertained by his oratory on the hustings.[25] A crowd might gather an hour or two early to get a good vantage point near the platform. When Randolph "was seen to move forward to the rostrum," as a witness recalled, "then the courthouse, every store, and tavern, and peddler's stall, and auctioneer's stand, and private residence, was deserted."[26] Some remember standing for hours as he spoke, scarcely noticing the passing time; others years later could recall scraps of his rhetoric to the word.[27] As he grew older, suffering from various physical maladies, becoming more eccentric and perturbed, though still a national figure, he became something of a rare spectacle, "a theatrical show, a circus as well,"[28] and even more of an attraction. At that stage of his life, as in all others, one must not forget that on election day in Jeffersonian Virginia, the poll was taken immediately after the oratory.

"Personal Courtship"

Making speeches in all corners of his district was only part of John Randolph's electioneering. His campaign arsenal contained other weapons equally as effective and conventional, if not so spectacular, as his rhetorical genius. Most of these other devices were used, as was his oratory, to implement his belief that "personal courtship is as necessary to success in Politics as in Love,"[29] a comment not without amusement coming from a lifelong bachelor. In the company of other Virginia politicians, the aristocratic Randolph "courted" while in fact regarding the practice with some distaste. "If electioneering were allowed in heaven," he once said, "it would corrupt the angels."[30]

Randolph conducted his "personal courtship" in a manner typical of the times. In election season, whether he had an opponent or not, Randolph generally canvassed for support. He attended military musters, court days, and other public gatherings. He mixed among the freeholders, renewed old friendships and made new ones, shook hands in all directions, and talked "freely and familiarly with the people on various subjects" while on his best behavior.[31]

A devout if erratic Episcopalian himself, he was arduous and skillful in courting other religious groups. In one election he praised the Presbyterians and their minister so lavishly, said a witness, that anybody "who did not know him might think he had a notion of joining that denomination." In another contest he sought Baptist affections by gathering with them in worship, in prayer, in conversation, and in exhortation, paying "marked attention to the elders."[32] Invited to a service where his opponent was also scheduled to appear, Randolph sent a personal note which said, in the words of a contemporary, "he should be glad to attend worship, but could not violate the Sabbath by profanely attending the house of God for electioneering purposes."[33] The message passed among the congregation and received its general approval.

Randolph employed all the standard techniques of publishing open letters to the freeholders in Southside and Richmond newspapers; disseminating handbills, essays, circulars, and his congressional speeches; and making use of his private correspondence.[34] If necessary, he could be more direct and personal in his appeals. He won over some voters, usually elder citizens, by extravagant praise and others by making them afraid to support anybody else.[35] Well known to the timid were Randolph's violent and volatile temper, his capacity for sarcasm and scorn, his phenomenal memory, his reputed implacability, and his intimate knowledge of most public and private matters in the district. They also knew that he had, on occasions, subjected an opponent's key supporters to public ridicule in an effort to weaken their influence. Randolph's face-to-face impact was particularly potent during this era of viva voce voting with candidates present at the polls.[36]

As did his fellow office seekers, Randolph often campaigned on the defensive. He frequently faced a hostile state press, antagonistic politicians living outside his district but having influence within it, and unfriendly local officials working against him on election day.[37] He also had to answer charges and smears injurious to his personal reputation and political career.[38] A good example of how Randolph handled these latter difficulties is found in his first race in 1799. A rumor circulated that young John if elected to Congress would introduce legislation to free the slaves. Randolph responded by denouncing categorically any interference with slavery in the states, corralling the men associated with the rumor and getting their denials, and publishing the particulars in the *Virginia Gazette* and in handbills disseminated throughout the district.[39] On other occasions Randolph used his platform talents to blunt if not refute the attacks of his adversaries.[40]

The congressional election in which Randolph campaigned hardest was, ironically, the only one he ever lost. His defeat by John Wayles Eppes in 1813, however, had little to do with his electioneering, which, if anything, narrowed the margin. He fell victim that year to a gush of wartime patriotism that muted or sidetracked dissenters, especially one so articulate and outspoken.[41] His fall brought

An Unlikely Prototype

jubilation to orthodox Republicans, some of national fame, who had been working against him in the district since his break with the party several years earlier. Their pleasure scarcely outlasted the war, however, as his constituents returned him to Congress in April 1815.[42] John Randolph was a hard loser. Although neither forgetting nor forgiving those freeholders who voted against him, he focused his wrath, not on them, but on his opponent and his opponent's friends outside the district. In private letters he accused his adversary of playing on popular passions, of spreading false charges, of using unfair methods, and of even canvassing "house to house," "day and night" among "the lowest of the people."[43] Apparently Randolph's courtship philosophy stopped at the point a rival adopted it—another representative attitude of the political elite.

Character and Conduct

Any explanation of a popular vote getter must include the traits of his character and conduct that stood out most clearly to the freeholders determining his political fate. A good family name and private reputation might get one started in Virginia politics, and electioneering talents might bring an initial victory, but success over the long run required day-to-day personal qualities that the voters found acceptable if not commendable.

A probing of Randolph the man must be done within the framework of three unusual considerations: (1) during the early part of his life he experienced a series of harsh personal tragedies; (2) for most of his years he was in miserable health, plagued by a variety of painful and disconcerting afflictions often driving him to desperate cures; and (3) from about 1818 until his death in 1833 he was beset by intermittent fits of insanity.[44]

Against such a background, what are the prominent characteristics of John Randolph's reputation among his district freeholders? In the first place, a strong case can be made that his essential disposition was a congenial one and that he not only enjoyed the company of others but earnestly sought it.[45] He felt a depressing loneliness, perhaps from having been cut adrift from his immediate family at an early age, perhaps from having been unlucky in love, or perhaps from the solitude of Roanoke, a place he compared to Robinson Crusoe's island. He reached out eagerly for companionship and relished the finding of it.[46] His notebooks, diaries, and personal correspondence reveal a busy and varied social schedule. He was an engaging, if domineering, conversationalist, an enthusiastic traveler, and one of the era's most prolific letter writers. He was fond of hunting, fishing, singing, playing whist and chess, going to horse races and dinner parties, visiting and being visited, all highly social pastimes.[47] With some stormy exceptions his relationship with his Tucker half brothers and half sisters was one of mutual respect and affection.[48] In normal health and unprovoked by an act he considered disrespectful, John Randolph of Roanoke stood as the antithesis of the misanthrope his enemies labeled him.

He could also be an extremely generous man. Randolph assumed paternal responsibilities for numerous fatherless charges, not only providing their financial support in whole or part but also conveying genuine guidance, love, and devotion. He often visited a local grammar school, encouraging the students and participating in their lessons and games. He delighted in little children and once wrote, "I do not believe that there is a man in the world so fond of children as myself," and they reciprocated his affection.[49] Nor was his kindness limited to the younger set. Without being asked to do so, he wrote letters of introduction, gave security on a friend's bond, took care of an absent neighbor's crop, helped sick acquaintances, and befriended an insane stranger.[50]

Randolph was known for his honesty, his integrity, and his courage. He admitted an "obstinate preference of the true over the agreeable,"[51] was called "the very scourge of intrigue and corruption,"[52] and on more than one occasion—in the face of a duelist's pistol, a hostile crowd, or a countervailing political current—exhibited physical and moral intrepidity.[53] He was also an industrious, imaginative planter who experimented with new methods, bought land, treated his slaves with benevolence, made a going concern from what had been a losing operation, and left a large estate on his death.[54]

After an early bout with infidelity, Randolph returned to the faith of the political elite, the Episcopal church or, as he called it, the Church of England, into which he had been "born and baptized." About 1815 he went through a rather severe but eventually satisfying conversion experience. Otherwise there was little unusual about his spiritual life, except perhaps its periodic fervor, so long as he maintained control of his mental faculties.[55]

Randolph also had, of course, an abundance of personal flaws. Perhaps his most vulnerable qualities were an extremely high-strung sensitivity, a volcanic temper, and the ability to deliver a stream of mordant, unchecked verbal abuse. He had been thin-skinned from his youth, had never learned to contain his feelings of rage, and when aroused could employ "his tongue as a jockey would his whip" against an adversary.[56] On a few occasions he responded in this fashion with good reason; on others his physical or mental ills may have been partially or wholly responsible. But many times his actions were either plainly unjustified or greatly in excess. Randolph also possessed self-respect and family pride to the degree of blatant arrogance. He was unusually candid, always the critic, and uncommonly impulsive. Many of these traits caused him to be feared and in some instances worked to his political advantage.[57]

Complex, neurotic character that he was, on the balance and on home grounds, he came close to being the type of person he himself "held in highest esteem," the worthy man, "who by the exercise of the faculties which nature and education have given him, asserts his place among his fellows; and whilst useful to all around him, establishes his claim to their respect, as an equal and independent member of society."[58] As such, he was the kind who earned the confidence of his fellow freeholders.

"Ask My Constituents"

While administering the oath of office to newly elected congressmen in the fall of 1799, the official in charge noticed one particularly young-looking gentleman in the group and doubted if he met the age requirement. "Ask my constituents," replied John Randolph, unwittingly providing indispensable advice for anyone wanting to understand his political success or an important dimension of Virginia politics in the period.[59]

From first to last, Randolph's constituency remained virtually the same Southside Virginia district of Buckingham, Cumberland, Charlotte, and Prince Edward counties, all among the oldest in the region. It was a rural area noted for the cultivation of tobacco. The population was homogeneous and nearly static; the number of white residents increased only about six hundred from 1800 to 1830. Suffrage was limited to property owners, and the traditional "gentlemen freeholder" system of selecting leaders persisted.[60] It was an ideal atmosphere for a man of Randolph's background, talents, and social values first to attain office and then to hold it, despite a career which led one scholar to call him "the most pertinacious and personally dreaded freelance in politics that this country has ever known."[61]

Although at variance with national party standards, Randolph's views harmonized closely with those customarily voiced in his district. Long before he championed "state sovereignty, the agricultural interest, economy in government, and freedom from foreign entanglements," those principles were rooted in the Anti-Federalist tradition of Southside Virginia.[62] Operating from the outset in a congenial political climate, Randolph saw his local reputation further enhanced—at little cost to principle—by his prominent, constructive national role in Jefferson's first administration. By casting his later break with Jefferson in terms of personal integrity and devotion to Old Republicanism, he maintained his local prestige.[63]

As time passed, except for the war election of 1813, the bond of interests and values between the master of Roanoke and his constituents grew stronger and stronger, and in 1817 Charlotte freeholders even gave him a majority despite his clear announcement that he would neither run nor serve that year.[64] In the decade of the 1820s his better qualities receded, some of his more eccentric and disreputable ones reached new excesses, his physical condition— real and perceived—made him more wretched, and his aberrations became more frequent. Yet his statewide prestige soared to new heights with the resurgence of Old Republicanism in the Commonwealth. Few men represented the principles of '98 or the conservative leanings of eastern Virginia better than the master of Roanoke. His local popularity was never higher, and after 1821 he had faced his last seriously contested congressional election. As he wrote a friend, "Like the long waists of our mothers . . . [he had grown] if not generally, at least somewhat, in fashion."[65]

In keeping with many of his fellow representatives from the Old Dominion, Randolph appreciated the devotion of his constituents and had a strict sense of accountability to them.[66] He made it his business to stay informed of developments in the district: "You say that '*all the world are amazed how the devil I know every thing before any body else.*' I got that piece of information from Lynchburg, a long while ago, through my silent, discreet friend, W. L. . . . I have paid more money of my own for intelligence than, I believe, any other public man living; but this came *gratis*."[67] Despite his often expressed desire "to secede" from public life, he felt obligated to serve as long as he was called and physically able to do so.[68]

He was reelected without opposition in 1823 and again in 1825. In the latter year the Virginia legislature chose him to fill an unexpired term in the United States Senate, but in 1827 it rejected him for a full term. Immediately after this was known, freeholders throughout his district adopted resolutions requesting that he again serve them in Congress. The incumbent representative concurred in a public letter, and in April John Randolph of Roanoke was returned almost unanimously to the national House.[69] He retired for reasons of health in 1829 but was elected against his wishes as a delegate from Charlotte, Halifax, and Prince Edward counties to the Virginia Constitutional Convention of 1829–30. In that gathering of notables, Randolph was a leader of the victorious conservatives and an outstanding crowd pleaser as well.[70]

In 1830 President Andrew Jackson appointed Randolph minister to Russia. He served briefly in that capacity before a breakdown in health forced his removal to England, then resignation, and return home in 1831. He was doubtlessly deranged for the better part of the 1831–32 winter but recovered the following summer and subsequently championed the adoption of resolutions in his district protesting Jackson's strong stand against South Carolina in the nullification crisis.

In April 1833, completely debilitated by advanced tuberculosis and other maladies, as well as by opium and drink, subject to fits of dementia, a pathetic shadow of his best self, Randolph was once more elected to Congress with only nominal opposition.[71] Even death, which came a month later, failed to break the spell he had cast over his constituency. Decades later the people still talked about him, recited bits of his speeches, tried to imitate his voice and style, and swore that never again in Southside Virginia would there be the like of John Randolph of Roanoke.[72]

Political Practices

The span of Randolph's congressional years is a historic bridge, anchored on the one side in the troubled heyday of the first party system, passing over years of Republican ascendancy and an Era of Good Feelings, to be anchored on the other side in the turbulence of Jacksonian Democracy. During that long and eventful period scores of political giants mounted the national stage, played their parts, and made their exits, gracefully or otherwise. And through it all John Randolph of Roanoke was being elected and reelected, over and over, by the freeholders of four counties in the heart of the Old Dominion.

What accounts for his amazing record? Or, more importantly, what does the record reveal about the political practices of Jeffersonian Virginia? In the first place, it provides a nearly perfect guide for a successful political debut. Candidate Randolph was available and partisan, and had all the advantages afforded Virginia's foremost families. In addition he had established a good reputation and a separate identity beyond family ties, had consulted with a retiring incumbent, and had the sponsorship of a local party leader.

Randolph's career demonstrates the power of oratory in a campaign as well as the full range of electioneering devices and personal appeals used by candidates in the period. It shows that elections were always held within the powerful context of what the freeholders already knew about a contender's character and that even when the relationship between an incumbent and his constituents was long-standing and familiar, a canvass was still in order.

Like many others east of the Blue Ridge, Randolph's district was traditional in its political views, conservative in its social values, and static or declining in its demographic and economic structure. As the Randolph example reveals, such a fixed environment offered security to the politician who mirrored in his own life the interests and sentiments of his constituents and who cemented that bond with the right combination of electioneering appeals.

The Squire of Roanoke well understood that to be a statesman one had first to be a politician. Master of the diverse political practices of the Dynasty era, Randolph also represented (at least in his own mind) another facet of Virginia's leadership class, namely, the commitment to a service role on behalf of constituents, state, and nation.

Part Three

The
Service
Role

———

IX

The Congressmen and
Their Constituents

D uring the Dynasty era ninety-eight individuals represented the
Old Dominion in one or both branches of what Jefferson termed
"the great commanding theatre of this nation," the United States
Congress.[1] These men had dual significance. They were influential
persons, and they held influential positions. And they were unique
among Virginia's leaders in being elected throughout the state for
a national responsibility. In an era of primitive transportation and
communication, they often became the eyes through which constituents saw events beyond their districts. Conversely, the congressmen reflected on a national stage the interests, needs, and attitudes
of the freeholders at the grass-roots level in the Commonwealth. In
these and other ways, the ninety-eight provided a vital link between state and country. They also served the executive branch
of the federal government in diverse roles and exercised a dispro-
portionate influence in legislative and party affairs. The scope and
importance of what these Virginians did is seen clearly in the relationships they established with their constituents, their Commonwealth, and their co-workers in the United States government.

"The Will of the People"

"An essential principle of representative government," wrote Edmund Pendleton, "is that it be influenced by the will of the people."[2]
In the Dynasty period that fundamental influence registered itself
in a variety of direct ways. Obviously the interest of constituent and
congressman could be identical. For example, Charles Fenton Mercer no doubt accurately interpreted the wishes of Virginians concerned with the Leesburg Turnpike Company, of which he was a

director, or the Chesapeake and Ohio Canal Company, of which he became president. He must have also recognized the expediency of his appointment and service on the House Committee on Roads and Canals.[3] Similarly, William A. Burwell, who depended "entirely upon agriculture for . . . [his] support," presumably understood the farming needs of his constituents, just as the prosperous merchant Hugh Caperton appreciated the mercantile interests of the Valley district he represented.[4] Questions of foreign trade should have had little mystery for Thomas Newton, who lived in the port city of Norfolk and served many terms as chairman of the House Committee on Commerce and Manufacturing. John George Jackson hardly had to be told that the western roads he supported would enhance not only his constituency but also his own direct property holdings, and John Baker, representing an upper Potomac region, knew instinctively the benefits of internal improvements for trade between the northern Valley and both Alexandria and Georgetown.[5] Other examples of clear, mutual economic interests could be cited, and it scarcely needs stating that strong partisan bonds often united a congressmen and a majority of his constituents.

Constituent attitudes also registered themselves in the many informal, personal associations each congressman had within his own district. These included neighbors, friends and enemies, kinsmen, business associates, and the like. Their interests and needs might be known intuitively or might be raised casually or heatedly over the dinner table, the property fence, or the tavern bar. At church, militia musters, weddings and funerals, and especially at the monthly court day or during election campaigns, representatives mingled with freeholders and heard their political sentiments.

The postal service provided another direct means for citizens to communicate their views. The practice of writing one's congressman began early, was frequently employed, and helped to transform the nature of representative government in the early Republic. In colonial times Virginia's political leaders were justices of the peace and burgesses (sometimes concurrently) and thus geographically close to the freeholders. Both positions reflected county-level constituencies, burgesses commonly met for short periods, and people had limited expectations about what the local or colonial government might do to meet their individual needs. In the subsequent age of the great continental congresses, the political system—and the country itself—necessarily shared a preoccupation with the transcendent questions of independence and war. In the 1780s Virginians in the Confederation Congress were chosen by the state legislature and fundamentally were accountable to it. After 1788, however, representatives were elected in local districts for service in a distant city perhaps for several months at a time and in a government soon with the authority and resources to aid many a citizen's special plight. Concurrently a near revolution occurred in the enlargement of postal services. The number of post offices boomed from 75 in 1790 to 8,000 in 1829, and the mileage in post roads soared from a mere 1,875 in 1790 to 115,000 in 1829. Delivery time and other services also improved. Ironically, just as government became more remote, it also came closer at hand, in the form of the local postmaster and his extended services.[6]

Virginia congressmen took advantage of the improved mails to request the epistolary sentiments of key freeholders, as did Leven Powell in the Jefferson-Burr deadlock of 1800–1801 and Wilson Cary Nicholas during the Embargo period.[7] More typically, constituents seized the initiative and took pen in hand to express a point of view or to ask a favor. Republican John Dawson was urged in 1798 to support John Adams in order to unite the country in a time of crisis, William A. Burwell was queried about the Embargo's duration, Senator James Barbour got advice from influential friends about his role in the Missouri Compromise, and the powerful Philip Norborne Nicholas bluntly informed Andrew Stevenson that Richmonders were "all against" the tariff of 1824.[8]

Letters often originated with clusters of constituents. At the outset of the War of 1812, for example, "about seventy citizens . . . associated as volunteers . . . offered their services to the President of the United States" through their congressman, General John Smith; and two years later "a great number of gentlemen of the first respectability in the Lower Counties of the Northern Neck of Virginia" got Senator Richard Brent to contact the president and the governor about "the deplorable and unprotected state of that part of the country."[9] The usual letter, however, came from an individual with a specific request. The extant copies of these communications are legion, but they fall easily into several basic categories.[10] Constituents frequently asked for help in settling claims against the state or national government and for gaining some minor political or military appointment for a friend, relative, or themselves. Such a letter could be inspirational. A certain Graves asked John Clopton to recommend him for "the principal assessors place"; shortly thereafter, Clopton wrote the commissioner of revenue on behalf of, not Graves, but Clopton's own son.[11] Another kind of request falls under the rubric of desired preferential treatment, such as the awarding of a mail contract or the promoting of a military officer.[12] Finally, some freeholders required rather specialized favors. John Baker was asked to deliver a letter, and John George Jackson to support the "petition of Robert Lowe Stobie, a noncitizen of the United States, who desired a patent for a ship's rudder and a pump for extracting foul air from the holds of ships." One Edward Graham wanted James Breckinridge to evaluate a new stove advertised in the Washington press and to recommend "whether it would be worth our while to procure."[13]

If letters represented a relatively new way of registering opinion, local meetings and the use of petitions both had deep roots in Virginia's past political culture. "Spontaneous" gatherings had been popular in Revolutionary times, were generally prearranged and held at court day, and often led to a public vote on resolutions that condemned, supported, or recommended a course of action on a particular issue. Closely related was the practice of circulating petitions. Colonial Virginians had been accustomed to direct representation; the thousands of petitions and resolutions filed with the General Assembly after 1776 confirm both the continuance and popularity of the practice. Virginia congressmen could attest to the seriousness with which freeholders took the First Amendment guarantee of "the right of the people peaceably to assemble, and to petition the Government for a redress of grievances."[14]

Although public meetings, resolutions, and petitions are found throughout the period, in all sections of the state, and on a wide variety of subjects, they came most frequently at the time of great national crises or issues. Examples of the former include 1793–96 (Genêt's mission and Jay's Treaty), 1797–1800 (the Quasi-War with France and the Alien-Sedition Acts and their aftermath), and 1807–8 (the Embargo).[15] After the War of 1812, most memorials concerned the pervading national economic questions—the tariff, bank, and internal improvements.[16] Often in the same county or city separate gatherings would be held and both sides of an issue would be expressed in partisan resolutions; sometimes the meeting of one group would be taken over by its rivals, who would vote down the original proposals and substitute their own. The groundwork for these "spontaneous" assemblies occupied some of the state's most astute and prominent political leaders.[17] Congressmen reacted variously to these grass-roots memorials. John Clopton expressed a typical response: "Though the [pro-Jay Treaty] petition came after the *business* was over; yet I deemed it a duty to present it; as I also have done with respect to the resolutions from the other *side*."[18] No congressman could ignore completely a petition bearing the names of a large number of the freeholders in his district or some of its most prominent men.

The party celebrations that arose after the Revolution also developed into a formal way of expressing local interests. In the guise of parades, barbeques, dinners, and the like, such occasions clearly articulated constituent, if partisan, views. No ambiguity obscured, for example, the attitude of the elaborate daylong festivities in Washington County on July 4, 1812. Two of the many toasts were:

John Randolph, D. Sheffey, &c. May their constituents furnish them with a suit of Tory uniform, tar and feathers! Rogue's March!

Randolph—Sheffey, &c.—May they be compelled to eat the crumbs that fall from republican tables.[19]

Across the state the Fourth of July often became a day not only for patriotic celebration but also for voicing partisan positions on the issues and personalities of the day.[20]

Virginia newspapers and the biennial congressional elections also registered grass-roots sentiment. It should be noted that a representative could be swayed by the results of other polls in his district. Andrew Stevenson in 1834 read into an election for the state legislature sufficient reason to resign his House seat since "it would be folly in me to now doubt" that "a decided majority . . . differ with me upon the subject of the Removal and Restoration of the Public Deposits."[21]

The Service Role

Congressional Accountability

A congressman was, of course, no mere passive recipient of the various expressions of constituent interest. He participated actively in what John Clopton called the "reciprocal intercourse and communication of sentiment between the Representative and the Constituent" and was constantly required "to give an account of his stewardship."[22] "Even in times the most tranquil, and under circumstances much less interesting, the trust reposed in a representative is solemn and important," said Clopton. "So great and multifarious are the concerns of this nation at all times, that no period can arrive, at which he could be justifiable in considering himself not bound to account for his execution of this trust."[23] Most congressmen publicly articulated their accountability; none would have publicly denied it. While each implemented it in his own way, certain common practices emerged in the Dynasty period.

A basic part of being accountable meant keeping the freeholders abreast of national developments. As a Virginia congressman phrased it, "one among the most essential duties of the representative of a free people, [is] to give them all the information in his power."[24] This was often done at various public occasions, during elections, and through informal relationships. "I have been to several of the courts," wrote John Randolph in 1808, "and addressed the people on the subject of public affairs, generally."[25] On the other hand, it might require a heavy use of the postal services and the congressman's franking privilege. A member of the state's first congressional delegation set the tone for such correspondence when he wrote a constituent, "What seems to be the present public sentiment in Virginia relative to the general as well as our particular interests?" He went on to suggest, "If I can be of any use to you here be pleased to command me."[26]

Exchanges of letters between representative and freeholder provided information and material benefit to both. The stakes are reflected in the extreme fear of several congressmen that some unknown or hostile person had diverted or opened their mail.[27] Of course, communications that reached their destination often had a broad ultimate audience. The people at Amherst court day in March 1808, for example, had read to them "a long and able letter from Col.

[Wilson Cary] Nicholas," no doubt in defense of Jefferson's foreign policy.[28] Lengthy letters about national questions frequently were passed throughout the district at the representative's request, along with franked newspapers, published speeches, and various official documents.[29] The range is suggested in a circular of Burwell Bassett, who expressed a deep sense of accountability and mentioned his attempts to provide information by "sending weekly into each county, one at least of the *Universal Gazette*; in large counties more . . . [and] to the clerk of the district court of Accomack, a copy of the journal of the last session, and of this as far as it is printed. I lodged a copy in Williamsburg last year and shall this, lodge one with the clerk of York, as a more central point for the use of the western shore. [Of public documents,] I have sent thirty copies of those on our foreign relations into various parts of the district, and I have some others that I will take with me."[30] Printed material may often have been sent with the request to "please give them publicity that the people may know the situation."[31]

However justified by an obligation to keep freeholders informed, such practices were also politically advantageous, even necessary. A friend sent James Breckinridge a list of influential persons, one of whom "is easily flattered, and might be affected by an occasional newspaper inclosed," and others of whom he "ought by no means to neglect writing . . . and sending . . . occasionally papers and documents of a proper character."[32] This combination of the dutiful and the politically astute congressmen is also seen in their very common practice of sending printed letters to the electorate. The device was convenient for gaining wide distribution and for making "public . . . [the congressman's] opinions of the policy of our Government."[33] A letter ranged from a single sheet to several dozen, but typically it was one page folded to allow up to four of print and was dispatched at or just after the completion of a session. Uniformly it began with the heading "To the freeholders of the Congressional District Composed of . . . ," with the county names attached. The salutation was either a printed "Dear Friend" or "Fellow Citizen," or a "Dear . . ." with space for a name to be written in. Depending on weight, it might fall within a congressman's franking privileges, thus giving an incumbent a decided advantage over a challenger paying normal postal rates.[34]

The Service Role

The format and content of the circular letters were rather standard. The introductory paragraph stated the letter's purpose, and it generally read like Thomas Gholson, Jr.'s: "Conforming to the practice by which I have been heretofore governed, I proceed to submit to you a view of the principal subjects which have engaged the attention of Congress at the long and important session about to close."[35] Alexander Smyth wrote, "In this address I will very briefly notice the principal measures adopted or proposed during this session of Congress," and John Claiborne, "The session of Congress being about to close, I make use of this method of communicating to you, and through you to your neighbors, a view of the most important measures adopted during its progress."[36]

Next followed several paragraphs describing "the important measures"—such as the Embargo or the tariff of 1816—in general and partisan terms, at times with canned material and statistics, and always with some indication of the congressman's position on them. The conclusion usually combined a platitudinous pledge of dutiful service with an effusive appreciation for past favors. Occasionally there were variations. William McCoy devoted the bulk of a pamphlet to defending his opposition to the Virginia and Kentucky Resolutions thirty years earlier and, for good measure, attached a nine-page reprint of pertinent proceedings from the Virginia House of Delegates. William Lewis stressed his own activity in Congress, cited part of a new law for the benefit of "those who have claims for pensions," and ended by giving "the local acts of Congress relative to this District," that is, the laws establishing three post roads, whose routes Lewis delineated.[37]

The letters often included comments about elections impending, in progress, or just past. An incumbent might add, as Anthony New did in 1803, the reminder that he was seeking reelection, or the notice—by John Stratton in 1803 and John Tyler in 1821—that he was not. And an incumbent might, after an unsuccessful campaign, issue a farewell circular addressed, as Thomas Evans put it, to his "quondam Constituents."[38] Printed letters were also used by persons who aspired to election and by former congressmen, like John Page, who sought to set the record straight and correct the "mistake" that had led to his defeat two years earlier.[39]

The precise number and distribution of the circulars are impossible to determine, but Anthony New in 1800 had 500 printed for a district in which 1,278 voters went to the polls in a presidential election that same year.[40] Congressmen employed a variety of modes for dissemination of the documents. Most obvious was a select mailing, or not so select in the case of the Virginian charged with sending them "with almost equal assiduity to his *dead* as well as living constituents."[41] The letters frequently contained an appeal like that from John Clopton: "I should be obliged by a communication of the contents of this . . . to your neighbors as far as convenient to you."[42] They lent themselves to posting in handbill or broadside fashion at the county courthouse, local mills, and elsewhere. Sometimes congressmen published them in the press; often one newspaper reprinted them from another.[43] The versatility of a circular is suggested by Clopton in a letter to his son. The congressman said he had just mailed "the manuscript of an address to the people of the district to [Samuel] Pleasants for him to publish in the [Richmond] Argus. I had prepared it for a circular letter, but owing to the printers here being too much engaged I could not get it printed." The son should pay the editor if necessary, but, the father added, "don't mention that to him unless he should suggest it."[44]

Congressional letters, personal or circular, had a significance beyond fulfilling a representative's need for accountability or reelection. They helped define party issues and ideology, to report and interpret national events to a provincial Virginia, and to educate the freeholders in the process of the republican experiment as well as in its problems and principles. The latitude for legitimate comment in a circular letter became a center of controversy in 1797 when a Federalist-leaning grand jury in Richmond found that those of Republican Samuel J. Cabell were "a real evil . . . endeavoring at a time of real public danger to disseminate unfounded calumnies against the happy government of the United States . . ." and thus create national disunity.[45] Obviously, the partisan climate of the times could cause the letters to be treated with great seriousness.

Deeds to Match Words

Constituents held their representatives accountable for more than talk and letters. Deeds had to match words, and congressmen could expect to be measured by how they met the needs of their districts by performing such petty or substantial favors as writing recommendations, assisting with pension problems, securing minor appointments, getting subscriptions for a constituent's publication, gaining or losing a post road for the district, and so on. On a larger scale, the congressman had to vote right on the issues of interest to his electorate.

Occasionally the district's confidence in its representative might allow such sentiments as were expressed in a letter to Leven Powell: "exercise *your* own Judgment on this Important Question, you being better informed, and a better judge of these things, and well knowing your Integrity and Abilities, [we] will rest Satisfied with your Vote let it be as it may."[46] A different attitude is suggested in a sentence from George Tucker's manuscript autobiography: "In the following spring [1819] . . . I was invited to become a candidate for Congress, John Kerr, the former representative having become unpopular by voting for changing the per diem compensation of $6 a day to a salary of $1500."[47] John Randolph's sole defeat, in 1813, came in the wake of his failure to support the administration position on the War of 1812.

There is no comprehensive tabulation and analysis of the votes of Virginia's congressmen covering the full Dynasty period, but Charles Ambler and Norman Risjord have discussed the subject within larger studies.[48] Although writing over a half a century apart, these two scholars hold complementary views. On the great questions from 1789 forward, the majority of the Old Dominion's delegation usually voted alike, but there was seldom unanimity. Aside from the peculiarities of personality and transient local conditions, the minority vote followed a fairly consistent, nationalistic pattern, differing from the majority more on sectional than party grounds, though the two overlapped somewhat. Federalist strongholds, mainly in the west, formed a generally distinct voting region throughout much of the period, and some nationalistic Republicans were also prominent in the west.[49]

Voting patterns, of course, had their individual peculiarities. Shifts in the political winds at home could alter a congressman's stance. Virginia's movement toward state's-rights particularism after the War of 1812, for example, carried former nationalists such as James Pleasants and William McCoy along with it.[50] George Tucker found a successful way of handling changes in local sentiment. As a young writer for the *Port Folio* he expressed nationalist views on a variety of questions, including support for the tariff; as a congressman, however, he advocated "the standard Virginia positions," including opposition to the tariff. He wrote a private letter stating that the tariff was "greatly overrated" as an issue, but a month later, in a circular to his constituents, he expressed vigorous opposition to it. His postcongressional years found him back in the nationalist camp. Politician watchers in the modern era might react cynically to such a chameleonlike performance, but Tucker gave his political opportunism a reasoned defense. Another of his early *Port Folio* essays, "On Instructions to Representatives," concluded that a congressman generally had to follow the wishes of his constituents on a vital issue. Thus Tucker subordinated his personal thoughts about the tariff to the feelings of his district.[51]

Tucker's view was also clearly endorsed in a congressional speech by John Tyler. He stated: "where no . . . violation of the Constitution is involved, I regard it as only necessary to know the wishes of my constituents in order that they may be obeyed. . . . I speak of the voice of a majority of the people, distinctly ascertained and plainly expressed."[52] This philosophy had its negative aspects, as identified by William Wirt, who wrote a friend: "In all cases, whatever may be his own opinion, the representative seems to think of himself a mere mirror to reflect the will of his constituents, with all its flaws, obliquities and distortion. Even when he knows that it will injure the country, he will but echo the popular voice, with the single motive of retaining his ill-deserved office rather than offend the people by honest service."[53]

What or whom did the congressmen in fact represent? The stock Virginia answer was given by Tucker and Tyler: the majority will should be followed so long as it was constitutional. This interpretation seemed ideally suited to the Old Dominion. Congressional districts were economically homogeneous, constituents had many ways of expressing their views, candidates were similar in biographical profiles, few elections reflected divergent opinions on the central issues of the day, and a vast majority of the congressmen had been born and raised among the freeholders they represented. And the philosophy was vague and flexible enough to handle most unpleasant contingencies. After all, the "voice of the majority" and "constitutional" tests were subjective. A congressman could say a given petition reflected either majority or minority views and could bend constitutional provisions equally as well. But few such controversies developed in the Dynasty era.

An exception to the Tucker-Tyler model was John Randolph. "His propositions are original," noted one observer; "they are brought forward without one enquiry of who is to support or who is to oppose them."[54] He refused, for example, to alter his antiwar position even after his constituents opposed it to the point of defeating him in 1813. Randolph, however, stood on the right side of other questions of importance to his district and was returned to Congress as soon as the war ended.

Recording a vote provided constituents with one means of measuring a representative's stance; making a speech was another. An era which saw the arrival in Congress of Webster, Clay, and Calhoun might suggest sophisticated standards of parliamentary oratory, but Virginia's delegation indicates otherwise. A perusal of the *Annals* reveals that most members said little if anything on even the most critical issues. Randolph became an oratorical spectacle, and James Barbour, William Branch Giles, and John Tyler established reputations as legislative speakers. Some of their colleagues, however, were known at best for their vigor and verbosity,[55] and most fell in the mold of Robert Allen, who served from 1827 to 1833. "When in Congress I never spoke," he later confessed, "preferring silence and work, to engaging in the *heated* and *partisan* debates of the times."[56]

Some Virginians made an effort to develop oratorical skills. For example, George Tucker went to great lengths to memorize his maiden speech, took pride in the compliments it elicited, and felt anguish at Randolph's lack of appreciation of it.[57] Well might the attempt be made, because a congressional address had potential political value back home. "Your friends would be glad to read a speech of yours occasionally," wrote a constituent to James Breckinridge. "It might promote the federal interest at another election and we feel fully convinced that you possess at least as much intellect and eloquence as any Democrat in your house." Despite this urging, Breckinridge rarely spoke in Congress.[58] Most Virginia congress-

The Congressmen and Their Constituents

men, in the phrase David Hackett Fischer applied to several Federalists, were simply "quiet backbenchers."[59] This reticence is remarkable given the prominence of stump-speaking as an electioneering device in the Old Dominion and the reputation many Virginians had as hustings orators. But even the most able of them often fell silent in Congress. As John Tyler wrote to a friend, "You have, no doubt, been looking out for my name at the head of some speech. Would you know the fact?—we have so many speech makers, and there is so great and unnecessary a consumption of time, that I almost feel it my duty to remain silent."[60] In a like vein, Jefferson wrote his son-in-law Representative John Wayles Eppes: "I observe that the H. of R. are sensible of the ill effect of the long speeches in their house on their proceedings. But they have a worse effect in the disgust they encite among the people and the disposition they are producing to transfer their confidence from the legislative to the Executive branch . . . These speeches therefore are less & less read, and if continued will cease to be read at all." Jefferson went on to recommend a parliamentary procedure whereby "the eternal protraction of debate" might be curtailed.[61]

Personal associations, elections, correspondence, congressional votes, and speeches all helped establish an image of performance by which a representative might be judged by his constituents. Other elements of this image might have included a person's committee work or congressional leadership and his party role or loyalty. Inactivity might also have been a factor. "Congress, it seems, has done nothing," wrote Governor John Tyler, "and this is doing good, some say."[62]

Tyler to the contrary, energetic, effective service enhanced a congressman's standing with his constituents, especially if that service contributed constructively not only to the district but also to the larger sphere of Commonwealth and country.

X

Congressmen, Commonwealth and Country

A representative's relationship with his district, although central, only partially defined his role in Washington. Congressmen also served and were responsible to larger constituencies—the Commonwealth of Virginia and the nation.

Relations with the Commonwealth

A notable part of the relationship between the legislators and the Commonwealth was the General Assembly's practice of advising or instructing Virginia delegations on important national questions.[1] This followed a deeply rooted tradition of constituents' submitting petitions to the legislature, which Hamilton J. Eckenrode called "the outcome of the old-fashioned habit of addressing the representative body in general rather than particular representatives."[2] These colonial antecedents gained additional force during the Confederation period when congressmen were elected by and dependent on the legislature. The state's first Assembly after ratification of the Federal Constitution proved especially insistent upon continuing the practice because it was dominated by Patrick Henry and an Anti-Federalist faction, while the congressmen, chosen in districts, were mostly Federalists.

The General Assembly continued to instruct the state's congressmen during the Dynasty era. The usual procedure and terminology are illustrated in its resolution of January 22, 1811: "That the Senators of this State in the Congress of the United States be instructed and our representatives most earnestly requested in the execution of their duties as faithful representatives of their country to use their best efforts in opposing by every means in their power the renewal of the charter of the Bank of the United States."[3] The distinction between "instructing" senators and "requesting," or more commonly "advising," representatives is noteworthy. United States senators owed their seats to the General Assembly and were seen as being responsible to it. Representatives, on the other hand, were selected in districts throughout the state and were not directly bound to the legislature. The legal argument for controlling senators required little explication: the Assembly could influence those whom it could elect. Lacking an equivalent constitutional authority over the representatives, the legislature took the less binding approach of "requesting" or "advising" them to act in accordance with the majority position in the Assembly. A deferential tone made this approach no less powerful, and wise congressmen reacted with caution. After all, the legislature passed election laws, reapportioned districts, had the prestige of the state's basic constituent assembly, and consisted of influential politicians, many of whom served simultaneously as local justices.

The practice of instruction linked Virginians in Richmond and Washington on many vexatious issues in the early Republic. In the 1790s the legislature instructed Senators John Taylor and James Monroe "to move a bill in the Senate ordering the sequestration of British debts from Americans"; in 1804 Senators William Branch Giles and Andrew Moore were told "to consult Congress on the possible use of Louisiana as a colony for emancipated slaves"; in the sessions of 1814–15 and 1815–16 Virginia congressmen were requested to ask "the legislature of the Union to manifest an interest in internal improvements"; and in 1819 and 1820 the General Assembly sent resolutions and instructions opposing *McCulloch* v. *Maryland*, the Bank of the United States, and the Missouri Compromise.[4]

Given the factors of sectionalism, party, and personal interests, it seems inevitable that the Assembly's wishes would be at times ignored or violated. Two occasions involving the Bank of the United States serve as examples of both the controversy inherent in such a system and the general principles most contemporaries saw at issue. After the General Assembly declared its opposition to the renewal of the BUS charter in 1811, Senator Richard Brent flatly violated his instructions by voting for renewal. Senator Giles, whom the legislature had just elected by a 123–5 margin, delivered what John Randolph called "the most unintelligible speech on the subject of the Bank of the United States that I have ever heard," in which he condemned the bank as unconstitutional and inexpedient. Giles then voted against renewal but went on to denounce the Assembly's instructions because they were phrased as though they were mandatory. He further argued that even advisory ones could be a mistake if overdone, adding that "he considered himself the representative of the people of the United States, delegated to that character by the Legislature of Virginia." Ironically, Giles as a member of the Assembly in 1800 had written a set of instructions similar in tone to those he now condemned.[5]

Giles was censured in Virginia by the *Richmond Enquirer* and by public meetings. In the legislature John Tyler, Andrew Stevenson, and Benjamin Watkins Leigh led a successful move for resolutions condemning Giles and Brent and affirming a strict interpretation of the right of instruction. Giles countered with "An Address . . . to the People of Virginia" defending his position on a number of controversial points, including "The Right of Instructing Representatives, an Unalienable right. To be executed by Man in his native, and not in his Representative character."[6] Although heated, the imbroglio only briefly tarnished the orator's popularity; fortunately for him the Old Dominion had failed a few years earlier in its attempt to amend the Federal Constitution to allow the removal of senators by a majority vote of a state legislature.

The controversy over the charter renewal is significant for articulating the theory that, except for cases of blatant constitutional doubts, legislative instructions bound a senator. It is also interesting because Tyler, Leigh, and Stevenson figured in similar controversies in the 1830s. They were joined by William Cabell Rives, who in 1820 had committed the political blunder of opposing the doctrine of instruction.[7] In 1834 the General Assembly requested Virginia representatives and required Senators Rives and Tyler to vote for restoration of the BUS deposits removed on President Jackson's order. Rives, a loyal Democrat, could not do so in good faith; nevertheless, reversing his position in 1820, he supported the doctrine of instruction. He resigned and defended his action in a congressional speech, saying,

I hold it, sir, to be a vital principle of our political system, one indispensable to the preservation of our institutions, that the representative whether a member of this or the other house, is bound to conform to the opinions and wishes of his constituents, authentically expressed; or, if he be unable to do so, from overruling and imperious considerations, operating upon his conscience or honor, to surrender his trust into the hands of those from whom he derived it, that they may select an agent who can better carry their views into effect.[8]

Virginia's representatives in 1834 reacted more on the basis of party lines than of political philosophy. Jacksonian Andrew Stevenson, former champion of the doctrine of instruction, paid lip service to the principle but declined to comply with the specific resolutions. He doubted the General Assembly expressed "the public voice of Virginia" and declared: "in the absence of instructions from a majority of those who have honored me with their confidence, I shall feel myself at liberty to discharge my duty in the manner that I think right, and best calculated to promote the safety, honor, and prosperity of my country."[9] Other Democratic representatives concurred with Stevenson. Anti-Jacksonian Charles Fenton Mercer, on the other hand, supported the resolutions.[10]

The 1834 controversy then went a step further. To replace Rives the General Assembly chose Benjamin Watkins Leigh, an advocate of instruction who faithfully worked to restore the bank deposits. In the meantime, Virginia's political winds shifted; in 1836 the legislature instructed Senators Tyler and Leigh to support the pro-Jackson resolutions of Thomas Hart Benton, who sought to expunge a censure of Old Hickory from the Senate records. Unable to comply, Tyler resigned, only to be succeeded by Rives. Leigh, on the other hand, would neither comply nor resign, and defended himself in a letter to the Assembly which argued, "if a State instructs its Senators to give a vote plainly unconstitutional, or to raise the standard of rebellion, the Senator is not bound to obey such instruction." Virginia demanded the former, in his opinion, and thus was not binding. Leigh's justification failed to satisfy even a majority of his own party; he remained under fire until forced to resign, solely, he said, due to the "imperious necessity [of] . . . private affairs."[11] The controversy suggests the variety of possible responses to legislative instructions. For some men (Tyler and Rives), the principle was binding; for others, it became secondary when linked to party concerns.

Congressional ties to the Commonwealth can be demonstrated in several other ways. On a number of occasions the delegation represented Virginia at large on federal-state matters, such as the reimbursement due the Old Dominion for the service of its militia during the War of 1812 and the long-standing attempt to redeem the "claims of the Virginia revolutionary *State* troops against the United States for lands."[12]

Congressmen also transmitted official or timely documents and information to the governor and the legislature. This diverse correspondence includes constitutional amendments, the Treaty of Ghent, notice of the death of a Virginia senator, news of congressional activity deemed injurious to the Commonwealth, requests for information to assist federal investigations, replies to inquiries about particular federal-state problems, and appeals for aid with specific difficulties.[13] Groups of congressmen made personal recommendations from time to time, such as those on behalf of Cary Selden as "agent of the State for the settlement of Accounts between the State and the Government of the United States" and John Floyd to fill an unexpired Senate term.[14]

The fact that a vast majority of Virginia's congressmen had prior service in the General Assembly provided a strong personal tie with the state government.[15] And, of course, the legislature elected the Old Dominion's senators. As important politicians in their own right and as holders of important political positions, the congressmen also exercised a powerful influence on state party affairs. The Richmond Junto, for example, included Wilson Cary Nicholas, William H. Roane, and Andrew Stevenson, as well as their kinsmen; and the Barbour brothers were close advisers, if not actual members.[16] Virginia's presidential electors always had a heavy complement of senators and representatives. The legislators maintained unique ties with national party leaders and served frequently as their instruments in state politics.[17] Prime examples of the latter role are the Embargo crisis and the election of 1808. Loyal Republicans in the Virginia delegation went to exceptional lengths to present the administration's case on the controversial "Dambargo,"[18] and William Branch Giles and Wilson Cary Nicholas shrewdly maneuvered the state's legislative caucus behind Madison (and against Monroe) in the presidential race of 1808.[19] Beyond supporting friends or constituents for political and military appointments, the congressmen also voiced opinions about federal patronage in the Commonwealth.[20]

Relations with the Dynasty Presidents

The many-faceted roles of the Virginia congressmen at the national level resulted from several circumstances, not the least of which was their association with the great triumvirate in power. Conversely, the Dynasty leaders benefited from relations with legislators from their native state.

This relationship was especially fruitful during the presidency of Thomas Jefferson. A more successful party leader than Madison, he also exercised much greater control over Congress than either Madison or Monroe. Aside from his own considerable political talent, Jefferson had the advantage of being a victorious opposition candidate whose enemies were still clearly defined and whose decline was hardly predictable in 1801.[21] Jefferson came to the presidency when congressional institutions were inchoate and when informal executive direction of legislative affairs through personal relationships was not only possible but natural and accepted.[22] Madison and Monroe, however, would face such rising and maturing institutional developments as the nominating caucus, a powerful Speaker of the House, and an elaborate system of standing committees.[23]

With an opportunity for direct personal influence, Jefferson depended heavily on men he knew well and trusted, including his fellow Virginians in Congress. They served in many ways—as advisers, floor leaders, party lieutenants, and sources of information. Temperamentally less assertive and constitutionally perhaps more sensitive, Madison faced a Congress, party, and nation divided over controversial issues of diplomacy and the reality of an unpopular war.[24] Monroe presided over an era of party decline, sought the politics of consensus, regarded himself as "head of a nation, not the leader of a party," and suffered from the factionalism caused by energetic and early rivals for the presidential succession.[25] Both Madison and Monroe also operated under the increased restraints of what Leonard White bluntly calls "the transfer of power from the executive to the legislative branch," as well as a concurrent sensitivity in Congress to charges of Virginia influence and executive interference.[26] As a result, Jefferson's two successors relied much less on Virginians in the House and Senate than did their friend from Monticello.

Close personal, even blood relations, formed a part of the Dynasty ties with congressmen from the Old Dominion. Jefferson is the strongest example. Among the Virginia representatives serving during his presidency were his two sons-in-law (John Wayles Eppes and Thomas Mann Randolph), his former private secretary (William A. Burwell), his close Albemarle County friend (Wilson Cary Nicholas), and his distant cousin (John Randolph). Except for the latter, all stood within his orbit and served him on more than one occasion, in spite of his perhaps inaccurate explanation about his sons-in-law, who lived in the White House with him: "No men on earth are more independent in their sentiments than they are, nor any one less disposed than I am to influence the opinions of others. We rarely speak of politics or of the proceedings of the House, but merely historically." Despite the fact that Eppes nearly fought a duel on the issue of his independence from the president, their loyalty was indeed demonstrable.[27]

Madison had a militant defender in his brother-in-law congressman John George Jackson, who was willing to duel in his defense and whose father and brother had been and would be representatives in the Dynasty era. Marriage ties also linked Madison to Congressman Richard Cutts of Massachusetts and to Andrew Stevenson of the Richmond Junto.[28] In the Virginia delegation Monroe had a close friend and former Albemarle County neighbor, Hugh Nelson, and another Albemarle resident, William Cabell Rives, to whom he had once offered the position of private secretary. Monroe's son-in-law George Hay, though not a congressman, held political office in Richmond and became an influential member of the Junto.[29]

Another side of Jefferson's personal leadership is seen in his efforts to recruit talented Virginians for Congress. He asked John Taylor of Caroline to engineer Monroe's election to the Senate (the letter arrived too late), his boyhood friend John Page to run for reelection (he lost), Wilson Cary Nicholas to return to the Senate (he declined) and later to seek the House seat vacated by Thomas Mann Randolph's retirement (he did), and William Wirt to "come into Congress . . . the threshold to whatever a man is qualified to enter" (he declined).[30]

One reason Jefferson wanted Nicholas in the House in 1807 was the need for him as a floor leader, "a rallying point" for party and executive affairs.[31] Duly elected, Nicholas served in that important capacity, being only one of several Virginians to do so. Once more, the record under Jefferson is especially full. During his administration the majority or floor leader was a key position. The men who held it functioned, in the words of a recent scholar, as "personal representatives of the President" and as such wielded power in the legislative branch and party councils.[32] First of the Virginians to serve Jefferson in this way was his kinsman John Randolph. As a very assertive if youthful chairman of the influential Ways and Means Committee, he had the role despite a mild challenge for it by another Virginian, the veteran William Branch Giles. Randolph performed with some efficiency until his break with the president in 1805–6, after which Jefferson adroitly neutralized him and later put Nicholas in the post. Jefferson's first Senate leader was the longtime partisan Stevens Thomson Mason. After his death in 1803 the reins shifted to Giles, who had the aid of Virginia-born John Breckinridge of Kentucky.[33] Another strategic position during the early Dynasty era fell to pioneer party manager John Beckley, late of the Old Dominion and William and Mary and formerly mayor of Richmond and clerk of the Virginia House of Delegates and of the United States House. In 1801 he again became clerk of the House of Representatives, an ideal slot for such an inveterate partisan.[34]

Virginians also compiled a strong record of committee leadership in the Dynasty years. Their representation often exceeded even what might be expected from the delegation's large size, and most of the major committees at one time or another had Virginians in the chair.[35] John Randolph spent several terms as head of Ways and Means, a post also held by Eppes for six sessions. The Committee of Commerce and Manufactures, "the second most influential"[36] in the House, had Thomas Newton as chairman from 1807 until 1819, when it was subdivided, and Newton continued as leader of the new Commerce Committee through the 1820s. Senate standing committees date from 1816, at which point James Barbour began almost ten years at the helm of the Foreign Relations Committee. During most of the Embargo crisis, Virginians had charge of three of the then-seven standing committees in the House; and when Madison became president, they had three of the nine committees.[37] Other leaders from 1801 to 1825 included Speaker of the House Philip P. Barbour and his brother, Senate President pro tem James Barbour.[38]

The purpose of such a catalogue of names and positions is not to suggest any premeditated Virginia scheme for controlling the national government. The point is simply to demonstrate the service role of Virginians in Congress and to suggest the possibilities of their assistance to the Dynasty, whom they in fact served in a variety of ways aside from the official leadership positions.

Less formal roles are seen in the example of William A. Burwell, Jefferson's former secretary. On becoming a congressman, Burwell told the president that "his former station required considerable caution to shield me from the suspicion of being under influence, but I should always give him faithful information upon every subject which would enable him to be useful and promote his happiness."[39] Burwell was equally adept in taking information. In 1806 "Decius" (John Randolph) attacked Jefferson in the *Richmond Enquirer*. Loyal editor Thomas Ritchie asked Burwell for a reply; Burwell wrote Jefferson, who answered: "These, my dear Sir, are the principal facts worth correction. Make any use of them you think best, without letting your source of information be known." Shortly afterwards, an anonymous two columns of "Important Facts" appeared in the *Enquirer*, with no indication of Jefferson's or Burwell's hand in the matter.[40] With extensive correspondence to and from influential persons throughout the Commonwealth and a lofty standing in Congress, Wilson Cary Nicholas also kept Jefferson posted on politically significant matters. "Be assured that I value no act of friendship so highly," Jefferson wrote Nicholas, "as the communicating facts to me, which I am not in the way of knowing otherwise."[41] Others offered behind-the-scenes assistance to the president. Having been instructed to burn the original, John Dawson received a bill drafted by Jefferson himself, and the president asked Thomas Mann Randolph to explain some administration measures to the citizens of Albemarle, adding: "I must not be quoted. You will be free however to mention that these are your own opinions."[42]

On other occasions Virginians defended Jefferson's administration more openly. Thomas Mann Randolph reviewed and supported the president's scheme to purchase West Florida; Eppes, Giles, and Nicholas, among others, backed the Embargo at critical times.[43] Representatives from the Old Dominion also introduced and steered party measures in Congress. Jefferson once suggested to Gallatin, his secretary of the treasury: "If you will prepare something on these or any other ideas you like better, Mr. Eppes will give them to Mr. [Thomas] Newton . . . and he will push them through the House." Virginians played central roles in the Chase impeachment proceedings in 1804–5. One scholar remarked, "As John Randolph considered himself responsible in the House, so Giles looked upon himself as the manager in the Senate." For his legislative program and foreign policy, Madison found a ready ally in his brother-in-law Jackson and in Ways and Means Chairman Eppes, though, of course, the president had difficulty with his quondam friend Giles, as well as with Old Republicans of the Randolph persuasion. Monroe worked closely, prudently, and constructively with Senator James Barbour during the heated Missouri controversy.[44]

These Virginians served as an extension of executive will in Congress, enabling presidents to influence what happened there in a direct, effective, and yet discreet manner which smoothly and efficiently bridged the constitutional separation of powers between the two branches. Other, more minor roles were also performed; for instance, Representative John Dawson served as an executive agent on at least two diplomatic missions, and Senator Richard Brent, in the capacity of an intermediary, contacted Monroe about joining Madison's cabinet.[45]

Party Matters

The Virginia congressmen were equally active in party matters. Noble Cunningham's detailed investigation of the Jeffersonian Republicans led him to conclude that "at the focal point of party formation was the Congress of the United States."[46] Implicit in Cunningham's writings is a related conclusion: the Old Dominion was crucial to the focal point. In the 1790s Madison, Giles, and Taylor, among others, helped to forge an opposition faction and then to lead it to victory. On the Federalist side in the late nineties, Marshall, Leven Powell, Daniel Morgan, and Henry Lee were all strongly partisan and influential and thus contributed to party definition and rivalry.[47]

The importance of the congressmen during the period of party formation continued into the Dynasty era. As Cunningham put it: "The Republican members of Congress provided the national party organization of the Jeffersonian party. They maintained close touch with their state party organizations and through their informal association in Washington supplied the leadership of a national party committee. The administration relied heavily on Republicans in Congress for contact with state organizations, for patronage recommendations, and for communicating the accomplishments of the administration to the voters."[48] As in the 1790s, the Old Dominion contributed greatly to this partisan activity. Few if any states surpassed its leadership in the prime institution for controlling presidential elections, the congressional caucus. Virginians participated prominently in each of the major caucuses of the period. The actions of Nicholas and Giles in 1808 were masterful in timing and coordination and helped contain the Monroe movement before it began.[49] James Barbour spearheaded the drive to nominate Monroe in 1816, and the last meaningful caucus, that of 1824, has been called "largely a New York–Virginia affair."[50]

A majority of legislators from the Old Dominion consistently defended the caucus against its critics and endorsed its nominees. At the same time, however, a minority of Virginia representatives led the fight against it.[51] As early as January 1808 Edwin Gray answered his formal caucus invitation with a vigorous condemnation of the practice, expressing an "abhorrence of the usurpation of power . . . —the mandatory style—and the object contemplated therein." He had not been elected to "consent either in an individual or representative capacity, to countenance by my presence, the midnight intrigues of any set of men, who may arrogate to themselves the right which belongs alone to the people, of selecting proper persons to fill the important offices of President and Vice President."[52] Randolph and others of the "Minority" denounced the system, and Federalist Charles Fenton Mercer boasted in an 1824 letter, "I never was at a caucus, a faro bank, or a cock fight."[53]

As for party matters on the state level, the Richmond Junto was closely associated with Republican corresponding committees established to supervise each presidential election.[54] The congressional influence within the Junto itself has been noted, as has the frequency of congressmen on electoral college slates and the congressional role in questions of executive appointments and patronage. Party loyalists like Giles and Eppes worked to isolate the dissident Randolph, even to the point of preventing his reelection, a feat accomplished by Eppes in 1813.[55] The legislators also helped to define and articulate the ideology of both "Old" and "Nationalistic" Republicans and provided a continuous interpretation and communication of party positions for their constituents. On a broader scale, a distinguished historian has called John Taylor, "the publicist of the Virginia triumvirate," a phrase to be taken lightly with regard to Madison at least.[56]

The Virginia Delegation

Influential as individuals in Washington, the Virginians also had significance as a group. For most of the era, the delegation was as large as or larger than that of any other state, and it remained relatively cohesive in its membership and voting behavior. The representatives of the Commonwealth had many traits and interests in common, generally sharing an elite profile in the gentry mold. The legislators rarely stood in complete agreement, but Federalists and dissident Republicans remained in the shadows as a distinct minority, with never over eight of twenty-two seats, thus assuring a solid majority bloc of party loyalists on any question not touching the sensitive nerve of local, sectional interests.

Some recent quantitative studies of Congress in the antebellum era make it possible to put the Virginians in historical perspective and to deal with them in comparative terms.[57] One immediate conclusion is that the state's delegation enjoyed exceptional stability (table 18). For the twelve Congresses from 1801 to 1825, the average percentage of Virginia's holdovers was almost 75, against an average for all the congressional delegations of only 56 percent.[58] In every session the Virginia legislators boasted a higher percentage of hold-

Table 18. Delegation stability: Virginia's biennial holdovers, 1801–25

Congress	Senate			House			Combined		
	Seats*	HO	%	Seats*	HO	%	Seats*	HO	%
7th (1801–3)	2	2	100	19	10	53	21	12	57
8th (1803–5)	2	2	100	19	13	68	21	15	71
9th (1805–7)	2	2	100	22	18	82	24	20	83
10th (1807–9)	2	2	100	22	20	91	24	22	92
11th (1809–11)	2	1	50	22	17	77	24	18	75
12th (1811–13)	2	2	100	22	15	68	24	17	71
13th (1813–15)	2	2	100	22	17	77	24	19	79
14th (1815–17)	2	1	50	23	17	74	25	18	72
15th (1817–19)	2	1	50	23	13	57	25	14	56
16th (1819–21)	2	2	100	23	16	70	25	18	72
17th (1821–23)	2	2	100	23	19	83	25	21	84
18th (1823–25)	2	2	100	23	19	83	25	21	84
Total							287	215	74.9

Source: Biographical Directory of the American Congress.

* This is the number of Virginia seats in the preceding Congress, that is, the number of possible holdovers; the Senate numbers are somewhat misleading because the senatorial term is six years and several senators resigned or died before their terms expired.

overs than did Congress at large, and in some instances the margin was substantial. The state's congressmen also had greater longevity. For the entire House, by decades, the median years of service ranged from two to four years, well below the five to eight years that constituted the collective median for the Commonwealth. Between 8 and 9 percent of all United States representatives had over eight years' tenure, but the Virginia figure is 45 percent.[59] Apropos is the comment of *Niles' Register*:

> The practice in Virginia of continuing the old members in congress, gives her a mighty moral power in the house of representatives, on many accounts—yet we like the custom in some other of the states, of returning the representatives to the people from whence they came, that they themselves may more sensibly feel the effects of their own measures, and see the operation of them on their fellow citizens—from the body of whom, as from a pure fountain, it is designed that the elements of our government should be derived.[60]

Virginia's congressmen from 1801 to 1825 were better educated and had more military experience than the other United States representatives of that period. Fifty-one percent of the state's members of the House had attended college, while only about 40 percent of the House at large could claim that distinction.[61] Fifty-nine percent of the Virginians had prior military service, and almost all of them had been officers; of members of the entire House by decades, between 27 and 54 percent were veterans, and of that group, between 76 and 86 had held commissions.[62] Congressmen from the Old Dominion also tended to be more tied to the occupations of farming and law than did the representatives from other states.[63]

The Old Dominion also had a clear advantage over its rivals in the House in terms of prior political experience and of congressmen-relatives. Eighty-eight percent of the Virginians had previously served in the state legislature, and virtually all of them had held one or more local positions. For the House at large by decades from 1789 to 1830, from 67 to 78 percent of the members had had some state-level experience, and from 27 to 34 percent had prior local service. Sixty percent of the Commonwealth's representatives were related to one or more other congressmen, in contrast to percentages ranging between 24 and 34 by decades for the entire House over the same period.[64] Finally, in a comparative vein, Virginia's House delegations tended to be younger in age than was the House in general.[65]

Beyond the quantitative comparisons, the Virginia delegation enjoyed additional advantages in its relationship with the Dynasty and with other Washington groups as well. Over 376 natives of the Old Dominion numbered among "the principal classes of officials and employees" of the federal establishment in 1801,[66] and between 227 and 232 native sons born before 1810 served other states as senators or representatives. Georgia, for example, had either one or two Virginia-born senators for twenty-three of the state's first thirty-five years under the Constitution. Most of the 227-plus had left the Commonwealth "in their young manhood"; many had attended its colleges and were members of prominent families or were related to congressmen in the state's delegation. Of these "expatriates," twelve in time held cabinet positions, and twenty-one had been or would become territorial or state governors.[67] The national scene also included key congressional officers like Beckley and cabinet members like Madison, Monroe, and Wirt. Present but withdrawn from Virginia politics were Chief Justice John Marshall and his fellow Federalist Justice Bushrod Washington.[68]

In a minor way geography further enhanced the delegation's influence. Congressmen from several states had to travel through the Old Dominion to get to and from Washington. They often visited their colleagues in the Commonwealth and were not immune to political persuasion mixed with gracious hospitality.[69] A final consideration about the Virginians as a group is that they operated within a context of inherited prestige and leadership on the national level and boasted enough individuals with the talents, training, and ties, such as had catapulted earlier Virginians into positions of command, to retain the traditional respect accorded the Old Dominion.

The Significance of the Service Role

What impact did this pervasive service role have on political affairs in the Dynasty era? First, on the national scene, the prominence of Virginians in Congress and elsewhere in the government provided the presidents, especially Jefferson, with a talented and devoted coterie within the federal establishment. Although these individuals from the Old Dominion gave counsel on occasion, they were more important for implementing rather than for making policy. Their lieutenants' role made it easier for the executives to work within rather than with (or against) the legislative branch and to control rather than merely to influence party operations. On the latter point, not the least of the legislators' contributions was their assistance, by leadership within the Republican caucuses, in perpetuating the Dynasty itself.

Second, on the state level, Virginia's national influence brought political rewards to the congressmen and their constituents. Several representatives and senators retired from congressional service to choice patronage positions, and the Commonwealth ranked near the top among states in the number of its citizens who received major presidential appointments.[70] On a smaller scale numerous requests for post roads, pensions, and the like were filled. The vital connection between congressional leaders and state matters has been discussed at length, but stress should be given the general prestige that Republican candidates in Virginia gained from Dynasty rule in Washington.

The association of local politicians with a national regime had the subtle but perhaps negative effect of giving a greater credibility to administration policy than on occasions it might have deserved. A good example is Jefferson's Embargo. Although the measure brought economic distress to the Old Dominion, most of its citizens nevertheless supported it with fidelity. Part of the explanation relates to the large number of prominent Virginians who helped to create, implement, enforce, and defend the act. Most of the state's political elite stood close to Jefferson; their prestige, and his, assured a fair trial for the measure from the outset and minimized criticism as time passed.[71]

Third, Virginia's prominence is noteworthy in retrospect for the way it masked the state's decline in national influence. Prestige and power reached a high tide with Jefferson; the prestige continued through other Dynasty presidents and other conspicuous leaders, but the power dissipated to a point in the 1820s when the question of a Virginia influence had become of as little concern beyond the state as it was a cause of deep despair within it.

If Virginia's earlier preeminence related directly to the caliber of its political leaders during the Revolution and immediately afterward,

The Service Role

in like fashion its elite can be examined for clues to the sad but central theme of decline in the Dynasty era. In this case, the focus rests on what had developed, imperceptibly, into an increasingly anachronistic generation of public men.

Epilogue

Evolution and
Decline

A central irony of the Dynasty period is that it suggests a sustained, powerful, even dominant national role for the Old Dominion when in fact the era was one of a steady and irreversible diminution of influence. On Jefferson's inaugural day in March 1801, few Americans would have questioned Virginia's leadership in the young nation, and some critics believed it had become so strong as to threaten seriously the interests of rival states or sections. When Monroe left office in March 1825, however, the issue of Virginia influence was largely historical.

The Decline Theme

"The old Revolutionary generation has passed away. The new presents so many who are equal or think themselves so (which is the same thing) that every section of the union will have its claims—except Virginia. She by common consent is to repose on the recollection of what she has done."[1] So wrote Senator James Barbour in 1820, sounding the tocsin of "nostalgia, pessimism, and malaise" that became the hallmarks of the "doomed aristocrat" in late-Jeffersonian Virginia and the fascination and pastime of generations of Virginians and scholars ever since.[2] The decline thesis, however, is easily overstated. It ignores the positive developments and the progressive and nationalistic voices of 1801–25. Those years saw, for example, antidueling legislation (1810); the establishment of a Literary Fund in 1810 and the passage in 1811 of "An Act to Provide for the Education of the Poor" (called the beginning of "publicly-financed common school education in Virginia")[3]; expanded internal improvements in the form of new projects and a

Epilogue

Public Works Fund and Board (1816); the state's leadership in the American colonization movement begun in 1817; the launching of the University of Virginia in 1819; and several milestones in the articulation of western Virginia's rights to reapportionment and a broad franchise.[4]

Among the vigorous political reformers of the Jeffersonian era stood James Barbour, John Breckinridge, Joseph C. Cabell, John George Jackson, and Charles Fenton Mercer, all of whom offered constructive leadership designed to meet new challenges and circumstances with state or federal support of a variety of social and economic programs. Barbour also ranked high as an agricultural reformer, as did John Taylor of Caroline and Thomas Mann Randolph.[5]

In Washington, D.C., from 1801 to 1825, Virginians could claim all three presidents, the chief justice of the United States, and a cohesive and influential delegation of congressmen. The latter group, similar in many traits to the Old Dominion's "great generation," remained relatively stable throughout the period.

Finally, a preoccupation with the decline argument obscures the national leadership of some prominent Virginians in the decades after 1825. The Old Dominion had one or more cabinet members under six of the ten presidents from John Quincy Adams through James Buchanan; Supreme Court appointments went to Philip P. Barbour (1836–41) and Peter V. Daniel (1841–60); and several congressmen attained the prestigious positions of Speaker of the House and president pro tem of the Senate.[6]

Nevertheless, even conceding a continued presence on the national level and random reform manifestations within the state itself, the theme of declining influence, kept in perspective, is certainly a correct one for Dynasty Virginia. Contemporaries saw it clearly and talked about it incessantly. Although many lamented its validity, few contested its reality.[7] In retrospect, the presidency itself provides the most dramatic illustration. Washington, Jefferson, Madison, Monroe: a Virginian was at the helm of the nation for thirty-two of the first thirty-six years of the Republic. But never again would a citizen of the Old Dominion even be the candidate of a major party for that office.[8]

Explaining this diminution of power is perhaps the premier

question about politics in Jeffersonian Virginia. Historians concur with contemporary observers on the erosion of influence, but there is no consensus on the reason for it.[9] Economic adversity is a logical villain. Unquestionably the state felt the effects of erratic markets in the Napoleonic years and the unsettling impact of the War of 1812 and the Panic of 1819, all of which compounded the ancient woes of soil misuse and a faulty credit structure. However, the Commonwealth shared many of these problems with other regions, and citizens west of the Blue Ridge escaped some of the distress. Furthermore, economic reforms began concurrently, and the strain of the Dynasty era appears no worse, if as bad, as that experienced during the Revolutionary period and immediately thereafter when Virginia's influence reached its zenith.

A relative loss in population is another common explanation for Virginia's decline. The Old Dominion stood without rival as America's most populous state in Revolutionary times and in the decades that followed. In the early 1800s, however, it fell behind much of the nation, as many Virginians departed and few immigrants arrived. These demographic patterns certainly had an adverse effect on the state's political standing, but the crisis came later. The Commonwealth, in fact, had the largest number of congressmen until the 1810 Census and the second largest until after 1820—that is, during the bulk of the Dynasty period. A fairly cohesive and well-prepared delegation, a general ticket law governing presidential campaigns, virtual one-party politics, the impressive number of native sons attaining prominence elsewhere, and the Dynasty incumbents themselves surely offset the initial impact of a decreasing population.

A third explanation is the acute internal stress felt by Jeffersonian Virginia as a result of an almost continuous state of crisis and alarm. No doubt Virginians found unsettling such events and disturbances as Gabriel Prosser's Revolt, the *Chesapeake* affair, the Embargo, the War of 1812, the Panic of 1819, and the passing of the Revolutionary giants, from Henry and Washington in 1799 to Jefferson in 1826. But the period also had its spells of tranquillity and of exultation; and stress hardly qualifies as a condition novel or peculiar to the Dynasty years. To the contrary, it seems almost a way of life for citizens of the Commonwealth. Were internal waters more calm during the French and Indian War of the 1750s, or the boiling revolutionary crises of the 1760s, or the independence and war decade of the 1770s, or the economic dislocations and political turmoil of the eighties, or the partisan warfare of the nineties? Virginia's earlier leaders thrived amid tension and distress and achieved their just fame for meeting the challenges of adversity and change.

Other sources of Virginia's decline? Writing in the 1840s, a pioneer historian identified them as the want of education and internal improvements and the presence of slavery.[10] Surely the analysis has merit, but, by the standards of the early 1800s, would the state rank poorly in education and internal improvements? Its public men surpassed their congressional colleagues en masse in educational achievements (in the era before the public school movement boomed in America), and the Old Dominion had been a pathfinder in the 1780s by launching the first comprehensive canal scheme on the continent, a scheme well ahead of the fabled Erie and one into which the state poured considerable funds in the early 1800s. In time, the Commonwealth would indeed suffer from its flawed "mixed enterprise" approach to public improvements and from its narrowly constricted educational system, but the Dynasty period seems early for these indictments. Slavery? Without question it was becoming a sensitive sectional issue within the state, and the Missouri Compromise elevated it momentarily into a divisive question on the national scene. But, again, the subject became burning and controversial within Virginia and beyond during a later era and not during the Dynasty years themselves.

Sectionalism? It did indeed become a divisive reality, one that eventually separated the state into two geographic and political entities when West Virginia broke away during the Civil War period. In the Jeffersonian decades, however, sectionalism would rank as an ominous, sensitive, relatively recent concern, to be weighed against the many commonalities that bound Virginians east and west. The peaks of sectional tension were the conventions of 1829–30 and 1850–51 and the great slave debate of 1831–32, all postdating the Dynasty years. Sectional animosity sharply declined in the 1850s, a decade of renewed prosperity and fulfilled western political goals. This suggests that east and west, though different in some particulars, could complement as well as compete with one another, and that sectionalism all along had been somewhat of a rhetorical and mishandled issue.

The Last Stand of the Old Elite

Without accepting any one or all of the traditional explanations of decline completely—and certainly without disregarding them either—it is possible to shed light on the question of decline by taking a close look at the political leadership of Jeffersonian Virginia. This emphasis on leadership, after all, has been used to account for the Old Dominion's earlier prominence. As Dumas Malone has written: "The most distinguished generation of public men in the history of the United States was the first one. . . . The famous sons of Virginia comprised the most conspicuous and important single group at that time, and they constituted a great generation in themselves."[11]

The Revolutionary elite generally perpetuated itself into and throughout the Dynasty era. Virginia congressmen from 1801 to 1825 came from the traditional leadership mold and had been shaped by traditional institutions, values, and political ideologies. In the Jeffersonian era, however, many of the institutions were crumbling, some of the values were under scrutiny, and much of the ideology was either under fire or had turned from a constructive creed to a defensive shibboleth. The prototype Dynasty leader—similar in many ways to the Revolutionary one and possessing many estimable qualities—increasingly became an anachronism. Whatever the appearance and reality of prestige, his time was passing. The Jeffersonian years marked the last stand of the old elite. It had served Virginia and the nation well, but by the 1820s the state had changed so much that a new leadership class would soon emerge with talents of a secondary order.

Far from being a virtual model of stability,[12] Dynasty Virginia is best understood as a bizarre mixture of change and continuity. The leadership class represents a continuance of a past elite, but the state's political milieu, and its social and economic foundations, were in the midst of a profound transformation. The process of change was deceptively evolutionary rather than drastic, violent, or even very conspicuous. But the end result would discourage some worthy citizens from entering politics, drive others out, and restrict the

Epilogue

vision and spirit of many who remained. In a larger perspective, the Dynasty years mark the end of an era and point toward a transferal of elites from the reluctant but dutiful public servant to the eager and available professional politician, from a commitment to the broad commonweal toward one of a narrow local constituency, from a class set apart and above the rank and file to one increasingly "from and of the people," and from a generation of orators often articulating political principles and issues to one "largely concerned with defending Virginia's [status quo] . . . and in glorifying her role in the history of the nation."[13] The Dynasty years, in short, saw changes that would lead, in time, to the diminution of the old elite and, correspondingly, of the Old Dominion itself.

Virginia's decline is admittedly a complex question, and it was likely the result of numerous converging factors. The Dynasty leaders, however commendable in many ways, did contribute somewhat to the pattern. Of greater significance, they can serve as a window for viewing certain additional causes otherwise difficult to perceive and especially potent in the post-Dynasty era. By the 1820s the anachronism of the Jeffersonian elite was clear, as demonstrated in virtually every category of the collective profile and in many facets of the Old Dominion's political culture.

The web of kinship was so basic a pattern in Virginia politics as to be accepted as axiomatic, and it was certainly characteristic of the Dynasty elite. For example, 62 percent of the congressmen had at least one other congressman as a relative. At the same time, however, the web had begun to unravel. Migration from the state affected great families along with lesser ones, while changing political demands and electioneering practices led to a new generation of officeholders; the system grew increasingly open, especially after the reform constitution of 1851 added scores of new elective positions. The percentage of congressmen with relatives in the House or Senate declined to 39 percent in the 1830s, then to 16 percent in the 1840s, and finally to a mere 8 percent in the 1850s.[14]

Over half the congressmen had been raised Anglicans and were tied to the prestige and authority of colonial Virginia's established church. But the Revolution and disestablishment left that venerable institution in shambles. "At the commencement of the War of Revolution," wrote Bishop Meade, "Virginia had 91 clergymen, offici-

Evolution and Decline

ating in 164 churches & chapels; at its close" there were only twenty-eight ministers active.[15] In 1792 a staunch Episcopalian lady in Richmond complained to a friend that "in our extensive State [there are only] three churches that are decently supported," and an English traveler a decade later noted a Tidewater church he thought not unusual with "the roof having fallen in and the floor broken down in every direction . . . since the War of Revolution, serving now but as a building place for birds, and a local mark of the downfall of the Anglican Church in this district of the state of Virginia."[16] As one scholar has noted, "so prostrate was the church in 1811 that a report to [its] . . . General Convention expressed doubt that it could be revived."[17] It did not disappear and soon enjoyed a mild renaissance, but its preemptive position had become largely historical. The booming denominations, though poorly represented among the congressmen, were the Baptists and Methodists. Highly evangelistic and closely attuned to the spiritual needs of the rank-and-file Virginian, these churches burgeoned in the Old Dominion—though again, the trend is masked by the reported faiths of the political elite.[18]

For over a century William and Mary had been a matrix of Virginia leadership, and it claimed about a third of the Dynasty congressmen as alumni. Despite an enlightened curriculum and the dedicated presidency of Bishop Madison, the college declined sharply in the post-Revolutionary years. The war had been disruptive, and independence terminated a healthy English endowment. When the capital moved to Richmond, Williamsburg slipped into decay. "This poor town has little to recommend it to a stranger," observed George Tucker, "except the memory of its ancient importance."[19] A rash of student duels and riots, a reputation for "deistic" teaching and a "dissipated" and "licentious" campus life, and the granting of diplomas after only two years' study all turned public opinion against the school. Enrollment at various times in the 1780s and 1790s ranged from thirty to forty students; for the entire decade after the War of 1812 it numbered only several hundred, "no less than seventy-eight [of whom] had been suspended, dismissed, or expelled";[20] and for 1824–25 it plummeted to less than twenty. Other schools, especially the University of Virginia, superseded it as the educational institution of the state's elite; but none could replace the unique political atmosphere and inspiration it had provided earlier generations of officeholders in the Old Dominion.[21]

The vast majority of Virginia congressmen had military experience, almost always as an officer, and had benefited from the leadership training and recognition, as well as from related political rewards. As the decades passed and the Revolution and War of 1812 receded in time, however, fewer and fewer veterans appeared on the political scene, as reported in statistics for Congress at large for the period 1800–1850.[22]

If the military pattern is predictable, a charting of service on the county court and in the state legislature reflects surprising change. In the "gentlemen freeholders" system so ably described by Sydnor, experience as a justice prepared one for tenure in the legislature, and acceptable service at both rungs trained Virginians to advance up the ladder of leadership toward a distinguished career on the national scene. That elementary sequence holds true for the Dynasty congressmen, half of whom were JPs and eighty-seven of ninety-eight of whom had prior terms in the General Assembly. Two trends from the Revolution to the Civil War, however, clearly altered the scenario. First, the JP and the delegate faced increasing criticism for flawed performance of their duties, and they suffered a distinct loss of power and prestige. Second, as the decades passed and the political system became increasingly open, both positions became less and less a province of the gentry or a part of the sequence of training and advancement for Virginia politicians.[23] Nearly every Dynasty congressman could claim prior political experience on the local or state level. The trend for Virginia congressmen with any political experience from 1831 to 1861, however, was away from that earlier standard. For 1831–49, 81 percent claimed such experience; for 1849–61, 76 percent; for 1859–61, only 56 percent.[24]

Great emphasis has been placed in this study—and in others—on the agricultural ties of Virginia's elite and the association of those ties with personal values and political beliefs. Note has also been made of how the life of a gentleman provided a measure of preparation as well as the financial resources for public service. Almost all the Dynasty congressmen lived in rural areas, and most earned their livelihood from the soil in some way and owned slaves in addition to their acres. Gradually, however, an urban Virginia began to emerge. The percentage of people in rural areas declined with each census from 1790 to 1860, as the urban population rose correspondingly, from 12,296 to 115,879.[25] Barely underway in the Jeffersonian era and uncompleted in the antebellum period, this demographic shift still had a disproportionately profound impact on the occupational and residential patterns of the leadership class. Through the decades there were more lawyers and fewer farmers in Congress, until by the 1850s the former exceeded the latter over two to one. The number of farmers with large holdings also declined—continuing a trend from late colonial times—and, perhaps most striking of all, the politicians increasingly moved from the country to the city. In the 1850s over 60 percent of the congressmen called urban Virginia their home.[26]

The slaveholders among Virginia congressmen of 1801–25 numbered at least ninety-four of the ninety-eight individuals, a third of whom owned twenty or more. Slave property had long been associated with the ruling class, and the "peculiar institution" had helped to sustain its way of life. Beginning with the Revolution, sporadic criticism was voiced until it exploded in the candid legislative debates of 1831–32. Recent scholarship documents the persistence of antislavery sentiment after 1832 even east of the Blue Ridge, while west of it a largely nonslaveholding region continued to increase its political power, especially as a result of the reform constitution of 1851. An almost predictable trend—though one obscured by the profile and one only in an early stage during the Jeffersonian years—was the decrease in slaveholding among congressmen and the increase in those completely without slaves until the nonowners constituted 40 percent of the Virginia delegation for 1859–61.[27]

As this review makes clear, an increasingly anachronistic pattern is revealed in many categories of the congressmen's collective biography. Of course, the degree of the anachronism varies with the category, from immediate and profound (the Episcopal church and William and Mary influences, for example) to moderate, as in the early stage of a trend (the switch from agriculture to the law, for example). Still, the support system of a leadership class was being undermined, and the class itself would soon decline in influence.

Epilogue

By the Monroe years, the political elite fully acknowledged the presence of unwelcome change; lamented the decline of traditional institutions, values, and influence; and increasingly looked to the past rather than to the present or future. As one critic-congressman noted about his fellow Virginians: "We have been too prone to repose upon the laurels of our ancestors, and to rely on *their* fame as dispensing us from the necessity of winning a character for ourselves in the World by our own meritorious deeds and exertions."[28]

As time passed, the Dynasty prototype would be replaced by another, one of a new and different leadership class. The emergent elite would be more diverse in religious affiliation, more legal than agricultural in occupation, and increasingly urban in residence, would have had less military service and prior political experience, and would own less slave property. Many of these changes reflected national patterns,[29] and others mirrored the increasingly democratic base of Virginia politics; but all moved the Old Dominion away from an earlier type of leader who had served both state and nation honorably and well.

A Transitional Political Culture

If the personal profile reflects an increasingly anachronistic elite, so does an examination of Virginia's political culture in the Age of Jefferson. Again one finds not stability or homogeneity but a blend of change and continuity, a transition from old to new which would weaken the national influence of the Commonwealth. Because of this transformation, increasing numbers of talented Virginians would find politics an unattractive pursuit and would refuse to enter the lists or, if elected, would voluntarily or prematurely terminate their public service. Into the vacuum came individuals more politically inclined but less able and with a vision often narrowly focused on the reelection process and also constricted by the reverence they accorded an anachronistic political ideology.

The Dynasty congressmen were products of what had been an oligarchical system of government with few elective offices and with entrenched interests in the county courts, an eastern-dominated legislature, and restricted suffrage. All aspects of this system were under attack but would survive the challenge of constitutional revision in 1829–30. However, the conservative triumph in that convention was not long sustained. Reform demands continued until constitutional changes in 1851 successfully remodeled the state's system of government and politics, casting them on a democratic foundation which largely erased the remaining vestiges of the old, restricted gentry rule. A foreshadowing of this transformation came during the Dynasty period when the legislature began to allow alternative polling sites, directly unsettling the traditional pattern of a gentleman appearing on court day to appeal to a fixed group of deferential constituents in a familiar milieu. With concurrent voting at different sites, electioneering took on new twists, some more indirect and organizational, as precinct polling and politics helped to democratize the system by bringing it closer to more of the people.[30]

Many of the Virginia congressmen from 1801 to 1825 had played central roles in developing the first party system in America, and many benefited from an association with the dominant Republicans. Some promising Federalists, however, no doubt had partisan ceilings placed on their ability to rise in national politics; James Breckinridge and Charles Fenton Mercer, for example, merited higher leadership posts. In time, of course, party battles receded, only to be revised in the 1820s by the emergence of fresh issues and leaders, which carried the Old Dominion into a genuine two-party system with an equivalent increase in party organization and enthusiasm, in competitive principles and electioneering practices. Many late-Dynasty congressmen, however, were caught between the first and second party systems and were a bit incongruous with both.

Though some sectional concerns were voiced in the Revolutionary generation,[31] the war of independence was fought by a largely united elite. The ideal of a common cause and commitment scarcely outlasted the fighting, however, as sectional alignments soon appeared within the General Assembly, often pitting a Northern Neck interest against a Southside bloc. In time the axis tilted, and problems emerged between Virginians east and west of the Blue Ridge. "The result of the struggle between the two sections of the country," observed a traveler to the Old Dominion in 1816, "will probably be the division of the state into two great parties . . . which will in a degree destroy its political weight in the general government."[32] Heirs to a consensual politics from the Revolutionary era,

Epilogue

Dynasty leaders lived in a climate of increasing sectional tension; the future held genuine conflict between east and west and divided Virginia's voice on many national issues.

An evolution in electioneering practices also placed Dynasty legislators in a somewhat anachronistic position and had an adverse impact on Virginia's national leadership. In the late colonial period candidates "treated" and deferred to in ritualistic ways a familiar local constituency. The creation of multicounty districts and the rise of partisan competition, to cite two conspicuous changes, led to an expansion of campaign techniques. Unknown in most colonial races, oratory now became a virtual prerequisite to success on the hustings. This broadening of campaign demands had at least two negative effects on the candidates. First, it discouraged some otherwise competent individuals from seeking or continuing in office. One example is that of Edmund Ruffin, later renowned as a scientific farmer and an arch southern nationalist. A well-educated, highly motivated young Virginia gentleman, Ruffin moved naturally toward a career in politics only to end it abruptly on discovering that he, in his own words, "had no talent for oratory, or to influence popular assemblies" and was unwilling to "pay the necessary price for popularity" by meeting the petty demands of constituents and legislators.[33] Popular rhetoric aside, there was at least some sincerity behind the antielectioneering sentiments of many politicians in the early Dynasty era, and it is significant to note a decline in those sentiments as the decades moved toward the Age of Jackson. Fortunately for the country, Jefferson and Washington had already established themselves in national posts before the need for hustings oratory took hold in Virginia.

The second adverse effect of expanded electioneering was the elevation in politics of men whose prime talents lay more in courting favor with a mass electorate than in statecraft. This pattern was well described by a disconcerted contributor to the Richmond *Virginia Gazette* in April 1809:

It appears from the manner of conducting elections, that the mass of the people do not think it absolutely necessary to send the best men which their county afford, to represent them in the General Assembly. . . , No! electioneering intrigues have arrived to such a degree of perfection in this state, that a man without any pretensions to Financering, Law, Justice, or any other requisite qualification may be elected, by riding through the county which he wishes to represent, making fair promises to the inhabitants to pass some local act for their benefit, to suppress the increasing burden of their taxes, (though in fact the taxes in this state are trifling indeed) and to treat them with a deluge of *whiskey* on the day of election; this last requisite, as a stimulant has a most powerful effect on the minds of the lower class of citizens; which class being the most numerous give by far the strongest vote. It seems to be the nature of man to confer favours on others, whose minds and habits are the nearest assimilated to his own. This method of electioneering has often been known to succeed in opposition to talents and real merit. Of course the man who is the best qualified is not always the choice of the people; yet if he willingly loosens his purse strings, treats with liberality, and drinks profusely with those who are to become his constituents, and appears to be "one of their own kidney," he then stands an equal chance of being elected; but people of elevated minds will seldom resort to such means to secure their election.[34]

Accustomed to a relatively simple and informal mode of electioneering, many Dynasty congressmen felt increasingly out of phase with the times. Of course, some Virginians, like John Randolph, became masters of the new politics and prospered accordingly. But others decreased their participation in public life, to the detriment of the Commonwealth and country.

The Ideal of Public Service

An examination of the Dynasty leaders reveals other notable transitions in Virginia's political culture, but few as profound as the change in the ideal of holding public office. The concept of a public life underwent a distinct transformation in the decades preceding the Age of Jackson. The American Revolution might be regarded as a unique and extraordinary crisis which brought forward the best leaders available in a generation of Virginians. As fortunes, life, and sacred honor had been pledged and indeed rode on the outcome, participation became a moral obligation, and the ultimate constituency for many individuals was the cause and the commonweal themselves. Even after the war ended, the survival of the new republican system seemed at stake and thus attracted the concerns and commitments of many Virginians until the question appeared settled by the election of Jefferson in 1801. At that point, most patriots believed the sacrifices of battle had not been in vain and the fruits of independence would be preserved.

In the meanwhile, the burden of public office greatly expanded. For many politicians in the Old Dominion, it no longer consisted of relatively calm deliberations among friends and neighbors on court day and a few weeks in the convivial atmosphere of Williamsburg or Richmond. If service came in an elective post at higher levels, say in Congress after 1789, the cost could be prohibitively high. Long and expensive separations from home and livelihood, difficult traveling conditions, constant petty requests from a growingly assertive constituency, the increased demands for electioneering—these and other mundane considerations became more and more obvious and burdensome. Concurrently, a prime motive for service dissipated as the Revolution receded and the new republic prospered; the urgency and preemptive need simply no longer existed.

The result was a redefinition of public service. The life of a congressman appeared unattractive to many ambitious and able young Virginians who were in the gentry mold and in times past would have risen to the top of the Commonwealth's political system. Some of these individuals, like Joseph C. Cabell and George Keith Taylor, chose careers in the state legislature and served there with distinction; others, like William Wirt, attained professional eminence and later enjoyed a less restrictive form of national service.[35] Still others, like Francis Walker Gilmer, who was once called "the *future hope of Virginia*—its ornament! its bright star!" turned to legal and intellectual pursuits, and still others, like Edward Coles, left the Old Dominion for noncongressional success in politics elsewhere.[36]

West Point called a number of young Virginians of "blood and breeding" who in earlier times might reasonably have entered politics. A Civil War galaxy well illustrates the pattern. Robert E. Lee had several congressmen in his immediate family (including, of course, his father); Stonewall Jackson was of the Trans-Allegheny Jacksons who were in Congress from 1795 to 1823; Jeb Stuart's father and cousin were United States representatives; Joseph E. Johnston's brother and nephew served in the Virginia delegation; and cousins Richard B. and Robert S. Garnett were of the Essex Garnetts. During the Civil War Lee's personal staff included aides bearing the honorable names of Garnett, Mason, Marshall, Taylor, and Washington.[37]

In addition to men of promise who entered fields other than national politics, an increasing number of Dynasty leaders voluntarily retired, often citing the press of private needs. Of Virginia's delegation in 1801–2, 43 percent died in office and 43 percent resigned or declined to seek reelection; of the 1823–24 group, 15 percent died in office and 73 percent resigned or declined to run again. Many other legislators refused offers of appointive positions within the federal government.

Who from the Old Dominion remained in national politics? Individual motivation defies exact explication, but one can speculate that the old pulls of noblesse oblige, patriotism, ambition, and prestige were being largely reduced to the latter two spurs. More and more officeholders were persons who enjoyed the new politics and who drew from it their own concrete and intangible rewards. By the Jacksonian era, this profound transformation was well along: the professional politician had basically replaced the public servant.

Littleton Waller Tazewell provides a useful example of the transformation in ideals of public service. A Virginian of the old school, well educated and connected, a giant in contemporary legal circles, a man of courage and integrity, Tazewell held the positions of state legislator, congressman, president pro tem of the Senate, and governor of the Commonwealth. This impressive list of offices is, however, quite deceiving. His public life was actually sporadic and represented few of his adult years. He resigned as senator and as governor and declined cabinet and diplomatic appointments. Tazewell never adjusted to the new era of mass politics, perhaps because he retained from his youth a contrasting model of the Virginia republican system.

In an autobiographical narrative prepared for his children, Tazewell recalled an incident from his schoolboy days which had fixed in his own mind a standard for public life. In 1788 the freeholders of York County had gathered to select two delegates for the ratification convention set for Richmond in June. Several contenders made speeches, after which a freeholder from the crowd spoke up and proposed that the voters reject all of the announced candidates (with their fixed opinions on the Constitution). He argued the people should choose instead two respected citizens "still open to conviction . . . well qualified to determine wisely . . . to examine impartially" the best available course. The immediate consensus settled on John Blair and George Wythe, neither of whom had sought the position or were even in attendance. The crowd next marched to Williamsburg, assembled in front of Wythe's home, and chanted, "Will you serve? Will you serve?"—thus startling the chancellor and also the eleven-year-old Tazewell, then "reciting a Greek lesson." On determining the circumstances and wishes of the group, Wythe lost control of his emotions and could only respond, "Surely— How can I refuse."[38]

This poll reflected the ideal of freeholders' selecting from the men they personally knew, the best one available for a particular responsibility, and, in turn, that individual's putting aside his personal desires for the public good. To this legacy, Tazewell years afterward added his own credo: "If I know myself, there is no situation within the power of government to bestow which I covet or desire, nor is there one which I would not accept, if the discharge of its duties by me was deemed necessary or useful to my country. I have no ambition to gratify, although I have duties to fulfill."[39]

The Tazewell model reflects an anachronistic ideal, in a sense, and one which led him and other worthy men to spend relatively little time in politics, given the absence of dramatic and transcendent crises that challenged their sense of public duty. Thus another Dynasty congressman who later wrestled with the cause of Virginia's decline decided: "It can only be because the faculties of her sons have not been strenuously exerted in *her* service and for *her* advancement. They have been unwisely devoted to other objects, or rusting in unprofitable inaction."[40]

The Ideology of "Second Generation Men"

Of all the areas in which anachronism can be demonstrated, that of ideology is perhaps most important, especially in explaining the decline in the Old Dominion's national influence. Two-thirds of the Dynasty congressmen might be called "second generation men," born after 1765 and thus too late to have participated in the most meaningful event in Virginia history to that point, the American Revolution. They were born, however, close enough to it to feel the

Evolution and Decline

immediate inspiration of its leaders and ideals and to grow up craving to understand and emulate both. These impressionistic young men would discover much of the meaning of the Revolution in the events that followed it in the 1780s and 90s.

In the minds of many contemporaries, establishing a new national government represented the culmination of Revolutionary purpose. The destruction of the political relationship with the mother country came at a great personal sacrifice to Americans, a sacrifice which could be vindicated only by the erection of an enduring republican system to replace the discarded colonial one. Virginians who led in the winning of independence also led in nation-making, and certain controversies and disagreements along the way provided opportunities for redefining the first principles to be fulfilled and for transmitting them to a younger generation. A prime example is the conflict over adopting the new Federal Constitution in 1787–88. With Madison and Henry leading opposing and nearly equal forces and with an assembly of notables in attendance, the state's ratification convention ranks high in American history for its articulation of popular, yet rival theories of government.

The losing Anti-Federalists feared the Constitution's consolidated and pervasive power might be turned against the interests or rights of specific individuals, classes, states, sections, or economic groups, and thus they championed a simple, limited national government and the retention of most essential powers by the states. The victorious Federalists, on the other hand, minimized the dangers of a representative and balanced—if potent—national government and established the necessity for central energy and authority to meet a young and growing country's needs. The convention settled the issue of accepting or rejecting the Constitution, but not the matter of its principles. The latter remained a viable question, especially given the new but related issues of the 1790s growing out of Hamilton's financial program and the foreign policy of Washington and Adams.

Party lines formed in Virginia around these pivotal national questions and personalities, with rough continuity from the earlier ratification struggle. Some leaders conspicuously changed sides, but the principles of the Anti-Federalists were generally championed by the Democratic-Republicans; those of the old Federalists by the new Federalists. Several specific controversies provided an opportunity for reaffirming party doctrine and denouncing the opposition's, but the most significant occasion came late in the decade, in the legislature's great debate over the Virginia Resolutions of 1798 and Madison's Report of 1800.

Both parties recognized the significance of those sessions, and both sought to elect their most able champions to the legislature even if it meant calling some from retirement (the Federalist Henry) or from a congressional seat (the Republican Giles, and later Madison). Although much has been written about the assemblies of 1798–1800, the intent of the resolutions remains partly shrouded in controversy. What seems clear, however, is that the debates provided an opportunity unmatched at the time in Virginia for expressing and defending, defining and refining, first principles of government, for seeking answers to the central question of what the Revolutionary experience should mean to future generations. The Republican victory was predetermined by a weighty majority in delegates, but that fact should not obscure the genuine debate that took place or the Federalists' worthy contribution to it.

Among the younger delegates in those dramatic sessions were twenty-eight future congressmen. The experience was formative and fundamental, as many later acknowledged. To see Revolutionary fathers—James Madison, John Taylor, Wilson Cary Nicholas, and Henry Lee—interpret and debate basic principles left its mark on the younger men. It established or reestablished categories of belief from which few ever departed. Years afterward a Dynasty congressman still referred to "the great cause I espoused in 1798 & of which I have never ceased to be the zealous advocate."[41] Indeed, the "principles of '98" became sacred doctrines in Republican Virginia during the Dynasty era and required neither explanation nor apology. "Those resolutions and that report," wrote John Marshall later, "constitute the creed of every politician, who hopes to rise in Virginia; and to question them . . . is deemed political sacrilege."[42] An expanded version of the Old Anti-Federalist arguments, the principles now included decentralization of power, frugality, agricultural interests over commercial ones, civil authority over the military, state sovereignty in the protection of individual rights, and strict construction of the Constitution—all natural beliefs for Virginia's landed aristocracy.

Those principles were also tailored for the minority status of Virginia's Republican party in the partisan nineties and served as points of departure, not blinders, for the Dynasty presidents, who modified or violated all of them. National responsibilities and power required a broad view congenial to Jefferson, Madison, and Monroe and to American interests. But few Virginians made the transition, and as time passed a gulf developed and widened between the presidents and their home-state lieutenants. Jefferson isolated and squelched a revolt by the purist John Randolph and a handful of his fellow Quids; Madison faced a more serious defection led by former party stalwart Giles; and Monroe drifted so far afield as to forfeit influence over the Junto and over the Commonwealth's politics in general.

The principles of '98 became increasingly rigid, less a persuasion and more a dogma, and eventually, after the War of 1812, even a sacred liturgy. The transformation seemed to fit Virginia's immediate needs. Surely Marshall's decisions, tariffs, national banks, and internal improvements benefited states other than the Old Dominion—and at its expense, as seen in its declining economy. The doctrines of '98 became a yardstick for measuring political performance, especially east of the Blue Ridge. It was reaffirmed in Spencer Roane's dry and legalistic arguments that were no more intelligible beyond Virginia than the abstruse prose of John Taylor or the fantastic oratory of John Randolph. But it had taken hold, and many politicians followed it as the true revelation of the Revolutionary experience.

The pattern and philosophy are neatly summarized in an obituary notice for Archibald Austin, a Dynasty congressman who died in 1837: "With the origin of the two great parties, Republican and Federalist, Mr. A. attached himself to the former party, believing they were the true friends of free, representative government, to be administered within the prescribed limits of the Constitution: from which principles he never deviated to the day of his death one jot or tittle, stedfastly opposed to a National Bank, a protective Tariff, and public improvements on the part of Congress as so many usurpations on their part."[43] Though "stedfastly" held by most of the state's leaders, by 1815–16 the Virginia political creed had become, for much of the nation, a model of obstruction and backward thinking. In a country bursting at the seams with westward expansion and economic growth, the Virginia ideology seemed inadequate and anachronistic. For the previous generation that ideology had fit the demands of a national minority headed for majority leadership and had dealt with general questions of concern to all Americans. But the pattern of the past seemed now to represent only a narrow, doctrinaire defense of eastern Virginia's economic self-interest.

Perhaps historian James Schouler best summarized the point: "the new school of Virginia statesman made much of constitutional points and questions of abstract political right, while for practical and economical legislation, such as develops industry and resources, they showed no aptitude. It is a profound statesman who can make a large State from a small one; but of Virginia policy, as it was said, the present effect appeared, on the contrary, to make a small State out of a large one."[44] That so many politicians in the Old Dominion clung to the pattern of the 1790s and even exalted it is understandable, yet tragic. It was a major cause of the state's decline in influence in the new nation, which an earlier generation of Virginians, who were broad in vision and preeminently men trained for their times, had played central roles in establishing.

Appendix
Notes
Index

Appendix

Virginia Congressmen 1801–1825

This appendix provides the name, political party, geographic section, and dates of service for each of the ninety-eight Virginia congressmen in the Dynasty era. Party ties are indicated by R (Republican), F (Federalist), M (the "minority," maverick party men), and "?" (the two congressmen whose affiliations have not been ascertained). Virginia's four main geographical regions are shown by TW (Tidewater), PM (Piedmont), V (Valley), and TA (Trans-Allegheny); subregions are designated by ES (Eastern Shore), SS (Southside), and UP (Upper Potomac). Congressional designations are HR (House of Respresentatives) and USS (United States Senate).

Alexander, Mark, Jr. (R, PM-SS). HR, 1819–33.
Archer, William Segar (R, PM-SS). HR, 1820–35. USS, 1841–47.
Austin, Archibald (R, PM-SS). HR, 1817–19.
Baker, John (F, V-UP). HR, 1811–13.
Ball, William Lee (R, TW). HR, 1817–24.
Barbour, James (R, PM). USS, 1815–25.
Barbour, John Strode (R, PM). HR, 1823–33.
Barbour, Philip Pendleton (R, PM). HR, 1814–15, 1827–30.
Bassett, Burwell, II (R, TW). HR, 1805–13, 1815–19, 1821–29.
Bayly, Thomas Monteagle (F, TW-ES). HR, 1813–15.
Breckinridge, James (F, V). HR, 1809–17.
Brent, Richard (R, TW). HR, 1795–99, 1801–3. USS, 1809–14.
Burwell, William Armistead (R, PM). HR, 1806–21.
Cabell, Samuel Jordan (R, PM). HR, 1795–1803.
Caperton, Hugh (F, TA). HR, 1813–15.
Claiborne, John (R, PM-SS). HR, 1805–8.
Claiborne, Thomas (R, PM-SS). HR, 1793–99, 1801–5.

Appendix

Clark, Christopher Henderson (R, PM). HR, 1804–6.
Clay, Matthew (R, M, PM-SS). HR, 1797–1813, 1815.
Clopton, John (R, TW). HR, 1795–99, 1801–16.
Colston, Edward (F, V-UP). HR, 1817–19.
Dawson, John (R, TW). HR, 1797–1814.
Eppes, John Wayles (R, PM-SS). HR, 1803–11, 1813–15. USS, 1817–19.
Floyd, John (R, TA). HR, 1817–29.
Garland, David Shepherd (R, PM). HR, 1810–11.
Garnett, James Mercer (R, M, TW). HR, 1805–9.
Garnett, Robert Selden (R, TW). HR, 1817–27.
Gholson, Thomas, Jr. (R, PM-SS). HR, 1808–1816.
Giles, William Branch (R, PM-SS). HR, 1790–98, 1801–3. USS, 1803–15.
Goodwyn, Peterson (R, PM-SS). HR, 1803–1818.
Gray, Edwin (F, M, TW). HR, 1799–1813.
Gray, John Cowper (R likely, TW). HR, 1820–21.
Griffin, Thomas (F, TW). HR, 1803–5.
Hawes, Aylett (R, PM). HR, 1811–17.
Holmes, David (R, V). HR, 1797–1809.
Hungerford, John Pratt (R, TW). HR, 1811, 1813–17.
Jackson, Edward Brake (R, TA). HR, 1820–23.
Jackson, George (R, TA). HR, 1795–97, 1799–1803.
Jackson, John George (R, TA). HR, 1803–10, 1813–17.
Johnson, James (R, TW). HR, 1813–1820.
Johnson, Joseph (R, TA). HR, 1823–27, 1833, 1835–41, 1845–47.
Jones, James (R, PM-SS). HR, 1819–23.
Jones, Walter (R, TW). HR, 1797–99, 1803–11.
Kerr, John (R, PM-SS). HR, 1813–15, 1815–17.
Leftwich, Jabez (R, PM). HR, 1821–25.
Lewis, Joseph, Jr. (F, PM). HR, 1803–17.
Lewis, Thomas (F, TA). HR, 1803–4.
Lewis, William J. (R, PM-SS). HR, 1817–19.
Love, John (R, PM). HR, 1807–11.
McCoy, William (R, TA). HR, 1811–33.
McKinley, William (R, TA). HR, 1810–11.
Mason, Armistead Thomson (R, PM). USS, 1816–17.
Mason, Stevens Thomson (R, PM). USS, 1794–1803.
Mercer, Charles Fenton (F, PM-UP). HR, 1817–39.
Moore, Andrew (R, V). HR, 1789–97, 1804. USS, 1804–9.
Moore, Thomas Love (?, PM). HR, 1820–23.
Morrow, John (R, V-UP). HR, 1805–9.
Nelson, Hugh (R, PM). HR, 1811–23.
Nelson,Thomas M. (R, PM). HR, 1816–19.
New, Anthony (R, TW). HR (VA.), 1793–1805. HR (Ky.), 1811–13, 1817–19, 1821–23.
Newton, Thomas, Jr. (R, TW). HR, 1801–33.
Nicholas, Wilson Cary (R, PM). USS, 1799–1804. HR, 1807–9.
Parker, Severn Eyre (?, TW-ES). HR, 1819–21.
Pegram, John (R, PM-SS). HR, 1818–19.

Virginia's Congressmen, 1801–25

Pindall, James (F, TA). HR, 1817–20.
Pleasants, James (R, PM). HR, 1811–19. USS, 1819–22.
Randolph, John (R, M, PM-SS). HR, 1799–1813, 1815–17, 1819–25, 1827–29, 1833. USS, 1825–27.
Randolph, Thomas Mann (R, PM). HR, 1803–7.
Rives, William Cabell (R, PM). HR, 1823–29. USS, 1832–34, 1836–39, 1841–45.
Roane, John, Jr. (R, TW). HR, 1809–15, 1827–31, 1835–37.
Roane, William Henry (R, TW). HR, 1815–17, 1837–41. USS, 1837–41.
Sheffey, Daniel (F, V). HR, 1809–17.
Smith, Arthur (R, TW). HR, 1821–25.
Smith, Ballard (R, TA). HR, 1815–21.
Smith, John (R, V). HR, 1801–15.
Smith, William (R, TA). HR, 1821–27.
Smyth, Alexander (R, V). HR, 1817–25, 1827–30.
Stephenson, James (F, V-UP). HR, 1803–5, 1809–11, 1822–25.
Stevenson, Andrew (R, TW). HR, 1821–34.
Stratton, John (F, TW-ES). HR, 1801–3.
Strother, George French (R, PM). HR, 1817–20.
Swearingen, Thomas Van (F, V-UP). HR, 1819–22.
Swoope, Jacob (F, V). HR, 1809–11.
Taliaferro, John (R, TW). HR, 1801–3, 1811–13, 1824–31, 1835–43.
Tate, Magnus (F, V-UP). HR, 1815–17.
Taylor, John (R, TW). USS, 1792–94, 1803, 1822–24.
Tazewell, Littleton Waller (R, TW). HR, 1800–1801. USS, 1824–32.
Thompson, Philip Rootes (R, M, PM). HR, 1801–7.
Trigg, Abraham or Abram (R, TA). HR, 1797–1809.
Trigg, John Johns (R, PM). HR, 1797–1804.
Tucker, George (R, PM-SS). HR, 1819–25.
Tucker, Henry St. George (R, V). HR, 1815–19.
Tyler, John (R, TW). HR, 1817–21. USS, 1827–36.
Venable, Abraham Bedford (R, PM-SS). HR, 1791–99. USS, 1803–4.
White, Francis (F, TA). HR, 1813–15.
Williams, Jared (R, V). HR, 1819–25.
Wilson, Alexander (R, V). HR, 1804–9.
Wilson, Thomas (F, TA). HR, 1811–13.

Notes

Abbreviations

CVSP	*Calendar of Virginia State Papers.* . . . 11 vols. Richmond, 1875–93.
Duke	Duke University Library, Durham, N.C.
LC	Library of Congress, Washington, D.C.
UNC	Southern Historical Collection, Library of the University of North Carolina at Chapel Hill
UVA	University of Virginia Library, Charlottesville, Va.
VHS	Virginia Historical Society, Richmond
VMHB	*Virginia Magazine of History and Biography*
VSL	Virginia State Library, Richmond
WM	Earl Gregg Swem Library, College of William and Mary, Williamsburg, Va.
WMQ	*William and Mary Quarterly*

Chapter I

[1] *Return of the Whole Number of Persons within the United States . . . [1800]* (Washington, D.C., 1801).

[2] Svend Petersen, *A Statistical History of the American Presidential Election* (New York, 1963), 3.

[3] Sir Augustus John Foster, *Jeffersonian America: Notes on the United States of America Collected in the Years 1805–6–7 and 11–12*, ed. Richard Beale Davis (San Marino, Calif., 1954), 163.

[4] *Biographical Directory of the American Congress, 1776–1961* (Washington, D.C., 1971), 47 (hereafter cited as *BDAC*).

[5] Thomas Jefferson, *Notes on the State of Virginia*, ed. William Peden (Chapel Hill, N.C., 1955), 89, 108; Charles H. Ambler, *Sectionalism in Virginia from 1776 to 1861* (Chicago, 1910). For a slightly earlier period, Norman K. Risjord identifies five basic sections, the Northern Neck, Middle Tidewater, Piedmont, Southside, and West, with other variations (*Chesapeake Politics, 1781–1800* [New York, 1978], 75, 595n).

[6] Josiah Quincy to Mrs. Josiah Quincy, Feb. 26, 1808, in Edmund Quincy, *Life of Josiah Quincy of Massachusetts* (Boston, 1869), 134.

Notes

[7] Edmund Randolph said this about his wife in a note to his children, in Bishop [William] Meade, *Old Churches, Ministers, and Families of Virginia*, 2 vols. (Philadelphia, 1906), 1:182.

[8] Arthur Singleton [Henry Cogswell Knight], *Letters from the South and West* (Boston, 1824), 66.

[9] Hugh Blair Grigsby to Thomas Ritchie, Mar. 14, 1854, "Ritchie Letters," ed. Charles H. Ambler, *John P. Branch Historical Papers of Randolph-Macon College* 4 (June 1916): misnumbered as p. 417.

[10] John Randolph to Josiah Quincy, July 1, 1814, Quincy, *Quincy*, 354.

[11] Avery O. Craven, *Soil Exhaustion as a Factor in the Agricultural History of Virginia and Maryland, 1606–1860* (Urbana, Ill., 1926), chap. 3; Winifred J. Losse, "The Foreign Trade of Virginia, 1789–1809," *WMQ*, 3d ser., 1 (1944): 161–78.

[12] Joseph C. Robert, *The Tobacco Kingdom: Plantation, Market, and Factory in Virginia and North Carolina, 1800–1860* (Durham, N.C., 1938), 15–19; Risjord, *Chesapeake Politics*, 46–51.

[13] Richard Beale Davis, *Intellectual Life in Jefferson's Virginia, 1790–1830* (Chapel Hill, N.C., 1964), esp. Chaps. 2 and 4; Thomas Jefferson to Spencer Roane, June 28, 1818, "Roane Correspondence, 1799–1821," ed. William E. Dodd, *Branch Historical Papers* 2 (June 1905): 133.

[14] Henry D. Gilpin to his father, Joshua Gilpin, Sept. 16, 1827, in Ralph D. Gray, ed., "A Tour of Virginia in 1827: Letters of Henry D. Gilpin to His Father," *VMHB* 76 (1968): 464.

[15] Jean Gottmann, *Virginia at Mid-Century* (New York, 1955), 80–83, 94–95, 109–14; Davis, *Intellectual Life*.

[16] Gerald W. Mullin, *Flight and Rebellion: Slave Resistance in Eighteenth-Century Virginia* (New York, 1972), 136, 141; *CVSP*, 9:140–74; Robert McColley, *Slavery and Jeffersonian Virginia*, 2d ed. (Urbana, Ill., 1973), 107–14, 219.

[17] Winthrop D. Jordan, *White over Black: American Attitudes toward the Negro, 1550–1812* (Chapel Hill, N.C., 1968), 574; McColley, *Slavery and Jeffersonian Virginia*, chap. 5.

[18] McColley, *Slavery and Jeffersonian Virginia*.

[19] James K. Paulding, *Letters from the South . . . 1816*, 2 vols. (New York, 1817), 1:114–15.

[20] Abel Parker Upshur to Francis Walker Gilmer, July 7, 1825, in Richard Beale Davis, *Francis Walker Gilmer: Life and Learning in Jeffersonian Virginia* (Richmond, 1939), 247–48.

[21] See Freeman H. Hart, *The Valley of Virginia in the American Revolution, 1763–1789* (Chapel Hill, N.C., 1942); Robert D. Mitchell, *Commercialism and Frontier: Perspectives on the Early Shenandoah Valley* (Charlottesville, Va., 1977); Klaus Wust, *The Virginia Germans* (Charlottesville, Va., 1969), pts. 2 and 3.

[22] See Otis K. Rice, *The Allegheny Frontier: West Virginia Beginnings, 1730–1830* (Lexington, Ky., 1970).

[23] Thomas C. Miller and Hu Maxwell, *West Virginia and Its People*, 3 vols. (New

York, 1913), 2:555; Lyon G. Tyler, ed., *Encyclopedia of Virginia Biography*, 5 vols. (New York, 1915), 2:50; David E. Johnston, *A History of the Middle New River Settlements and Contiguous Territory* (Huntington, W.Va., 1906), 389.

[24] Rice, *Allegheny Frontier*, 360.

[25] Except as otherwise noted, the analysis here rests heavily on Harry Ammon, "The Republican Party in Virginia, 1789 to 1824" (Ph.D. diss., University of Virginia, 1948); Richard R. Beeman, *The Old Dominion and the New Nation, 1788–1801* (Lexington, Ky., 1972), chap. 2; Fletcher M. Green, *Constitutional Development in the South Atlantic States, 1776–1860* (Chapel Hill, N.C., 1930), 62–65, 139–141; Charles S. Sydnor, *Gentlemen Freeholders: Political Practices in Washington's Virginia* (Chapel Hill, N.C., 1952), and *The Development of Southern Sectionalism, 1819–1848* (Baton Rouge, 1948), esp. chap. 2; Anthony F. Upton, "The Road to Power in Virginia in the Early Nineteenth Century," *VMHB* 62 (1954), esp. 266–70; Ralph A. Wooster, *Politicians, Planters, and Plain Folk: Courthouse and Statehouse in the Upper South, 1850–1860* (Knoxville, Tenn., 1975), 2–6, 55–56, 87–88. For a detailed critique of the Virginia structure of government, see *Proceedings and Debates of the Virginia State Convention of 1829–30* (Richmond, 1830); pertinent extracts are in Merrill D. Peterson, ed., *Democracy, Liberty, and Property: The State Constitutional Conventions of the 1820's* (Indianapolis, 1966), pt. 3.

[26] Beeman, *Old Dominion*, 46.

[27] Irving Brant, *The Fourth President: A Life of James Madison* (Indianapolis, 1970), 37.

[28] Thomas Mann Randolph, in William H. Gaines, Jr., *Thomas Mann Randolph, Jefferson's Son-in-Law* (Baton Rouge, 1966), 133, 127; Dice R. Anderson, *William Branch Giles: A Study in the Politics of Virginia and the Nation from 1790 to 1830* (Menasha, Wis., 1914), 220; Brant, *Fourth President*, 37.

[29] See the notables listed, with dates of service, in Earl Gregg Swem and John W. Williams, comp., *A Register of the General Assembly of Virginia . . .* (Richmond, 1919), ix-x.

[30] Harry Ammon, *James Monroe: The Quest for National Identity* (New York, 1971), chap. 10; Katherine Elizabeth Merryman, "John Page, Governor of Virginia, 1802–1805" (M.A. thesis, University of North Carolina, 1951); Elinor Janet Weeder, "Wilson Cary Nicholas, Jefferson's Lieutenant" (M.A. thesis, University of Virginia, 1946).

[31] Strongly partisan considerations about appointments to the county courts can be found in numerous letters in volumes 9 and 10 of *CVSP*.

[32] John Taylor to the Vice-President [Thomas Jefferson], Feb. 15, 1799, "John Taylor Correspondence," ed. William E. Dodd, *Branch Historical Papers* 2 (June 1908): 278–79.

[33] Gov. William H. Cabell to Wilson Cary Nicholas, Jan. 9, 1808, William H. Cabell Papers, LC.

[34] For examples, see the *CVSP* for this period and the papers of Governor William H. Cabell, LC.

Notes

[35] Thomas Jefferson to John Taylor, July 21, 1816, in Jefferson, *The Writings of Thomas Jefferson*, ed. Paul Leicester Ford (New York, 1892–99), 10:53. See also Tadahisa Kuroda, "The County Court System of Virginia from the Revolution to the Civil War" (Ph.D. diss., Columbia University, 1969).

[36] Sydnor notes that "in the three sessions of 1819–1820, 1831–1832, and 1844–1845, which were chosen as samples, the justices constituted between 42 percent and 56 percent of the membership of each house and senate" (*Southern Sectionalism*, 50). The JP's decline is a theme in A. G. Roeber, *Faithful Magistrates and Republican Lawyers: Creators of Virginia Legal Culture, 1680–1810* (Chapel Hill, N.C., 1981).

[37] For the Virginia system of gentry politicians and its screening process, see Sydnor, *Gentlemen Freeholders*, chaps. 5–7. A strongly dissenting view is Robert E. and B. Katherine Brown, *Virginia, 1705–1786: Democracy or Aristocracy?* (East Lansing, Mich., 1964), esp. chaps. 6–10.

[38] A good introduction to Virginia politics in this period is the work of Harry Ammon, Norman K. Risjord, and Richard R. Beeman, as well as Lisle A. Rose, *Prologue to Democracy: The Federalists in the South, 1789–1800* (Lexington, Ky., 1968); David Hackett Fischer, *The Revolution of American Conservatism: The Federalist Party in the Era of Jeffersonian Democracy* (New York, 1965); and James H. Broussard, *The Southern Federalists, 1800–1816* (Baton Rouge, La., 1979). Also essential are Noble E. Cunningham's volumes, *The Jeffersonian Republicans: The Formation of Party Organization, 1789–1801* (Chapel Hill, N.C., 1957) and *The Jeffersonian Republicans in Power: Party Operations, 1801–1809* (Chapel Hill, N.C., 1963).

[39] The most cogent argument for a continuity in parties and regional divisions is Risjord, *Chesapeake Politics*.

[40] John Taylor to Creed Taylor, April 10, 1799, Creed Taylor Papers, UVA; Daniel Morgan to his son-in-law Presley Neville, 1798, in William Couper, *History of the Shenandoah Valley*, 3 vols. (New York, 1952), 1:697.

[41] John Randolph to Citizen Creed Taylor, 16th Sept. 23rd of Independence [1798?], Creed Taylor Papers, UVA; J. S. Watson to David Watson, Dec. 24, 1799, "Letters from William and Mary, 1798–1801," *VMHB* 29 (1921): 151–52.

[42] Creed Taylor to Ch. Clarke, Feb. 1805, Creed Taylor Papers, UVA; *Norfolk Herald*, April 18, 1821; Frances Norton Mason, ed., *My Dearest Polly: Letters of Chief Justice John Marshall to His Wife* (Richmond, 1961), 245.

[43] Various aspects and ramifications of party spirit are covered in J. S. Watson to David Watson, Mar. 2, 1801, "Letters from William and Mary," 161–62, and "Party Violence, 1790–1800," *VMHB* 29 (1921): 171–79. The disunion views are expressed in Littleton W. Tazewell to Henry Tazewell, Jan. 5, 1797, Tazewell Papers, VSL, and Maude Howlett Woodfin, "Contemporary Opinion in Virginia of Thomas Jefferson," *Essays in Honor of William E. Dodd*, ed. Avery Craven (Chicago, 1935). These intense partisans did agree on at least one point, the evils of partisanship! See the remarks of John Marshall, in Albert J. Beveridge, *The Life of John Marshall*, 4 vols. (Boston, 1916–19), 2:410. But, as Andrew Stevenson said, "Party . . . is a bloody Idol, and spares not; and yet without Parties, there

can be no political principles" (Francis F. Wayland, *Andrew Stevenson* [Philadelphia, 1949], 247). Samples of press partisanship are the *Richmond Examiner* account, April 13, 1803, of the Prince William congressional race in which Richard Brent "the enlightened republican candidate" defeated Joseph Lewis, "the ignorant tory candidate," and the Richmond *Virginia Argus* listing of returns for Anthony New "Democrat" and John Taylor ("Demagogue"), on May 14, 1803.

[44] Beeman, *Old Dominion*, chaps. 7–9; Risjord, *Chesapeake Politics*, 524–42, 546–62; Myron F. Wehtje, "The Congressional Elections of 1799 in Virginia," *West Virginia History* 29 (1968): 251–73. An excellent articulation of the contemporary Republican creed is Edmund Pendleton's "The Danger Not Over," Oct. 5, 1801, *The Letters and Papers of Edmund Pendleton*, ed. David John Mays, 2 vols. (Charlottesville, Va., 1967), 2:695–99, and Pendleton's addresses of Nov. 1798 and Feb. 20, 1799, ibid., 2:650–66.

[45] Federalist membership in the Virginia General Assembly, 1800–1816, is shown in Broussard, *Southern Federalists*, 294, table 9. See also his map (p. 406) depicting the party's geographic strength in the Old Dominion.

[46] Cunningham, *Republicans: Formation*, 144–46. Federalist hostility to the act can be seen in a printed protest in the William Austin Folder (along with other party literature), John Cropper Papers, VHS, and in Thomas Evans's letter to Col. Leven Powell, Oct. 30, 1800, in William E. Dodd, ed., "The Leven Powell Correspondence," *Branch Historical Papers* 3 (June 1903): 54–46. A hint of a general ticket law for congressional elections is found in Leven Powell to Major Burr Powell, Dec. 14, 1798, ibid., 233–34.

[47] Broussard, *Southern Federalists*, believes the party was better organized in Virginia than in any of the four states he surveyed (pp. 263–68). His typical Virginia Federalist politician was "a town-dwelling lawyer or commercial man" (p. 199).

[48] Alexander B. Lacy, "Jefferson and Congress: Congressional Method and Politics, 1801–1809" (Ph.D. diss., University of Virginia, 1963), 144–89, 198–99.

[49] See John Taylor of Caroline to Congressman James Garnett, Dec. 14, 1807, John Taylor Papers, Duke.

[50] Harry Ammon, "James Monroe and the Election of 1808 in Virginia," *WMQ*, 3d ser., 2 (1963): 33–56.

[51] Jan. 21, 1817.

[52] Hugh Nelson to Dr. Charles Everett, Dec. 2, [1817], Risjord, *Old Republicans*, 182; see also ibid., 181.

[53] See, for example, the foreboding letter of George Tucker to Gen. H. St. G. Tucker, Mar. 6, 1820, Tucker Family Papers, UNC.

[54] See especially Ammon, "Republican Party in Virginia," chap. 8.

[55] See Broussard, *Southern Federalists*, 200–201; Joseph C. Cabell to Wilson Cary Nicholas, Jan. 18, 1809, Wilson Cary Nicholas Papers, LC.

[56] Samuel Mordecai, *Richmond in By-Gone Days*, 2d ed. (Richmond, 1860), 235.

[57] *Southern Federalists*, 6.

⁵⁸ James Mercer Garnett to John Randolph, Sept. 12, 1808, Randolph-Garnett Transcripts, John Randolph Papers, LC.

⁵⁹ Of seventeen Virginia newspapers with party affiliations on Oct. 1, 1800, only six were Federalist (Fischer, *Revolution*, app. 3, table 1).

⁶⁰ Beeman, *Old Dominion*; Sydnor, *Gentlemen Freeholders*. Continuity is also a theme in Upton, "Road to Power," and in the Virginia portion of Paul Goodman's "The First American Party System," in *The American Party Systems: Stages of Political Development*, ed. William Nisbet Chambers and Walter Dean Burnham, 2d ed. (New York, 1975), 81–84.

⁶¹ Richard P. McCormick, *The Second American Party System: Party Formation in the Jacksonian Era* (Chapel Hill, N.C., 1966), 178–79.

⁶² The Jacksonian era is treated by McCormick, *Second Party System*, 178–99. For an argument deemphasizing the differences between the Jeffersonian and Jacksonian eras on the national level, see Edward Pessen, "We Are All Jeffersonians, We Are All Jacksonians: or A Pox on Stultifying Periodizations," *Journal of the Early Republic* 1 (1981): 1–26.

⁶³ Morgan P. Robinson, *Virginia Counties: Those Resulting from Virginia Legislation* (Richmond, 1916); Cynthia Miller Leonard, comp. *The General Assembly of Virginia, 1619–1978* (Richmond, 1978), 88–90.

⁶⁴ Lucille Griffith, *Virginia House of Burgesses, 1750–1774* (Northport, Ala., 1963), 72, 74.

⁶⁵ Ibid., 75.

⁶⁶ Ibid., 71.

⁶⁷ Miller, *General Assembly*, 137–39, 219–21.

⁶⁸ See chap. 7 below.

⁶⁹ Quoted in Wayland, *Stevenson*, 39.

⁷⁰ McCormick, *Second Party System*, 198.

⁷¹ McCormick, "New Perspectives on Jacksonian Politics," *American Historical Review* 65 (1960): 288–301, tables 1, 3, and *Second Party System*, 197–98; J. R. Pole, "Representation and Authority in Virginia from the Revolution to Reform," *Journal of Southern History* 24 (1958): 49.

⁷² McCormick, *Second Party System*, 198–99. See also the election coverage by the Richmond press in 1799 and 1831.

⁷³ Craven, *Soil Exhaustion*, chap. 3; Lewis Cecil Gray, *Agriculture in the Southern United States to 1860*, 2 vols. (Washington, D.C., 1933), 2: 760–62; Robert, *Tobacco Kingdom*, 131–43. See especially Creed Taylor to Eldred Simpkins, July 1, 1803, Creed Taylor Papers, UVA.

⁷⁴ Gov. William H. Cabell, Annual Message, Journal of the Senate, Session of 1808/9, VSL.

⁷⁵ Robert Gamble to Thomas Massie, Jan. 5, 1808, Massie Family Papers, VHS. See also Daniel P. Jordan, "Virginia and Jefferson's Embargo," paper presented at the annual meeting of the Organization of American Historians, New York City, 1978.

⁷⁶ Ambler, *Sectionalism*, 112. "Madison's credit and the prospects of Virginia

agriculture were so poor by 1825," writes Ralph Ketcham, "that even his personal appeal to Nicholas Biddle failed to procure a $6,000 loan" (*James Madison* [New York, 1971], 624).

[77] Robert Colin McLean, *George Tucker: Moral Philosopher and Man of Letters* (Chapel Hill, N.C., 1961), 19; Malcolm Lester, "George Tucker: His Early Life and Public Service, 1775–1825" (M.A. thesis, University of Virginia, 1946), 55; Joseph C. Robert, "William Wirt, Virginian," *VMHB* 80 (1972): 387–441.

[78] Anderson, *Giles*, 213.

[79] Richard Beale Davis, "The Jeffersonian Virginia Expatriate in the Building of the Nation," *VMHB* 70 (1962): 49. Although based on admittedly incomplete research, this article has astounding figures about native Virginians who became political leaders in other states. See also John M. Jennings, "Virginia's People in the Eighteenth and Nineteenth Centuries," in *Exploring Virginia's Human Resources*, ed. Roscoe D. Hughes and Henry Leidheiser, Jr. (Charlottesville, Va., 1965), 27.

[80] William Cabell Bruce, *John Randolph of Roanoke, 1773–1833*, 2 vols. (New York, 1922), 2, 119; Jennings, "Virginia's People," 26.

[81] Gaines, *Randolph*, 46–47; William Wirt to Dabney Carr, Mar. 20, 1803, in John Pendleton Kennedy, *Memoirs of the Life of William Wirt, Attorney-General of the United States*, 2 vols. in 1, rev. ed. (Philadelphia, 1860), 1: 96. Even that monarch of the Virginia bar Littleton Tazewell seriously considered going "to the Western Country" to practice law in Kentucky, as noted in his "Sketch of His Own Family," ed. Lynda R. Heaton (M.A. thesis, College of William and Mary, 1967), 193.

[82] John Taylor to Wilson Cary Nicholas, Mar. 13, 1803, May 23, 1804, April 4, 1805, April 14, May 14, 1806, Edgehill-Randolph Collection, UVA; William A. Burwell to [Major William Dickerson, of Bedford?], Nov. 20, 1808, William A. Burwell Papers, LC; Charles Fenton Mercer to Major Burr Powell, July 1, 1814, Tucker Family Papers, UNC.

[83] See Carter Goodrich, "The Virginia System of Mixed Enterprise: A Study of State Planning of Internal Improvements," *Political Science Quarterly* 64 (1949): 355–87; Joseph C. Robert, *The Road from Monticello: A Study of the Virginia Slavery Debate of 1832* (Durham, N.C., 1941); Charles W. Turner, "Virginia State Agricultural Societies, 1811–1860," *Agricultural History* 38 (1964): 167–77.

[84] Ambler, *Sectionalism*, chap. 4; Ammon "Republican Party in Virginia," chap. 8; Rice, *Allegheny Frontier*, chap. 14; Risjord, *Old Republicans*, 177–78.

[85] Examples are Wilson Cary Nicholas (and the Norfolk collectorship), Thomas Mann Randolph (United States Senate or Richmond postmastership), John Clopton (Privy Council), and St. George Tucker (federal judgeship). See Wilson Cary Nicholas to the Governor, May 22, 1804, *CVSP*, 9:397–98; Weeder, "Nicholas," 60–62; Gaines, *Randolph*, 146–47; John Clopton to John B. Clopton, Nov. 22, 1808, John Clopton Papers, Duke; St. George Tucker's draft letter, Jan. 27, 1813, in Mary Haldane Coleman, *St. George Tucker: Citizen of No Mean City* (Richmond, 1938), 155.

[86] Commentary of John Pendleton Kennedy in his *Wirt*, 1:192–93.

[87] Edwin M. Gaines, "The *Chesapeake* Affair . . . ," *VMHB* 64 (1956): 134, 138.

[88] Weeder, "Nicholas," 96–97; Norman K. Risjord, "1812: Conservatives, War Hawks, and the Nation's Honor," *WMQ*, 3d ser., 18 (1961): 196–210.

[89] Lyon G. Tyler, *The Letters and Times of the Tylers*, 2 vols. (Richmond, 1884), 1:279.

[90] Bruce, *Randolph*, 1:413–14; Wayland, *Stevenson*, 32.

[91] Samuel Taylor to Creed Taylor, Oct. 31, 1824, Creed Taylor Papers, UVA.

[92] The toast was given at Yorktown (Edgar E. Brandon, comp., *Lafayette, Guest of the Nation . . . as Reported by Local Newspapers*, 3 vols. [Oxford, Ohio, 1950–57], 3:62).

[93] Henry Adams, *John Randolph* (Boston, 1882), 91; Francis Walker Gilmer to Peter Minor, Mar. 25, 1821, Davis, *Gilmer*, 153.

[94] John Randolph to James Mercer Garnett, Feb. 10, 1815, Randolph-Garnett Transcripts, LC.

[95] James Schouler, *History of the United States of America under the Constitution*, 7 vols. (New York, 1880–1913), 3:233.

[96] Robert P. Sutton, "Nostalgia, Pessimism, and Malaise: The Doomed Aristocrat in Late-Jeffersonian Virginia," *VMHB* 76 (1968): 41–55; see also Robert R. Howison, *A History of Virginia*, 2 vols. (Philadelphia, 1846–48), 2:510–11.

Chapter II

[1] Compare *DAB* sketches; see also Charles H. Ambler, *Thomas Ritchie* (Richmond, 1913); Carol M. Tanner, "Joseph C. Cabell, 1778–1856" (Ph.D. diss., University of Virginia, 1948); Edwin M. Gaines, "The Political Career of Governor William H. Cabell" (M.A. thesis, University of Virginia, 1954); and Joseph H. Harrison, "Oligarchs and Democrats—The Richmond Junto," *VMHB* 78 (1970): 184–98, which is excellent on family ties.

[2] The data for these categories, analyzed in the tables in this chapter, have been compiled in App. 1, "Biographical Profiles: Virginia Congressmen, 1801–1825," in the MS version of this study, deposited at UVA and VSL; the congressmen are listed in the appendix below. Except as otherwise noted, comments on the Virginia context follow the sources cited in chapter 1; Davis, *Intellectual Life*, was especially useful.

[3] Paul Goodman, "Social Status of Party Leadership: The House of Representatives, 1797–1804," *WMQ*, 3d ser., 25 (1968): 467.

[4] Ralph Ketcham noted that "Madison was 'connected' with most of the landowners in Orange County," often "had multiple ties" with a relative, and left in his will property "to his thirty-odd nieces and nephews" (*Madison*, 6).

[5] Henry G. Ellis, "Edmund Ruffin: His Life and Times," *Branch Historical Papers* 3 (June 1910): 100.

[6] Davis, *Intellectual Life*, 8.

[7] This sequence does not apply to a frontier hero like George Jackson whose "only education had been instruction given him by the first sergeant of his militia company, schooling soon ended when the sergeant was killed by Indians" (Dorothy Davis, *John George Jackson* [Parsons, W.Va., 1976], 13).

[8] The uncommonness of a college education is demonstrated by Sidney H. Aronson, *Status and Kinship in the Higher Civil Service . . .* (Cambridge, Mass., 1964), 122–23.

[9] Jefferson to Richard Price, Aug. 7, 1785, in Julian P. Boyd, ed., *The Papers of Thomas Jefferson* (Princeton, N.J., 1950—), 8:357.

[10] See Davis, *Intellectual Life*, esp. 49–54; Sydnor, *Gentlemen Freeholders*, 15; Steven J. Novak, *The Rights of Youth: American Colleges and Student Revolt, 1798–1815* (Cambridge, Mass., 1977), esp. 96–106.

[11] Davis, *Intellectual Life*, 53.

[12] Davis, *Intellectual Life*, has much to say about Bishop Madison.

[13] Novak, *Rights of Youth*, 44; Richmond *Virginia Argus*, April 14, 1801; J. S. Watson to David Watson, Dec. 24, 1799, and Mar. 2, 1801, "Letters from William and Mary," 151–52, 161–62. See also Creed Taylor to Eldred Simpkins, July 1, 1803, Creed Taylor Papers, UVA.

[14] For William and Mary graduates who attained prominence in other states, see Davis, "Jeffersonian Virginia Expatriate," 56.

[15] Another instance of this breach is noted in Gaines, *Randolph*, 43.

[16] Joining the Episcopal church were Mark Alexander and James Breckinridge, both of Scotch-Irish Presbyterian stock, and Lutheran-connected Daniel Sheffey, whose father had immigrated from Germany.

[17] Norman K. Risjord, "Virginians and the Constitution: A Multivariant Analysis," *WMQ*, 3d ser., 31 (1974): 616.

[18] See Fischer, *Revolution*, 225; and also, to a lesser extent, Broussard, *Southern Federalists*, 395.

[19] John B. Boles, *The Great Revival, 1787–1805: The Origins of the Southern Evangelical Mind* (Lexington, Ky., 1972), 10.

[20] Ibid., 171.

[21] Meade, *Old Churches*, 2:32.

[22] William A. Burwell to Letitia Burwell, Jan. 27, 1813, Burwell Papers, LC. Stevenson once wrote a friend that he "hoped . . . to be able to save my own soul, and that is the important matter. That however is not to be done by Church discipline" (to John Hartwell Cocke, Wayland, *Stevenson*, 240–41).

[23] Elisha Boyd to the Governor, April 4, 1813, *CVSP*, 10:219–20.

[24] The four were Armistead T. Mason, Charles Fenton Mercer, John Pegram, and Alexander Smyth.

[25] On Tucker's lack of support, see the letter from the officers of the 31st Regiment of Virginia militia to the Governor, Nov. 1815, *CVSP*, 10:425. The Morgan story and quotation are in J. E. Norris, *History of the Lower Shenandoah Valley* (Chicago, 1890), 251.

[26] Sydnor, *Gentlemen Freeholders*, 15–16.

[27] McColley, *Slavery and Jeffersonian Virginia*, 48–56.

[28] Jefferson to Thomas Mann Randolph, Jr., May 30, 1790, Boyd, *Papers of Jefferson*, 16:449. See also E. Lee Shepard, "Lawyers Look at Themselves:

Notes

Professional Consciousness and the Virginia Bar," *American Journal of Legal History* 25 (1981): 1–23.

[29] Ketcham, *Madison*, 36.

[30] For life among the lawyers of the county courts, see George Tucker, *The Valley of the Shenandoah, or Memoirs of the Graysons*, introd. Donald R. Noble, Jr. (Chapel Hill, N.C., 1970), 224–30.

[31] Some individuals no doubt owned property in more than one county.

[32] See Jordan, "Congressional Returns by County, 1799–1825," App. 2, in the MS version of this study at UVA and VSL.

Chapter III

[1] An exception is Charles Fenton Mercer, whose profile is almost archetypically eastern but whose Loudoun residence no doubt linked him on many issues with the western position of the Upper Potomac region.

[2] The emphasis on sections is not intended to relegate parties to a level of unimportance. On their significance in the Virginia political system, see pages 16–21. Also arguing that state issues were usually contested along sectional rather than party lines in the Old Dominion are Beeman, Broussard, and Risjord. Diplomatic questions were more likely to reflect party alignments, as stressed in Broussard, *Southern Federalists*, esp. pp. 402–3, and as suggested by the public pronouncements of the Virginia congressmen.

[3] See Risjord, *Old Republicans*; Stephen W. Brown, "Congressman John George Jackson and Republican Nationalism, 1813–1817," *West Virginia History* 38 (1977): 93–125; Katherine K. McNulty, "James Breckinridge" (M.A. thesis, Virginia Polytechnic Institute and State University, 1970).

[4] See table 15 below. One could argue that the low number of contested elections also reflects the weakness of the Virginia Federalists as an opposition party. In turn, the Federalists were likely no stronger because the western Republicans adequately expressed regional needs, at least on domestic issues.

[5] *Norfolk Herald*, April 6, 1821.

[6] Quoted in Wayland, *Stevenson*, 39. See also Tyler, *Letters and Times*, 1:282.

[7] Compare *DAB* sketches; on James Barbour's essentially ideological turn toward a nationalistic brand of Republicanism, see Charles D. Lowery, "James Barbour, a Politician and Planter of Antebellum Virginia" (Ph.D. diss., University of Virginia, 1966), esp. chap. 5 and pp. 425–526.

[8] Jack P. Greene, "Foundations of Political Power in the Virginia House of Burgesses, 1720–1776," *WMQ*, 3d ser., 16 (1959): 485–506; Griffith, *Virginia House of Burgesses*, esp. chap. 7; Jackson Turner Main, *Political Parties before the Constitution* (Chapel Hill, N.C., 1973), 246–47, table 9.1; Beeman, *Old Dominion*, apps. 1–3; and my own working paper, "A Quantitative Analysis of Virginia Congressmen, 1789–1801."

[9] Greene, "Foundations of Political Power," 492.

[10] Boles, *Great Revival*, 174.

[11] See pp. 143–48.

¹²For example, see John Randolph to Nathan Loughborough, April 30, 1828, typescript, William Cabell Bruce–John Randolph of Roanoke Collection, VSL; John W. Eppes to Thomas Jefferson, Mar. 9, 1804, Edgehill-Randolph Collection, UVA.

¹³Captain Basil Hall, of the Royal Navy, *Travels in North America in the Years 1827 and 1828*, 3 vols. (Edinburgh, 1829), 3:72.

¹⁴Elbridge Gerry, Jr., in Dorothy Davis, *History of Harrison County, West Virginia* (Clarksburg, W.Va., 1970), 794.

¹⁵See McColley, *Slavery and Jeffersonian Virginia*, 38; Davis, *Jackson*, 224.

¹⁶Randolph, in Harold Kellock, *Parson Weems of the Cherry Tree* (New York, 1928), 66.

¹⁷Lewis P. Summers, *History of Southwest Virginia* (Baltimore, 1966). The unfortunate congressman was Charles C. Johnston (brother of the future Confederate general Joseph E. Johnston); the accident occurred on June 17, 1832.

¹⁸Captain Thomas Anburey, of the British army, in McColley, *Slavery and Jeffersonian Virginia*, 37–38.

¹⁹Nathaniel Macon to Joseph H. Nicholson, Mar. 1, 1813, typescript, Bruce-Randolph collection, VSL; the Irish poet Thomas Moore on his trip on the mail stage in 1804, in Kellock, *Weems*, 66.

²⁰Jabez Leftwich to Joel Leftwich, Dec. 7, 1821, Joel Leftwich Papers, UNC; Raymond C. Dingledine, Jr., "The Political Career of William Cabell Rives" (Ph.D. diss., University of Virginia, 1947), 64; John Roane (writing for John Clopton) to John B. Clopton, Feb. 25, 1814, John Clopton Papers, Duke.

²¹Davis, *Jackson*, 151.

²²Quoted in Davis, *Harrison County*, 794.

²³John George Jackson, in Davis, *Jackson*, 104.

²⁴Jabez Leftwich to Joel Leftwich, Dec. 7, 1821, Joel Leftwich Papers, UNC; John Clopton to John B. Clopton, Feb. 28, 1813, John Clopton Papers, Duke.

²⁵For representative examples, see Beveridge, *Marshall*, 2:378; Manning J. Dauer, "The Two John Nicholases . . . ," *American Historical Review* 45 (1940): 341; Francis Preston to John Preston, Feb. 1, 1797, Preston Family Papers, VHS.

²⁶Oliver O. Trumbo, "Charles Fenton Mercer, 1778–1858" (M.A. thesis, Madison College, 1966), 69; William H. Roane, in James C. Jewett, "The United States Congress of 1817 and Some of Its Celebrities," *WMQ*, 1st ser., 17 (1908): 141n.

²⁷Tucker, "To the Citizens of . . . ," *Richmond Enquirer*, Nov. 21, 1816. His kinsman George Tucker made a similar decision in 1824 (George Tucker, "Autobiography," 63, UVA; McLean, *George Tucker*, 25–28), the same year in which he penned a letter to Peachy Gilmer trying to recruit him into Congress and describing in rosy terms the financial side of living in Washington (Tucker to Gilmer, May 12, 1824, Peachy Gilmer Papers, VSL). Tucker suggested, "You can live here without your family for $15 or $16 a week—exclusive of clothes."

²⁸Ammon, *Monroe*, 203; William Wirt to Benjamin Edwards, May 12, 1816, in Ninian W. Edwards, *History of Illinois . . . and Life and Times of Ninian Ed-*

wards (Springfield, Ill., 1870), 444; Wirt to Thomas Jefferson, Jan. 14, 1808, Kennedy, *Wirt*, 1:209–10.

²⁹ William Wirt to Dabney Carr, Feb. 13, 1803, Kennedy, *Wirt*, 1:93–94.

³⁰ Tucker, "Autobiography," 63; see also the letters of John Clopton (at Duke) and of Daniel Sheffey, in the Sheffey Papers, VHS, and Daniel Sheffey to Robert Preston, April 3, 1812, Preston Family Papers, VHS. For overseers' difficulties, see Davis, *Jackson*, 95–96; Eliza Madison to John Preston, Dec. 8, 1794, Preston Family Papers, VHS. Business difficulties are noted in Davis, *Jackson*, 270–71, and Brown, "Congressman John George Jackson," 124.

³¹ Abraham B. Venable to the Governor, July 5, 1804, *CVSP*, 9:410. A contemporary noted that David Garland had "resigned his seat in Congress . . . to arrange and take care of his affairs at home" (Elijah Fletcher to [?], Nov. 29, 1811, in Elijah Fletcher, *The Letters of Elijah Fletcher*, ed. Martha von Briesen [Charlottesville, Va., 1965], 45).

³² Hugh Nelson to Charles Everett, Nov. 13, 1811, Hugh Nelson Papers, LC.

³³ See the letters between John George and Mary Jackson, Davis, *Jackson*, 214, 256.

³⁴ John Clopton to William Edmund Clopton, Mar. 3, 1808, Clopton Papers, Duke.

³⁵ Henry Tazewell to Richard Cocke, Esq., Dec. 10, 1797, Henry Tazewell Papers, typescripts in the possession of WM.

³⁶ On the thorny problem of whether seniority on the county court was forfeited by service as a congressman, see Walter Jones to the Governor, Aug. 10, 24, 1799, and John Taliaferro to the Governor, April 23, 1806, *CVSP*, 9:45, 129, 480.

³⁷ John Clopton to John B. Clopton, Jan. 18, 1815, John Clopton Papers, Duke.

³⁸ Thomas Evans to John Cropper, Jan. 16, 1801, John Cropper Papers, VHS.

³⁹ Harriet R. Stratton, *A Book of Strattons*, 2 vols. (New York, 1918), 2:348.

⁴⁰ John Randolph to James Mercer Garnett, Feb. 7, 1811, Randolph-Garnett Papers, LC; Randolph to Francis Walker Gilmer, Dec. 24, 1820, Davis, *Gilmer*, 176.

⁴¹ William Wirt to Dabney Carr, Aug. 11, 1811, Kennedy, *Wirt*, 1:288. James Sterling Young suggests this negative view of Washington reflected an antipower, proconstituency bias (*The Washington Community, 1800–1828* [New York, 1966], chaps. 2 and 3).

⁴² Dingledine, "Rives," 31–33, 35.

⁴³ Davis, *Jackson*, 229.

⁴⁴ Brown, "Congressman John George Jackson," 124.

⁴⁵ Examples of health problems in Washington are found in Wilson Cary Nicholas to the Governor, Nov. 27, 1809, *CVSP*, 10:77; William P. Cresson, *James Monroe* (Chapel Hill, N.C., 1946), 365–66; and Tyler, *Letters and Times*, 1:335, 339. Truly "desperate" remedies are described in Dingledine, "Rives," 79–80.

⁴⁶ Henry Tazewell to Richard Cocke, Esq., Sept. 30, 1798, Henry Tazewell Papers, typescript, WM; John Clopton to John B. Clopton, Feb. 16, 1816, John Clopton Papers, Duke.

Notes

⁴⁷ See John Tyler to Dr. Henry Curtis, Dec. 18, 1818, and Dec. 8, 1820, Tyler, *Letters and Times*, 1:303, 335.

⁴⁸ John Taylor of Caroline to James Mercer Garnett, Feb. 7, 1823, James Mercer Garnett Letters, VSL.

⁴⁹ John George Jackson, in Davis, *Jackson*, 171.

⁵⁰ John Page to Col. John Cropper, April 7, 1794, John Cropper Papers, VHS.

⁵¹ "The Virginians are fierce marksmen," observed one traveler to the state, "and duelling is not discountenanced" (Knight, *Letters*, 66). See also *Richmond Enquirer*, June 17, 1806.

⁵² Tucker, "Autobiography," 66.

⁵³ John Clopton to Sally Clopton, Jan. 13, 1804, John Clopton Papers, Duke.

⁵⁴ Wayland, *Stevenson*, 101. See also William Wirt to Benjamin Edwards, Jan. 10, 1806, Edwards, *History of Illinois*, 420.

⁵⁵ James Holland, circular letter, Philadelphia, May 7, 1796, in Noble E. Cunningham, Jr., ed., *Circular Letters of Congressmen to Their Constituents, 1789–1829*, 3 vols. (Chapel Hill, N.C., 1978), 1:57.

⁵⁶ For a humorous yet pathetic account of a backwoodsman from Kanawha County who tried to play the "proper" role in dress and manners among his fellow state legislators, see George W. Atkinson, *History of Kanawha County* (Charleston, W.Va., 1876), 159–60.

⁵⁷ See Leonard D. White, *The Federalists: A Study in Administrative History, 1789–1801* (New York, 1948), 317–18, 322.

Chapter IV

¹ William W. Hening, comp., *The Statutes at Large: Being a Collection of All the Laws of Virginia . . .* (13 vols., Richmond and Philadelphia, 1819–23), 12:654.

² John Randolph to Creed Taylor, Sept. 16, 1798, Creed Taylor Papers, UVA; Robert S. Garnett, *To the Freeholders of the Congressional District Composed of the Counties of Caroline, Essex, King & Queen, and King William*, Essex County, Mar. 20, 1817, circular, UVA; Wayland, *Stevenson*, 56; James Madison to Thomas Jefferson, Dec. 8, 1788, in Madison, *The Papers of James Madison*, ed. William T. Hutchinson et al. (Chicago and Charlottesville, Va., 1962—), 11:381–84; James Monroe to Jefferson, Feb. 15, 1789, in Monroe, *The Writings of James Monroe*, ed. Stanislaus M. Hamilton, 7 vols. (New York, 1898–1903), 1:199.

³ See chap. 10 below.

⁴ John Randolph to Creed Taylor, Sept. 16, 1798, Creed Taylor Papers, UVA; John George Jackson to James Madison, April 19, 1813, UVA; Jackson, in Davis, *Jackson*, 306; John W. Campbell to James Breckinridge, Feb. 21, 1807, McNulty, "Breckinridge," 39; John Eyre to Col. John Cropper, July 13, 1808, and Thomas Griffin to Cropper, Feb. 7, 1803, John Cropper Papers, VHS.

⁵ Davis, *Jackson*, 295–96, 306; Robert A. Brock, *Virginia and Virginians, 1606–1888*, 2 vols. (Richmond, 1888), 1:222.

⁶ For Breckinridge, see *Norfolk Gazette*, Mar. 2, 1809; Morrow: Charles Town

Farmer's Repository, Sept. 23, 30, 1808; Stephenson: ibid., Sept. 16, 1808; Jackson: Cunningham, *Republicans in Power*, 186; Baker: Broussard, *Southern Federalists*, 266; Blackburn: Joseph A. Waddell, *Annals of Augusta County* (Bridgewater, Va., 1958), 392; White: Broussard, *Southern Federalists*, 266; Mason: *Richmond Enquirer*, Nov. 16, 1816, and John Littlepage et al., *To the Citizens of . . .* , [n.p., 1815?], broadside, Rare Book Room, Duke; Colston: *Richmond Enquirer*, Mar. 25, 1817; Fitzhugh: ibid., Oct. 26, 1816. See also the speech of Magnus Tate, in F. Vernon Aler, *Aler's History of Martinsburg and Berkeley County, West Virginia* (Hagerstown, Md., 1888), 105–6. Robert B. Taylor was perhaps nominated for Congress by Norfolk Federalists in 1809 (*Norfolk Gazette*, April 24, 1809).

[7] James Mercer Garnett to John Randolph, Sept. 17, 1810, Randolph-Garnett Transcripts, LC. See also Brock, *Virginia*, 1:222; *Richmond Enquirer*, April 10, 1807, April 19, 29, May 6, 20, 1815.

[8] Tucker, "Autobiography," 65.

[9] John Randolph to James Mercer Garnett, Sept. 25, 1808, Randolph-Garnett Transcripts, LC. See also Richmond *Virginia Argus*, Sept. 27, 1808; *Richmond Enquirer*, Sept. 27, 1808; Randolph to Garnett, Aug. 2, 1812, Randolph-Garnett Transcripts, LC.

[10] Gaines, *Randolph*, 49–51. See also John Wayles Eppes's report on Cabell's displeasure, in Eppes to Thomas Jefferson, April 14, 1803, Edgehill-Randolph Collection, UVA.

[11] Gay Neale, *Brunswick County, Virginia, 1720–1975* (Richmond, 1975), 134.

[12] Brown, "Congressman John George Jackson," 93; Higginbotham, *Morgan*, 195.

[13] John Taylor to Wilson Cary Nicholas, Mar. 13, 1803, typescript, Edgehill-Randolph Collection, UVA; *Petersburg Intelligencer*, May 20, 1803.

[14] *Richmond Enquirer*, April 15, 1817; *Richmond Enquirer*, April 18, May 6, 1817.

[15] Washington *National Intelligencer*, April 10, 1817; Norfolk *American Beacon*, April 19, 1817.

[16] See especially John Clopton to Thomas Ritchie, Feb. 4, 1815, Clopton Papers, Duke.

[17] John Marshall, *An Autobiographical Sketch*, ed. John Stokes Adams (Ann Arbor, Mich., 1937), 15–16.

[18] Davis, *Jackson*, 187–88.

[19] Knight, *Letters*, 67–68.

[20] April 18, 1821.

[21] James H. Bailey, "John Wayles Eppes, Planter and Politician" (M.A. thesis, University of Virginia, 1942), 80–81. See also Randolph's analysis in Randolph to James Mercer Garnett, Mar. 19, 1811, Randolph-Garnett Transcripts, LC.

[22] Louise P. DuBellet, *Some Prominent Virginia Families*, 4 vols. (Lynchburg, Va., 1907), 3:39. Smith ran for the state legislature in the 1830s.

[23] *Richmond Enquirer*, Mar. 11, 1808.

[24] "To the Freeholders of the County of Loudoun," Leesburg *The Genius of Lib-*

erty, Mar. 24, 1818, in Charles P. Poland, Jr., *From Frontier to Suburbia* (Marceline, Mo., 1976), 99–100.

[25] Dingledine, "Rives," 54; Lester, "Tucker," 81–82.

[26] Littleton Waller Tazewell to Henry Tazewell, Feb. 16, 1798, Tazewell Papers, VSL. In this instance the former was seeking election to the Virginia Assembly.

[27] Bushrod Washington, in Martin Van Buren, *Autobiography*, ed. John C. Fitzpatrick, *Annual Report of the American Historical Association, 1918*, 2 (Washington, D.C., 1920): 178; Hugh Nelson to the Governor, Mar. 30, 1811, *CVSP*, 10:102.

[28] For examples, see Joseph C. Cabell to Wilson Cary Nicholas, Jan. 18 and Jan. 31, 1809, Wilson Cary Nicholas Papers, LC; John Randolph to Creed Taylor, Sept. 16, 1798, Creed Taylor Papers, UVA.

[29] John Floyd to James Breckinridge, May 18, 1824, Breckinridge Family Papers, VHS.

[30] See Archibald McRae to John Clopton, May 9, 1806, Clopton Papers, Duke.

[31] Gardner, "Stevenson," 269. "Make sure of your election before you declare yourself," wrote Henry Tazewell to his son Littleton, "and say to Mr. Ambler if he will offer, you will not" (Jan. 18, 1798, Tazewell Family Papers, VSL).

[32] *Richmond Enquirer*, April 5, 1825.

[33] The ploy of containing competition this way could break down by election time, as seen in Allen Taylor to James Breckinridge, Jan. 1, 1808, Breckinridge Papers, UVA.

[34] Allen Taylor to James Breckinridge, Jan. 20, 1813, Breckinridge Papers, UVA.

[35] John Patterson to [John] Cropper, Mar. 12, 1803, Feb. 16, 1819, John Cropper Papers, VHS. John Marshall felt his son Thomas would "lose some Federal votes who had en[ga]ged themselves before his being known as a candidate" (John Marshall to his wife, April 11, 1823, Mason, *My Dearest Polly*, 245).

[36] Robert Gamble to James Breckinridge, Jan. 19 and 23, 1823, Breckinridge Family Papers, VHS.

[37] Of course, this could be done without the person's consent or knowledge, as in the case of an infuriated William Wirt (Wirt to Judge Carr, June 16, 1830, Kennedy, *Wirt*, 2:265–66). After a man's name had been mentioned in print, his extrication from the race could be difficult. See the example cited in Davis, *Gilmer*, 248.

[38] John Randolph to James Mercer Garnett, July 20 and Aug. 9, 1812, Randolph-Garnett Transcripts, LC.

[39] Ibid., July 24, 1808, Mar. 19, 1811.

[40] Wehtje, "Congressional Elections of 1799," 254; Tom Molloy to John Breckinridge, undated, 1786, in Lowell H. Harrison, "A Young Virginian: John Breckinridge," *VMHB* 71 (1963): 31–32.

[41] Spencer Roane to William H. Roane, Mar. 10, 1815, "Roane Correspondence," 125–26.

[42] John Clopton to John B. Clopton, April 14, 1812, Clopton Papers, Duke; John H. Cocke to Joseph C. Cabell, Dec. 26, 1809, Cabell Family Papers, UVA; John Tyler to Dr. Henry Curtis, 1819, Tyler, *Letters and Times*, 1:308.

[43] See, for example, the county-by-county calculations in Burgess Ball to James Madison, Dec. 8, 1788, and George Nicholas to James Madison, Jan. 2, 1789, Madison, *Papers*, 11:385–86, 406–8; John Patterson to [John] Cropper, Mar. 12, 1803, John Cropper Papers, VHS.

[44] This was done by Edmund W. Hubard of Buckingham for a possible congressional race in 1841, as noted in Herbert Bradshaw, *History of Prince Edward County, Virginia* (Richmond, 1955), which prints the poll list with full annotations in app. 3.

[45] Thomas Mann Randolph to Major [Josiah] Ellis, Dec. 14, 1809, Ellis Family Papers, VHS. See also Josiah Parker to "The Representatives of Accomack County," May 29, 1790, John Cropper Papers, VHS.

[46] Francis Preston to John Preston, Feb. 2, 1795, Preston Family Papers, VHS.

[47] Both are in the Rare Book room, Duke. Smyth published a one-page *Postcript* [sic] dated Feb. 18, 1817; his opponent, Benjamin Estill, countered with five pages, dated Mar. 18; and Smyth rebutted with three more (ibid.).

[48] Anthony New, circular letter, City of Washington, Feb. 18, 1803, UVA; William McCoy, *To the Citizens* . . . , [1829?], pamphlet, VHS. These circulars and the others cited here are now accessible in Cunningham, *Circular Letters*.

[49] Six of these circular announcements are in the Letters of John Clopton, 1799–1806, and John Clopton Papers, both in the VSL. Examples of circular letters to constituents that announce an incumbent's retirement are those of John Stratton (1803), WM, and Charles F. Mercer, in James Mercer Garnett, *Biographical Sketch of Hon. Charles Fenton Mercer, 1778–1858* (Richmond, 1911), 69–80.

[50] Spencer Roane to William H. Roane, Mar. 10, 1815, "Roane Correspondence," 125. He also noted, "I think we will have the notification published also in the Fredericksburg paper."

[51] A few examples are the letters or notices of John Dawson, Washington, D.C., *Universal Gazette*, Mar. 19, 1801; Thomas Claiborne, *Petersburg Intelligencer*, Mar. 8, 1803; Samuel Tyler, Richmond *Virginia Argus*, Mar. 27, 1801; and John Eyre, Richmond *Virginia Gazette*, July 15, 1808.

[52] See the letters of Jerman Baker and John Guerrant, both in the Richmond *Virginia Argus*, Jan. 20, 1809.

[53] Magnus Tate, *To the Freeholders* . . . , Jan. 1815, in Aler, *Aler's History*, 105–6.

[54] Joseph C. Cabell speech, Mar. 26, 1810, Tanner, "Cabell," 86–87.

[55] James Monroe to Richard Brent, Feb. 25, 1810, Monroe, *Writings*, 5:111–12. See also Ammon, *Monroe*, 280–81.

[56] John Mercer, *To the Freeholders of the Congressional District Composed of the Counties of Spotsylvania, Orange, Louisa and Madison*, May 3, 1806, broadside, Rare Book Room, LC.

[57] John Randolph to James Mercer Garnett, July 20, 1812, Randolph-Garnett

Notes

Transcripts, LC. Spencer Roane wrote his candidate-son William, "I entirely concur with you that a publication of y'r intentions promptly may keep down opposition" (Mar. 10, 1815, "Roane Correspondence," 125–26).

⁵⁸ Aler, *Aler's History*, 107–8.

⁵⁹ John Taylor to James Monroe, May 10, 1812, "Taylor Correspondence," 338–39. Just how powerful that "Roane interest" was is clear from Spencer Roane to William H. Roane, Mar. 10, 1815, "Roane Correspondence," 125–26, and Harrison, "Oligarchs and Democrats," 190.

⁶⁰ Thomas Mann Randolph, *To the Freeholders of Albemarle, Amherst and Fluvanna*, Mar. 1803, Rare Book Room, LC.

⁶¹ The kind of connections a young delegate or senator might make in Richmond is suggested by the associations of William Cabell Rives and his young bride when the Assembly was in session: "Staying at a fashionable hotel, they enjoyed a society which included the Wickhams, Leighs, Stanards, Johnsons, Calls, and the venerable John Marshall," according to Dingledine, "Rives," 47.

⁶² Lester, "Tucker," 56.

⁶³ John W. Campbell to James Breckinridge, Feb. 3, 1810, Breckinridge Papers, UVA. See also S. L. Campbell to James Breckinridge, Feb. 15, 1810, ibid.

⁶⁴ Spencer Roane to William H. Roane, Mar. 10, 1815, "Roane Correspondence," 125–26.

⁶⁵ See, for example, Clopton's numerous letters of Dec. 1798, on the eve of his battle with John Marshall, in John Clopton Papers, Duke.

⁶⁶ Upton, "Road to Power," 262; John B. Clopton, *To the Freeholders . . .* , Oct. 9, 1816, Duke and UVA.

⁶⁷ Moreover, she was a member of the Church of England, and Coles compounded his error by going to New York for the marriage (Maud C. Clement, *The History of Pittsylvania County, Virginia* [Lynchburg, Va., 1929], 202).

⁶⁸ Waddell, *Augusta*, 383. Swoope also "dressed in German fashion," according to a contemporary (John W. Wayland, *A History of Rockingham County, Virginia* [Dayton, Va., 1912], 110). See also Wust's chapter on "Bilingual Politics" in his *Virginia Germans*.

⁶⁹ John H. Cocke to Joseph C. Cabell, Dec. 27, 1809, Cabell Papers, UVA; Gaines, *Randolph*, 70. Garland's claims to the common man's mantle are dubious. In the year he took office he owned 46 slaves, 29 horses, and 5,488¾ acres (Amherst County Tax Records for 1810, VSL).

⁷⁰ Sydnor, *Gentlemen Freeholders*, 52.

⁷¹ Davis, *Jackson*, 67–68; Brown, "Jackson," 17–20.

⁷² Gaines, *Randolph*, 57; Norris, *Lower Valley*, 258–59; Richard L. Jones, *Dinwiddie County* (Richmond, 1976), 109–10.

⁷³ McNulty, "Breckinridge," 2; Grigsby, "Sketches," 328.

⁷⁴ This is clearly shown in the series of printed circulars issued by Smyth and Estill in the Rare Book Room, Duke.

⁷⁵ John Tyler to Dr. Henry Curtis, 1819, Tyler, *Letters and Times*, 1:308; Pleasants's obituary, Richmond *Constitutional Whig*, Nov. 18, 1836.

Notes

[76] Cunningham, *Republicans in Power*, 278.

[77] Littleton Waller Tazewell to Henry Tazewell, April 10, 1798, Tazewell Papers, VSL. In a similar case, Federalist John Nicholas optimistically had predicted he would carry Charlottesville by all but two votes; in fact he lost Albemarle by a 416 to 125 margin (V. Dennis Golladay, "Jefferson's 'Malignant Neighbor,' John Nicholas, Jr.," *VMHB* 86 [1978]: 314; *Richmond Examiner*, May 3, 1799).

[78] William Wirt to Judge Dabney Carr, June 16, 1830, Kennedy, *Wirt*, 265–66. Wirt also said: "the people require a courtship which they will never receive from me. I have not the pride of Coriolanus, but I shall never stoop to ask an office."

Chapter V

[1] "Robert Munford's *The Candidates*," introd. Jay B. Hubbell and Douglass Adair, *WMQ*, 3d ser., 5 (1948): 231; Henry St. George Tucker to St. George Tucker, Mar. 1, 27, April 2, 7, 1807, April 4, 1815, Sydnor, *Gentlemen Freeholders*, 49; James Mercer Garnett, *To the Freeholders of Essex*, Essex, Mar. 29, 1798, UVA; John Taylor to Creed Taylor, April 10, 1799, Creed Taylor Papers, UVA, referring to a House of Delegates election; James Madison to Edmund Randolph, Oct. 17, 1788, to Thomas Jefferson, Dec. 8, 1788, Madison, *Papers*, 11:304–5, 381–84. See also Madison's letter in the Fredericksburg *Virginia Herald*, Jan. 29, 1789.

[2] John Page, *An Address to the Citizens of the District of York in Virginia*, June 20, 1794, VHS. This thorough condemnation of a variety of electioneering devices was, of course, an electioneering device itself. Page also campaigned by way of lengthy pamphlets, such as the two now in the VHS dated 1796 and 1799. For a candidate-incumbent accused of electioneering by a hard-electioneering opponent, see Joseph Johnson, *Circular*, Mar. 25, 1825, C. S. Morgan Collection, West Virginia State Archives, Charleston.

[3] James Madison to George Washington, Jan. 14, 1789, to his father, Aug. 14, 1790, Madison, *Papers*, 11:418, 13:292. James Monroe, Madison's adversary in 1789, likewise used "epistolary means." According to one strategically placed (or just plain nosy) observer, "Mr. Munroe is writing Myriads of Letters to the different Counties [;] their contents I know not—but the direction in his hand-writing I have seen" (George Lee Turberville to Madison, Dec. 14, 1788, ibid., 11:396).

[4] Charles Fenton Mercer to Major Burr Powell, Mar. 3, 1814, Tucker Family Papers, UNC; John Clopton to James Apperson, April 4, 1796, John Clopton Papers, Duke; John Randolph to James Mercer Garnett, May 27, 1808, Randolph-Garnett Transcripts, LC.

[5] Davis, *Jackson*, 47.

[6] Francis Preston to John Preston, Feb. 10, 1795, Preston Family Papers, VHS.

[7] John P. Preston to John Smith, Feb. 11, 1792, typescript, ibid. In a Valley race in 1799, incumbent David Holmes circulated a letter "in great numbers both in Dutch [German] and English" (*Winchester Gazette*, April 3, 1799). Holmes's letter may have been in printed form.

[8] See chap. 9 below and, for example, the several circulars in the John Clopton

Papers, VSL. Detailed rates for handbills, pamphlets, etc., are listed on the broadside *Prices for Printing in the City of Richmond*, May 18, 1818, Broadside Collection, VHS; for a printer's itemized statement, with costs given by different quantities produced, see Joseph C. Cabell to James Breckinridge, Feb. 24, 1829, VSL.

⁹Thomas Mann Randolph, *To the Freeholders of Albemarle, Amherst, and Fluvanna*, Mar. 1803, UVA; Thomas M. Nelson, *To the Freeholders . . . Mecklenburg*, Aug. 1, 1816, broadside, Edward Dromgoole Papers, UNC; George Nicholas to James Madison, Jan. 2, 1789, Madison, *Papers*, 11:406. The full letter (pp. 406–8) provides both a rationale for the use of printed circulars and insight into their distribution.

¹⁰Arthur Lee, *To the Freeholders . . . Fredericksburg*, [1789], broadside, Rare Book Room, LC; John B. Clopton, *To the Freeholders . . .* , Oct. 9, 1816, Duke and UVA.

¹¹Critics included Republican incumbent John Clopton in his circular letter, Philadelphia, Feb. 22, 1799, Clopton Papers, Duke; and candidate John Page, in his pamphlet, *An Address . . .* , April 24, 1799, VHS. A defense was offered by Federalist candidates [Thomas Evans], *An Address to the People of Virginia . . .* (Richmond, 1798), pamphlet, VHS, and [Henry Lee?], *The Address of the Minority . . .* (Richmond, 1799), pamphlet, VHS.

¹²Roger H. Brown, *The Republic in Peril: 1812* (New York, 1964), 63.

¹³Wust, *Virginia Germans*, 154. See also the letter of David Holmes cited in n. 7.

¹⁴John Page, circular letter, Philadelphia, May 12, 1794, VHS; John B. Clopton, *To the Freeholders . . .* , Oct. 9, 1816, Duke and UVA; James Mercer Garnett, *Substance of an Address . . .* , April 17, [1815], circular, Rare Book Room, LC. See also the lengthy circular by Francis Preston, *To the People of the Congressional District Composed of . . .* , Feb. 13, 1797, typescript, Preston Family Papers, VHS, in which Preston sought to refute a variety of charges leveled against him by Alexander Smyth.

¹⁵The full exchange is available in the Virginia Broadsides Collection, Rare Book Room, Duke. See also Daniel P. Jordan, ed., "Congressional Electioneering in Early Western Virginia: A Mini-War in Broadsides, 1809," *West Virginia History* 33 (Oct. 1971): 61–78.

¹⁶For committee-sponsored circulars, see the Tomlinson, Hammond, and McKinley items in Jordan, "Congressional Electioneering," and John Littlejohn et al., *To the Citizens . . .* , [1815], Duke. Samples of anonymous broadsides are *To the Enemies of Jefferson and Madison in This District*, Norfolk, April 22, 1809, and "Several Freeholders," *The Following Letter . . .* [Attacking Andrew Stevenson], both in the Rare Book Room, LC.

¹⁷Spencer Roane to William H. Roane, Mar. 10, 1815, "Roane Correspondence," 125–26.

¹⁸Joseph Tomlinson et al., *Address to the Freeholders of Ohio County, Virginia*, Wheeling, Mar. 6, 1809, and Charles Hammond et al., *To the Citizens of Ohio County*, 1809, both in Jordan, "Congressional Electioneering."

¹⁹Cunningham, *Circular Letters*, 1:xxiv–xxx; chap. 9 below.

Notes

[20] April 14, 1803. See also Richard Rummager, Esq., "The Junket," *Wheeling Repository*, Feb. 25, 1808.

[21] See, for example, John Tyler to Dr. Henry Curtis, Feb. 28, 1819, Tyler, *Letters and Times*, 1:306; John Page, of Rosewell, *An Address to the Freeholders of Gloucester County* . . . , April 24, 1799, VHS. The Virginia Republican scheme to distribute 20,000 pamphlets containing a large variety of public documents, short and long, is described in the "confidential" letter from John Taylor to Henry Tazewell, Dec. 14, 1798, Simms, *Taylor*, 93.

[22] Spencer Roane, to William H. Roane, Mar. 10, 1815, "Roane Correspondence," 125–26. On the subject of disseminating circulars throughout a district, see John Claiborne, circular letter, April 18, 1806, Washington City, Rare book Room, Duke; John Clopton, circular letters, Jan. 24, 1797, and April 4, 1806, with a note to his wife Sarah, dated April 6, 1806, and John Clopton to John B. Clopton, June 29 and July 6, 1812, John Clopton Papers, Duke; Robert Gamble to Col. John Preston, April 4, 1796, Preston Family Papers, VHS.

[23] A sampling from this vast literature includes "A Freeholder" writing to the Richmond *Virginia Argus*, Mar. 24, 1801, to contradict the report that Samuel Jordan Cabell would not seek reelection and to add effusive praise of his candidacy; the sparring match between supporters of John Clopton and his rival, Richard Morris, that developed in letters in the *Richmond Enquirer*, April 26, 1813; and the long and issue-oriented public letters addressed "To Burwell Bassett," *Norfolk Herald*, April 12, 1803, and to "Mr. Snowden," *Alexandria Gazette*, April 10, 1807.

[24] Examples include Roger West, "To the Freeholders," Alexandria *Columbian Mirror*, Feb. 15, 1799; "A Farmer," *Winchester Gazette*, April 3 and 17, 1799; and the exchange between West and Col. Leven Powell, *Alexandria Times*, April 19–27, 1799.

[25] James Mercer Garnett to John Randolph, Mar. 29, 1811, and Randolph to Garnett, April 7, 1811, Randolph-Garnett Transcripts, LC; *Richmond Enquirer*, Mar. 25, 29, April 1, 5, 8, 15, 16, 1815.

[26] Beveridge, *Marshall*, 2:386–87. The exchange is quoted in full in John P. Roche, ed., *John Marshall: Major Opinions and Other Writings* (Indianapolis, 1967), 29–32.

[27] For a charge that a candidate subsidized a newspaper to print "falsehoods," see *Alexandria Gazette*, April 23, 1817. See also Cunningham, *Circular Letters*, 1:xvii.

[28] *Alexandria Advertiser*, April 14, 1803.

[29] James Douglass, "To the Freeholders of Fairfax County," ibid.

[30] *Norfolk Gazette*, Mar. 29, 1809. The law in question was the Embargo.

[31] William Heth to George Washington, July 30, 1798, Wehtje, "Congressional Elections of 1799," 253.

[32] Elijah Fletcher to his father, Jan. 11, 1811, Fletcher, *Letters*, 26; [George Tucker], *Letters from Virginia, Translated from the French* (Baltimore, 1816), 203. Tucker said Virginia was "literally overrun with orators of all sorts and sizes, almost as numerous and noisey as the frogs in the plague of Egypt" (pp. 203–4).

He classified the orators as (1) "Political Spouters" who are "found in every hole and corner of the favoured land; but particularly the court yard and tavern"; (2) "County Court Lawyers" who "follow rules of eloquence entirely of their own invention," and (3) "Fourth of July Orators" and "Self styled Orators of the Human Race" who "once a year, (generally in very hot weather,) . . . proclaim their independence with a loud voice, and abuse the British *con amore*" (pp. 204–7). The style of oratory could reflect a political philosophy, as argued by Dickson D. Bruce, "The Rhetoric of Conservatism in Virginia: The Early National Period," paper presented at the Annual Meeting of the Society for Historians of the Early Republic, 1979.

³³ John Randolph to James Mercer Garnett, Sept. 14, 1812, Randolph-Garnett Transcripts, LC. In this letter Randolph was already calculating the votes he would receive by counties against Eppes in the April election.

³⁴ George R. Gilmer, *Sketches of Some of the First Settlers of Upper Georgia* (New York, 1855), 241.

³⁵ R. N. Venable Diary, Jan. 16, 1792, Woodfin, "Contemporary Opinion of Jefferson," 47.

³⁶ *Richmond Enquirer*, May 1, 1829. The election took place in the city of Norfolk. See also the long reports of Frederick County elections in the *Richmond Enquirer*, April 13, 1821, and April 15, 1825. The latter account changed little more than the candidates' names and their respective votes from the former and repeated much of the language verbatim, thus suggesting the ritualistic nature of the proceedings.

³⁷ This occurred at the Accomack poll in 1813, as described in Case **XXXIII** (*Bassett* v. *Bayley*), in M. St. Clair Clarke and David A. Hall, comps., *Cases of Contested Elections in Congress, from the Year 1789 to 1834, Inclusive* (Washington, D.C., 1834), 256. A proxy speaker is noted in a Kanawha election in Atkinson, *Kanawha*, 171.

³⁸ Quoted in Barton H. Wise, *The Life of Henry A. Wise of Virginia, 1806–1876* (New York, 1899), 37. The race occurred in the spring of 1833.

³⁹ See, for instance, the various gatherings noted in "To the Freeholders . . . ," *Richmond Enquirer*, April 6, 1813.

⁴⁰ Summers, *Southwest Virginia*, 490–91; see also Goodridge Wilson, *Smyth County History and Traditions* (Kingsport, Tenn., 1932), 106–7.

⁴¹ Dingledine, "Rives," 29, 60–62; handwritten copies of Cabell's speeches in the Cabell Family Papers, UVA; Davis, *Jackson*, 82; and, on Randolph's oratorical style, chap. 9 below.

⁴² Powhatan Bouldin, *Home Reminiscences of John Randolph of Roanoke* (Richmond, 1878), 27. See also Bailey, "Eppes," 90.

⁴³ April 14, 1803.

⁴⁴ John Page, circular letter, Philadelphia, May 12, 1794, VHS.

⁴⁵ Brock, *Virginia*, 1:170. This comment refers to Tazewell's courtroom "style of address."

⁴⁶ Francis Walker Gilmer, in Davis, *Gilmer*, 165; Sir Augustus John Foster in

Foster, *Jeffersonian America*, 165–66. On balance, Foster was unimpressed with Randolph's oratory.

[47] Ralph H. Rives, "A History of Oratory in the Commonwealth of Virginia Prior to the War between the States (Ph.D. diss., University of Virginia, 1960), 136. Irving made his remark in 1813 apparently in regards to Randolph's congressional oratory.

[48] Lowery, "Barbour," 159, 161.

[49] *DAB*, citing Bruce, *Randolph*, 2:202. On Philip P. Barbour, see also Tyler, *Letters and Times*, 1:291.

[50] Wyndham B. Blanton, *Medicine in Virginia in the Eighteenth Century* (Richmond, 1931), 236. According to his obituary, Jones "seldom spoke in public, though he had all the materials of the orator" (*Richmond Enquirer*, Feb. 13, 1816). On Roane, see the recollections of Frank G. Ruffin in "Roane Family," *WMQ*, 1st ser., 18 (1910): 274.

[51] Tucker, *Letters from Virginia*, 205–6.

[52] Bradshaw, *Prince Edward*, 179; Bruce, *Randolph*, 2:190–91, 196; Wayland, *Stevenson*, 239.

[53] Atkinson, *Kanawha*, 171–73.

[54] Gilmer, *Sketches*, 243.

[55] This concerns a General Assembly election in Norfolk, as reported in the *Richmond Enquirer*, April 26, 1805.

[56] Edward James Woodhouse, "The Public Life of George C. Dromgoole," *Branch Historical Papers* 4 (June 1904): 281–82. The race was for a seat in the Thirtieth Congress.

[57] Recollections of Frank G. Ruffin, in "Roane Family," 274.

[58] James Mercer Garnett to John Randolph, Aug. 12, 1808, Randolph-Garnett Transcripts, LC.

[59] Rives, "History of Oratory," 301.

[60] Said of Samuel Jordan Cabell, in General B. W. S. Cabell to N. F. Cabell, Brown, *Cabells*, 204. See also Richmond *Virginia Argus*, April 26, 1813; and *Richmond Enquirer*, April 25, 1817.

[61] Kennedy, *Wirt*, 1:250. For a similar, yet more hostile, contemporary analysis of the irresistible appeal of oratory to Virginians, see Tucker, *Letters from Virginia*, 203–12. See also the excellent chapter on "Law and Oratory," in Davis, *Intellectual Life*, 351–86.

[62] For example, James Waddel, the famous blind minister-teacher, had a great oratorical influence on his pupil James Barbour, as related in Lowery, "Barbour," 21. See also Rives, "History of Oratory," 308.

[63] Robert S. Garnett, *To The Freeholders . . .* , 1817, UVA.

[64] Joseph Bryan to John Randolph, June 3, 1806, Cunningham, *Republicans in Power*, 231. See also the *Wheeling Repository* (Mar. 31, 1808) announcement that Joseph Doddridge would be at the polls on election day to explain his conduct to the voters.

⁶⁵ James Madison to George Washington, Jan. 14, 1789, Madison, *Papers*, 11:418; John Randolph to James Mercer Garnett, April 16, 1811, Randolph-Garnett Transcripts, LC. An example of a convincing defense made after the poll is that of Edward Colston (1825), in Aler, *Martinsburg*, 166.

⁶⁶ James Mercer Garnett to John Randolph, Aug. 18, 1812, Randolph-Garnett Transcripts, LC.

⁶⁷ See Tyler, *Letters and Times*, 1:237; and H. Peter Pudner, "People nor Pedagogy: Education in Old Virginia," *Georgia Review* 25 (Fall 1971): 263–85, which places oratory in the tradition of "oral instruction" for the common folk.

⁶⁸ John Tyler, Sr., to John Tyler, Mar. 1, 1807, Tyler, *Letters and Times*, 1:203.

Chapter VI

¹ James Madison, "Autobiography," ed. Douglass Adair, *WMQ*, 3d ser., 2 (1945): 199; Edmund Pendleton to James Madison, April 7, 1789, in Pendleton, *Letters*, 2:556. The material for this chapter on "personal solicitation" is gleaned from the more spirited of the elections in the Jeffersonian period; no doubt numerous polls were dull, fairly routine, and ritualistic, especially when a candidate had no opponent.

² William H. Cabell to Joseph C. Cabell, Mar. 9, 1810, Tanner, "Cabell," 86.

³ Tom Molloy to John Breckinridge, undated, 1786, Harrison, "Young Virginian," 31–32.

⁴ Ibid., 26; Francis Preston to his brother John Preston, Feb. 1, 1797, Preston Family Papers, VHS.

⁵ John Neville to Daniel Morgan, Higginbotham, *Morgan*, 196.

⁶ William Brockenbrough [a successful candidate for the House of Delegates] to Joseph Cabell, June 18, 1801, Cunningham, *Republicans in Power*, 277–88. A two-month canvass by Peter Carr for the state senate is noted in E[lizabeth] Trist to [?], April 3, 1809, Trist Papers, UNC; and one of "four or five weeks" is mentioned in Elijah Fletcher to his brother, April 24, 1812, Fletcher, *Letters*, 52–53. Randolph appears to have been on the campaign trail eleven months before an election, as indicated in his letter to James Mercer Garnett, May 27, 1808, Randolph-Garnett Transcripts, LC.

⁷ Wehtje, "Congressional Elections of 1799," 264; see also Davis, *Jackson*, 47.

⁸ See, for example, Allen Taylor to James Breckinridge, Jan. 31, 1813, Breckinridge Papers, UVA; Rose, *Prologue to Democracy*, 156; Bouldin, *Home Reminiscences*, 50.

⁹ Wilson, *Smyth*, 106–7. See also Summers, *Southwest Virginia*, 490–91.

¹⁰ John Randolph to Josiah Quincy, April 19, 1813, Quincy, *Quincy*, 329–30.

¹¹ Bailey, "Eppes," 89–90. For attendance by a candidate at a Baptist political meeting in 1789, see Benjamin Johnson to James Madison, Jan. 12, 1789, Madison, *Papers*, 11:414–15.

¹² Richmond *Virginia Argus*, Aug. 9, 1808.

[13]George C. Taylor to John Preston, Oct. 6, 1798, Preston Family Papers, VHS.

[14]Wehtje, "Congressional Elections of 1799," 265.

[15]Davis, *Jackson*, 43. In a House of Delegates election in 1800, "civic duty" was encouraged by bribes of land (Brown, "John George Jackson," 42; Rice, *Allegheny Frontier*, 361).

[16]Thomas Evans to John Cropper, Dec. 6, 1796, John Cropper Papers, VHS.

[17]Sydnor, *Gentlemen Freeholders*, 51–59; Ferdinand-M. Bayard, *Travels of a Frenchman in Maryland and Virginia . . . in 1791*, ed. Ben C. McCary (Williamsburg, Va., 1950), 65.

[18]Chapman Johnson to David Watson, Feb. 20, 1801, "Letters to David Watson," 271.

[19]Madison felt secret balloting was "the only radical cure for those arts of Electioneering which poison the very fountain of liberty" (Ketcham, *Madison*, 183). For a long and humorous defense of "treating," see the Richmond *Virginia Argus*, Mar. 27, 1807, in which "A Friend to the Good Old Way" claimed, "If it had not been for the judicious management of these two articles [brandy and barbecue], my talents, and a heart burning with patriotism might have been buried in obscurity."

[20]For example, Charles Fenton Mercer to Major Burr Powell, Mar. 3, 1814, Tucker Family Papers, UNC; Spencer Roane to William H. Roane, Mar. 10, 1815, "Roane Correspondence," 125–26.

[21]George Mason, undated memorandum, Miller, *Mason*, 201. See also Davis, *Jackson*, 42.

[22]John P. Preston to John Smith, Feb. 11, 1792, typescript, Preston Family Papers, VHS. Preston was running for a seat in the Virginia senate.

[23]See, for example, the Alexandria *Columbian Mirror*, April 18, 1799; Charles Town *Farmer's Repository*, Sept. 16, 23, 30, Oct. 21, Dec. 9, 1808, Mar. 3, 24, 1809; *Norfolk Gazette*, Mar. 2, April 21, 1809.

[24]Waddell, *Augusta*, 383.

[25]"To the Freeholders . . . ," *Richmond Enquirer*, Mar. 31, 1813.

[26]For a sampling, see n. 23; and Aler, *Aler's History*, 97, 189; John Randolph to James Mercer Garnett, July 24, Sept. 25, 1808, Aug. 2, 1812, Randolph-Garnett Transcripts, LC. Postelection dinners are noted in W. Asbury Christian, *Richmond, Her Past and Present* (Richmond, 1912), 109.

[27]*Richmond Enquirer*, April 13, 15, 1825; see also Bayard, *Travels*, 66.

[28]Mrs. John Tyler, in Tyler, *Letters and Times*, 1:297.

[29]*Richmond Enquirer*, April 15, 1825.

[30]George Wythe Munford, *The Two Parsons . . .* (Richmond, 1884), 208–11.

[31]John Randolph to James Mercer Garnett, Mar. 19, 1811, Randolph-Garnett Transcripts, LC; Thomas Mann Randolph to Wilson Cary Nicholas, Mar. 30, 1805, Edgehill-Randolph Collection, UVA.

[32]Alexander Macrae [McRae?], "To the Freeholders . . . ," Richmond *Virginia*

Gazette, April 23, 1799; John Clopton to James Apperson, Dec. 23, 1798, John Clopton Papers, Duke; Beveridge, *Marshall*, 2:409–10; Benjamin Henry Latrobe to Thomas Jefferson, Sept. 22, 1798, in Latrobe, *The Virginia Journals of . . . , 1795–1798*, ed. Edward C. Carter II et al., 2 vols. (New Haven, 1977), 2:432.

[33] B. Estill to Daniel Sheffey, Nov. 21, 1812, Daniel Sheffey Papers, VHS; Thomas Evans to John Cropper, Dec. 6, 1796, John Cropper Papers, VHS; James Mercer Garnett to James Hunter, Jan. 24, 1823, James Mercer Garnett Letters, VSL.

[34] William E. Stokes, Jr., "Randolph of Roanoke, A Virginia Portrait: The Early Career of John Randolph of Roanoke, 1773–1805" (Ph.D. diss., University of Virginia, 1955), 153–57; Wehtje, "Congressional Elections of 1799," 265; Charles Fenton Mercer to John Randolph, Randolph-Garnett Transcripts, Dec. 26, 1814, LC. On the burning of Washington controversy, see the *Richmond Enquirer*, Mar. 25, April 1, 5, 8, 1815.

[35] John Randolph to James Mercer Garnett, April 20, 1811, Randolph-Garnett Transcripts, LC; Randolph to Josiah Quincy, April 19, 1813, Quincy, *Quincy*, 330; Randolph to Harmanus Bleecker, April 22, 1813, Randolph-Bleecker Letter Book, UVA.

[36] On "withdrawals," see John Kearsley, "To the Freeholders . . . ," Norris, *Lower Valley*, 249; the letter of "Freeholder," Richmond *Virginia Argus*, Mar. 24, 1801. Other tactics are covered in the *Alexandria Gazette*, April 17, 1817; *Richmond Virginia Gazette*, April 23, 1799; Alfred H. Powell to Burr Powell, April 6 and 15, 1827, Tucker Family Papers, UNC; *Berkeley County Election*, 1831, broadside, Duke.

[37] *Wheeling Repository*, Mar. 24, 1808. Chalmers was strongly defended by Republican William McKinley in the same issue.

[38] George Jackson to Gov. [Beverley] Randolph, July 5, 1791, *CVSP*, 5:339–40.

[39] Wehtje, "Congressional Elections of 1799," 266.

[40] William Allason to J. S. Woodcock, Esqr., Jan. 29, 1789, "The Letters of William Allason, Merchant of Falmouth, Virginia," ed. Dice R. Anderson, *Richmond College Historical Papers* 2 (June 1917): 174.

[41] See chap. 8 below, and Garnett, *Substance of an Address . . .* , April 17, [1815], Rare Book Room, LC.

[42] Randolph to James Mercer Garnett, Mar. 1809, April 15 and 20, 1811, Randolph-Garnett Transcripts, LC.

[43] John Littlejohn et al., *To the Citizens . . .* , [1815?], Duke.

[44] "To the Freeholders . . . ," *Richmond Enquirer*, April 2, 1813.

[45] Tucker, "Autobiography," 60–61; Alexander Smyth, *To the Electors of the Congressional District . . .* ," Duke. See also the statement signed by Sgt. John North, [1807?], in the Charles William Dabney Papers, UNC.

[46] "Freeholder," *Virginia Argus*, Mar. 24, 1801; James Mercer Garnett, *Substance of an Address . . .* , April 17, [1815], Rare Book Room, LC.

[47] Jordan, "Congressional Electioneering."

Notes

[48] See, for example, the *Norfolk Gazette*, April 15, 1809, and Richmond *Virginia Gazette*, April 5, 23, 1799.

[49] Charles Town *Farmer's Repository*, Dec. 2, 1808. Other ways of countering rumors or charges are represented by or noted in "To the Freeholders of Fairfax County," *Alexandria Advertiser*, April 14, 1803; John Clopton to [?], Mar. 25, 1802, John Clopton Papers, Duke; Samuel Richardson statements, July 24, 1807, Charles William Dabney Papers, UNC; John Randolph to James Mercer Garnett, April 16, 1811, Randolph-Garnett Transcripts, LC.

[50] *Alexandria Daily Gazette*, April 7, 1809.

[51] Beveridge, *Marshall*, 2:413; John B. Clopton, *To the Freeholders . . .*, Oct. 9, 1816, Duke and UVA; Thomas Mann Randolph, *To the Freeholders . . .*, [Mar. 1803], Rare Book Room, LC.

[52] For example, see John Clopton to John B. Clopton, Mar. 14, 1812, John Clopton Papers, Duke; Leven Powell to Major Burr Powell, Mar. 5, 1800, "Leven Powell Correspondence," 237–39.

[53] Gaines, *Randolph*, 70; see also *Alexandria Advertiser*, April 14, 1803; John Randolph to Harmanus Bleecker, April 22, 1813, Randolph-Bleecker Letter Book, UVA.

[54] S. J. Quinn, *The History of the City of Fredericksburg* (Richmond, 1908), 154–55.

[55] Charles Hammond et al., *To the Citizens of Ohio County, 1809*, Rare Book Room, LC; Magnus Tate, *To the Freeholders . . .*, Jan. 1815, in Aler, *Aler's History*, 105–6.

[56] See Beeman, *Old Dominion*, 25–26; Wust, *Virginia Germans*, 115–18; and chap. 8 below.

[57] George M. Betty, "William Branch Giles," *Branch Historical Papers* 3 (June 1911): 175; quoted in "Roane Family," 275; Sir Augustus John Foster, *Jeffersonian America*, 124–25; Waddell, *Augusta*, 383.

[58] Meriwether Jones to Creed Taylor, April 9, 1799, Creed Taylor Papers, UVA.

[59] S. L. Campbell to James Breckinridge, Feb. 15, 1810, Breckinridge Papers, UVA.

[60] Dingledine, "Rives," 37, 60–62. Partisan allegiance is stressed, for example, in Andrew Stevenson's announcement letter, Mar. 25, 1811, Wayland, *Stevenson*, 19.

[61] For example, see John Randolph to James Mercer Garnett, Sept. 14, 1812, Randolph-Garnett Transcripts, LC. This was, of course, a familiar charge against Randolph; see ibid., Mar. 18, 1809, and *Richmond Enquirer*, Mar. 31, 1809.

[62] See, for example, "A citizen," *To the Voters . . . Norfolk . . .*, [1833?], broadside, UVA, which argues: "What man of common prudence, or common sense, would employ an agent, hostile in every view to the individuals with whom he was to negotiate. The question is, will you give Mr. [Miles] King [the anti-Jackson congressional candidate] an opportunity to indulge his opposition at your expense?" See also Joseph Tomlinson et al., *Address to the Freeholders of Ohio County, Virginia . . .*, Mar. 6, 1809, Rare Book Room, LC.

Notes

[63] James Mercer Garnett, *To the Freeholders of Essex*, Mar. 29, 1798, UVA. Garnett was seeking election to the General Assembly.

[64] Waddell, *Augusta*, 392; Writers' Program of the Works Projects Administration in the State of Virginia, *Dinwiddie County* (Richmond, 1942), 101. The latter ticket was devised in 1839 by local Democrats with national elections in mind.

[65] Leesburg *The Genius of Liberty*, April 3, 1821, Poland, *Frontier*, 100.

[66] See Editorial Note: "Madison's Election to the First Federal Congress . . . ," Madison, *Papers*, 11:301–4; Higginbotham, *Morgan*, 200; Alexandria *Columbia Mirror*, Feb. 15, 1799; *Alexandria Times*, April 19–27, 1799; *Winchester Gazette*, April 3, 17, 1799; *Norfolk Gazette*, Mar. 2, 3, 31, 1809; Richmond *Virginia Argus*, Jan. 20, 1809; Jordan, "Virginia and Jefferson's Embargo"; John Taylor to James Monroe, May 10, 1812, "Taylor Correspondence," 338–39; John Randolph to James Mercer Garnett, Sept. 14, 1812, Randolph-Garnett Transcripts, LC; Robert Gamble to Gen. James Breckinridge, Mar. 17, 1813, Breckinridge Family Papers, VHS; John Love, "To the Freeholders . . . ," *National Intelligencer*, April 6, 1813; Armistead T. Mason to John T. Mason, July 15, 1816, Armistead T. Mason, "Letters of . . . 1813–1818," *WMQ*, 1st ser., 23 (1915): 233; *Richmond Enquirer*, Nov. 26, 1816, April 18, 1817; Tucker, "Autobiography," 60; Davis, *Jackson*, 269.

[67] The letter was ostensibly on behalf of the challenger, Richard Morris, and against incumbent John Clopton, but it appears to have been intercepted by the latter's supporters and published to embarrass the former's.

[68] Charles Town *Farmer's Repository*, Aug. 5, 1808.

[69] Ambler, *Sectionalism*, 65; *Berkeley and Jefferson Intelligencer*, issues for Mar. and April 1803; Davis, *Jackson*, 106; *Alexandria Gazette*, April 10, 1807; Mason, *Dearest Polly*, 245.

[70] *Norfolk Gazette*, Mar. 31, 1813.

[71] John George Jackson to James Madison, April 29, 1805, Madison Papers, LC. Jackson added "and in conformity with custom I was obliged to attend the various elections." See also Davis, *Jackson*, 151. Sample itineraries are found in the diaries of John Randolph for Sept. and Oct. 1812 and Mar. 1817, respectively in the Randolph-Bruce Collection, VSL, and the Randolph material, VHS.

[72] *Richmond Enquirer*, April 13, 1821.

[73] Beveridge, *Marshall*, 2:414, relying heavily on Munford, *Two Parsons*, 208–11.

[74] Various aspects of election-day activity are noted in John Randolph to James Mercer Garnett, Oct. 1, 1812, Randolph-Garnett Transcripts, LC; John W. Eppes to Thomas Jefferson, Feb. 10, 1803, Edgehill-Randolph Collection, UVA; Spencer Roane to William H. Roane, Mar. 10, 1815, "Roane Correspondence," 125–26; and Woodfin, "Contemporary Opinion of Jefferson," 47.

[75] George Lee Turberville to James Madison, Nov. 10, 1788, David Jameson, Jr., to Madison, Jan. 14, 1789, Madison, *Papers*, 11:341, 419.

[76] Mass voting by military units in various elections is described in Clarke and Hall, *Contested Elections*, Case VII (*Trigg* v. *Preston*), 79–84; Couper, *Shenandoah Valley*, 1:579; DuBellet, *Prominent Virginia Families*, 3:39; and Gardiner, *Berke-*

ley, 222. The matter of countering false or misleading information is included, for example, in James Madison to Edmund Randolph, Nov. 23, 1788, Mar. 1, 1789, Madison, *Papers*, 11:363, 453. William H. Cabell advised his brother Joseph: "Had you not better take a trip up the County, a day or two before the Election, in order to be early apprised of, & to be prepared to defeat any adverse step" (April 5, 1808, Cabell Family Papers, UVA).

⁷⁷ Garland, *Randolph*, 1:310–11.

⁷⁸ James Madison to the marquis de Lafayette, Feb. 20, 1828, Madison, *Writings*, 9:308–9; *Richmond Enquirer*, April 13, 1821. For intense, violent activity during elections, see also Elijah Fletcher to his brother [?], April 24, 1812, Fletcher, *Letters*, 52; Woodfin, "Contemporary Opinion of Jefferson," 47, 56.

⁷⁹ Munford, *Two Parsons*, 208. For a stout condemnation of alcoholic "treating," see the Caroline County Petition (n.d.) in Meade, *Old Churches*, 1:415–16.

⁸⁰ Hugh Nelson to Charles Everette, Dec. 12, 1808, Hugh Nelson Papers, LC; James Madison to Thomas Jefferson, Mar. 29, 1789, Madison, *Writings*, 5:334. Monroe's similar view is expressed in his letter to Jefferson, Feb. 15, 1789, Monroe, *Writings*, 1:199.

⁸¹ Higginbotham, *Morgan*, 201. Another winner, Thomas Griffin, wrote a letter of appreciation to supporter John Cropper (May 7, 1803, John Cropper Papers, VHS).

⁸² Joseph Jones to James Madison, Mar. 22, 1795, in Joseph Jones, "Letters from . . . to James Madison, 1788–1802," ed. W. C. Ford, *Proceedings of the Massachusetts Historical Society* 35 (1901–2): 150.

⁸³ Ibid.

⁸⁴ John Randolph to Joseph Quincy, June 20, 1817, Quincy, *Quincy*, 332; Randolph to James Mercer Garnett, May 15, 1813, Randolph-Garnett Transcripts, LC. For a first-rate piece of sarcasm on the subject of Randolph's loss, see Francis Walker Gilmer to Peter Minor, May 4, 1813, Davis, *Gilmer*, 116.

⁸⁵ H. B. Powell to Burr Powell, Feb. 6, 1819, Tucker Family Papers, UNC; see also Harrison Williams, *Legends of Loudoun* (Richmond, 1938), 188–90. Mercer himself declined a challenge from Mason (Trumbo, "Mercer," 33). For other election-spawned duels, see *Berkeley County Election*, 1831, Duke; Kuroda, "County Court System," 163.

Chapter VII

¹ Hening, *Statutes*, 12:653–65. Earlier election laws, also in Hening, are discussed in several secondary accounts, including those by Brown and Brown, Griffith, and Sydnor, as well as Chilton Williamson, *American Suffrage from Property to Democracy, 1760–1860* (Princeton, N.J., 1960), 112–14.

² Hening, *Statutes*, 13: 331–35; State of Virginia, *A Collection of All Such Acts of the General Assembly of Virginia . . .* (Richmond, 1803), chap. CCCIV; [Benjamin W. Leigh, comp.], *The Revised Code of the Laws of Virginia*, 2 vols. (Richmond, 1819), 1: chap. 50; State of Virginia, *Supplement to the Revised Code . . .* (Richmond, 1833), chap. 87. For "gerrymandering" or apportionment controversy, see Burgess Ball to James Madison, Dec. 8, 1788, Madison, *Papers*, 11:385

(among several letters which could be cited from that volume); Francis Preston to John Preston, Oct. 24, 1792, Preston Family Papers, VHS; "To Burwell Bassett, Esq.," *Norfolk Herald*, April 12, 1803, and editorial comment, ibid., April 30, 1803; *Berkeley and Jefferson Intelligencer*, June 17, 1803; William [?] Naylor to John Baker, Feb. 21, 1812, VSL; House of Delegates, *Journal for 1812–1813* (Richmond, n.d.), 75.

[3] *Documents, Containing Statistics of Virginia, Ordered to Be Printed by the State Convention Sitting in the City of Richmond, 1850–51* (Richmond, 1851). See also the Virginia material in Stanley B. Parsons, William W. Beach, and Dan Hermann, *United States Congressional Districts, 1788–1841* (Westport, Conn., 1978).

[4] May 25, 1803.

[5] In the post-Jeffersonian period, the election month moved in 1831 from April to Aug. (*Richmond Enquirer*, Aug. 2, 1831) but after that year back to April and on a standardized day, the fourth Thursday (Kuroda, "County Court System," 163, 167, 169n).

[6] *Richmond Enquirer*, Mar. 25, 1824; see also Cunningham, *Republicans: Formation*, 133–34.

[7] Kuroda, "County Court System," 186–87. Kuroda believes the development of a precinct system over time greatly altered the Virginia style of politics. The problem of living a long distance from the courthouse voting site is described in Miller and Maxwell, *West Virginia*, 1:623; Rice, *Allegheny Frontier*, 361; and Summers, *Southwest Virginia*, 467. Although complaints often rose from voters in the large western counties with poor transportation facilities, petitioners from Accomack County on the Eastern Shore also wanted a second polling place, noting the courthouse was 30 miles away and that voting took two days away from farming (legislative petition dated Dec. 20, 1825, Williamson, *American Suffrage*, 231).

[8] Kuroda, "County Court System," 145–56.

[9] Tucker, *Valley of Shenandoah*, 1:217.

[10] Kuroda, "County Court System," 156–62; Sydnor, *Gentlemen Freeholders*, 34. Kuroda concludes: "The active participation of the citizenry in court day activities rivalled that of the town meetings of New England" (p. 157). Sydnor states: "the day was a social institution in itself—one of the most important in the ante-bellum South" (p. 34).

[11] The German Johann Schoepf, in McColley, *Slavery and Jeffersonian Virginia*, 40.

[12] Robert Hunter, Jr. (ibid., 39).

[13] Beeman, ed., "Trade and Travel," 181.

[14] Elkanah Watson, *Men and Times of the Revolution; or, Memoirs of Elkanah Watson*, ed. Winslow C. Watson (New York, 1856), 60, also cited in Sydnor, *Gentlemen Freeholders*, 27.

[15] Quoted in Kuroda, "County Court System," 161–62. Again the caveat must be added: the surviving accounts are likely to overemphasize the exciting or unusual polls and thus fail to indicate that many elections were no doubt dull and ritualistic.

[16] Elijah Fletcher to his brother [?], April 24, 1812, Fletcher, *Letters*, 52.

[17] Reminiscence of Samuel Williams, in Atkinson, *Kanawha*, 171–72. During an election in 1789, a clerk appended a pithy characterization by each name recorded to include:

Thos Cannon, squints
Reuben Douge, very long
Thos Lovett Sr., pork maker
Jno Smith (son of Deaf Jno)
Robt. R. Keeling, some doubt
Abel Camonds, very old
Wm. White, lame of the gout
Thos Bonny, don't know him
Peter Singleton, alias Czar

Rogers D. Whichard, *The History of Lower Tidewater Virginia* (New York, 1959), 79.

[18] See Beeman, *Old Dominion*, 35–36; Kuroda, "County Court System," 174–75. Kuroda notes that "Virginia was the only state in the Union in 1824 expressly *requiring* oral voting as opposed to the ballot" (p. 174).

[19] James Schouler, "Evolution of the American Voter," *American Historical Review* 2 (July 1897): 671.

[20] Mordecai, *Richmond*, 93–94.

[21] Munford, *The Two Parsons*, 208–10, describing the contest in Richmond between John Marshall and John Clopton in 1799 and providing a basis for Beveridge's account in *Marshall*, 2:414–16. Norman K. Risjord praises the electorate as being actively involved in the political system and discriminating in judgment ("How the 'Common Man' Voted in Jefferson's Virginia," in John B. Boles, ed., *America, the Middle Period: Essays in Honor of Bernard Mayo* [Charlotteville, Va., 1973]).

[22] Washington *National Intelligencer*, April 25, 1803.

[23] J. H. Newton, *History of the Pan-Handle* (Wheeling, W.Va., 1879), 415–16.

[24] Beveridge, *Marshall*, 2:415.

[25] Diary of R. N. Venable, in Woodfin, "Contemporary Opinion of Thomas Jefferson," 47.

[26] Edmund Pendleton to Thomas Jefferson, Feb. 24, 1799, Pendleton, *Letters*, 2:667. Good running accounts of congressional polls lasting several days are in the *Richmond Enquirer*, April 13, 1821, and April 15, 1825.

[27] Beeman, *Old Dominion*, 34; Kuroda, "County Court System," 69–71, 168–77, 189–90. Press announcements of upcoming elections are in the *Norfolk Herald*, April 20, 1799; *Berkeley and Jefferson Intelligencer*, Mar. 4, 1803. A reopened poll is noted in the *Richmond Enquirer*, May 1, 1829.

[28] Examples of sheriff's certificates are in *CVSP*, 9:22, 281, 425, and 10:110. For a communication about a problem in comparing polls which also helps explain the custom and the law, see David Holmes to the Governor, May 15, 1799, ibid., 9:24. On the use of couriers, see Francis Earle Lutz, *The Prince George-Hopewell Story* (Richmond, 1957), 111, which notes a rider who charged "10 cents a mile and . . . furnished his own mount"; and Wehtje, "Congressional Elections," 269.

Notes

Tie-breaking is covered in Kuroda, "County Court System," 189. Pay vouchers compensating sheriffs for their election duties are in the Auditor's Office Records, item no. 151, VSL. A governor's notification of Congress is seen in Gov. John Tyler to the Honorable Speaker of the House of Representatives of the United States, May 16, 1809, Executive Letterbook, VSL.

[29] In this instance the official, the mayor of Williamsburg, was indicted by a grand jury for "preventing the people from exercising the right of suffrage" (*CVSP*, 9:205). See also Washington *National Intelligencer*, May 22, 1801; *Philadelphia Aurora*, May 22, 1801.

[30] John Randolph to James Mercer Garnett, April 11, 1811, Randolph-Garnett Transcripts, LC. See also *Alexandria Gazette*, April 23, 1817; Washington *National Intelligencer*, April 27, 1807; Summers, *Southwest Virginia*, 475; and the Virginia elections listed in Clarke and Hall, *Contested Elections*.

[31] *Journal of the House of Delegates, 1801–1802* (Richmond, 1802), 28.

[32] Entries in Randolph's diary, microfilm copy, UVA. Foster thought this system of "intervals . . . and the having the election at different places makes it more convenient to the voters and less subject to disorders than ours are [in England], and as the court house is small in which the poll is held, a number could not well assemble sufficiently great to cause confusion" (*Jeffersonian America*, 124).

[33] *Alexandria Advertiser*, May 3, 1803. This circumstance prompted a protest by citizens of Augusta County, who petitioned the legislature: "The political strength of a particular candidate . . . in an election which has passed, in one or more counties, being ascertained, the political machinery of others, yet to follow is set in motion to defeat him; combinations are formed—compromises made—the passions of the people are aroused—county is arrayed against county—and . . . a state of things revolting to every honorable and patriotic mind, is engendered" (Kuroda, "County Court System," 176).

[34] *Richmond Enquirer*, April 26, May 3, May 6, 1825.

[35] Foster, *Jeffersonian America*, 159; Phocion [pseud.], *To the Freeholders of Essex, Caroline, King-and-Queen, & King William* [Fredericksburg?, 1803?], broadside, UVA.

[36] Hening, *Statutes*, 12:654; see also Sydnor, *Gentlemen Freeholders*, chap. 3 and apps. 1 and 2.

[37] Thomas Jefferson, *Notes,* ed. Peden, 118; Jackson Turner Main, "The Distribution of Property in Post-Revolutionary Virginia," *Mississippi Valley Historical Review* 41 (Sept. 1954): 248; Main, *Social Structure*, 45, 47, 50, 51, 54; Sydnor, *Gentlemen Freeholders*, 39 and app. 2.

[38] Sydnor, *Gentlemen Freeholders*, 37.

[39] Brown and Brown, *Virginia*, 146. The Browns argue that 85 percent or more of the adult white males were eligible to vote in at least some portions of Virginia (ibid., 142).

[40] Pole, "Representation in Virginia," 34; Williamson, *American Suffrage*, 224.

[41] Beeman, *Old Dominion*, 3, 39, 155, 127. The two counties were Essex and Brunswick.

[42] Risjord, "How the 'Common Man' Voted," 50, 62–63.

⁴³ McCormick, *Second Party System*, 179; Jefferson to John H. Pleasants, April 19, 1824, Sydnor, *Southern Sectionalism*, 47; Williamson, *American Suffrage*, 223 (who believes roughly 40 to 50 percent of the adult white males could vote in the 1820s); Julian A. C. Chandler, *The History of Suffrage in Virginia* (Baltimore, 1900), 22, 40.

⁴⁴ J. R. Pole, *Political Representation in England and the Origins of the American Republic* (London, 1966), 562. See also Richard P. McCormick, "New Perspectives on Jacksonian Politics," *American Historical Review* 65 (1960): 288–301, esp. table II.

⁴⁵ Weather problems for other elections are noted in, for example, the *Alexandria Gazette*, May 3, 1803, April 10, 1817. In one election, at Dumfries in 1803, the low participation was explained in terms of "many of the inhabitants being at this season engaged in the fisheries" (Richmond *Virginia Argus*, April 13, 1803). There is some evidence of lawful plural voting (for example, see the *Norfolk Gazette*, April 26, 1809, and Robert Gamble to Gen. James Breckinridge, April 7, 1813, Breckinridge Family Papers, VHS), but Kuroda is correct in regarding the practice as insignificant ("County Court System," 165). For illegal voting, see the following section.

⁴⁶ As the *Richmond Enquirer* correctly observed in 1820: "The Election of the President of the United States has . . . excited very little interest" (Nov. 7). The pathetically (and abnormally) low turnout makes it a poor choice for analysis here, but it was the only presidential race coinciding with a complete set of applicable census returns and reasonably complete congressional data.

⁴⁷ Hening, *Statutes*, 12:655; Roeber, *Faithful Magistrates*, 180–81; Sydnor, *Gentlemen Freeholders*, 38–40; Miller and Maxwell, *West Virginia*, 1:626; Whichard, *Tidewater*, 79.

⁴⁸ The figures suggest that Chandler underestimated the problem in arguing that "five to ten percent" bad votes were "cast at every election" (*History of Suffrage*, 44–45).

⁴⁹ Thomas Mann Randolph to Thomas Jefferson, April 29, 1803, Edgehill-Randolph Collection, UVA, based "on a scouting [?] of the Amherst polls only" by another party on Randolph's behalf; Rose, *Prologue to Democracy*, 119–20.

⁵⁰ Richmond *Virginia Gazette*, May 4, 1803. The candidate, Republican Thomas Claiborne, was elected to Congress.

⁵¹ April 26, 1817. Seeking evidence of "irregularities, Mason went to various taverns in northern Virginia" (Poland, *Frontier*, 99n) and eventually fought and died in a duel caused by the election turmoil (see above, pp. 131–32).

⁵² John George Jackson reminiscing in 1824 about a House of Delegates race, in Brown, "Jackson," 25–26.

⁵³ *Alexandria Advertiser*, May 13, 1803.

⁵⁴ Clarke and Hall, *Contested Elections*, Case XXXII (*Taliaferro v. Hungerford*), 250–51.

⁵⁵ Madison noticed a sectional pattern in this regard: "West of the Blue Ridge the votes of non-freeholders are often connived at, the candidates finding it unpopular to object to them" (Madison to Joseph C. Cabell, Jan. 5, 1829, Williamson, *American Suffrage*, 230). Williamson believes the east tried harder to enforce

suffrage requirements than did the west (ibid.), and Kuroda notes the absence of any "system of voter registration until 1884" ("County Court System," 171).

⁵⁶ Clarke and Hall, *Contested Elections*, 247. See also Kuroda, "County Court System," 171–72.

⁵⁷ As of Aug. 1979 the Inter-University Consortium for Political and Social Research at Ann Arbor, Mich., had only scattered holdings for Virginia congressional races and none for state legislative elections before 1824 (Janet Vavra to the author, Aug. 6, 1979).

⁵⁸ Federalist displeasure about the Assembly's choices can be seen, for example, in Thomas Evans to John Cropper, Dec. 6, 1796, John Cropper Papers, VHS; and Robert Gamble to Gen. James Breckinridge, Jan. 2, 1810, Breckinridge Family Papers, VHS. Exceptions to the usual lack of competition in senatorial elections were (1) William Wirt's loss to James Barbour, 107–80, described in great detail in Wirt to Dabney Carr, Dec. 10, 1814, VSL; and (2) the contest of Dec. 1824 to fill the vacancy caused by Taylor's death. For the latter, there were various candidates, but the final vote was 139 for Littleton Waller Tazewell, 80 for John Tyler, 20 "scattered." It was a contest Lyon G. Tyler said was "one not of principle, but of age," Tazewell's being sixteen years the elder man (*Letters and Times*, 1:363). Perhaps suggestive of a paucity of candidates was the selection of Armistead T. Mason, a man able enough perhaps but only age twenty-nine when his tenure began, and thus constitutionally ineligible for the position.

⁵⁹ Some of the men—John Taylor, for instance—served on more than one occasion; others, such as Giles, served more than one consecutive term. Taylor was elected to the Senate on three different occasions but only served a total of four years.

⁶⁰ William Branch Giles to the Governor, Nov. 23, 1815, *CVSP*, 10:426. See also the public justification for resigning in Littleton Waller Tazewell to the Governor, Oct. 22, 1832, ibid., 579–80, and his private one, in John Floyd, "Diary," ed. Charles M. Amber, *Branch Historical Papers 5* (June 1918): 195–96.

⁶¹ See, for example, *CVSP*, 9:60, 10:40, 97, 412, 620; James Pleasants, Jr., Clerk, House of Delegates, to The Clerk of the Council, Jan. 7, 1809, Executive Papers, VSL.

⁶² Andrew Moore to the Governor, Sept. 20, 1804, *CVSP*, 9:414. Conventional responses are found in ibid., 9:360 (Taylor), 9:413, 434 (Giles), 10:565 (Tazewell), and 10:584 (Tyler).

⁶³ Merryman, "Page," 20–21.

⁶⁴ An interesting but abortive attempt to get a western senator, in the person of John Floyd, was made by several Virginia congressmen when incumbent James Barbour was expected to resign to join John Quincy Adams's cabinet in Feb. 1825 (*CVSP*, 10:519).

⁶⁵ For examples see *CVSP*, 11:115–16, 10:77, 90–91, 317, 492, 495, 506.

⁶⁶ Ibid., 10:493; see also ibid. 9:412, and Gov. William H. Cabell's correspondence with the sheriffs of John Claiborne's former district, July 8, Oct. 3, 1808, Executive Papers, VSL.

⁶⁷ Clarke and Hall, *Contested Elections*.

Notes

[68]See the Virginia reports, ibid.

[69]Ibid., Case VII (*Trigg* v. *Preston*), 79. See also the equally "voluminous" correspondence on the subject during 1793 and 1794 in the Preston Family Papers, VHS.

[70]Ibid., 134; Gaines, *Randolph*, 52.

Chapter VIII

[1]James W. Alexander, *The Life of Archibald Alexander* (New York, 1854), 188–89; Bruce, *Randolph*, 1:142–54; Garland, *Randolph*, 1:129–41; William Maxwell, *A Memoir of the Rev. John H. Rice, D.D.*, (Philadelphia, 1835), 21.

[2]Maxwell, *Memoir of the Rev. John H. Rice*, 21.

[3]Exceptions to the prototype were Randolph's bachelor status and his not having held public office before running for Congress.

[4]John Randolph (hereafter JR) to Creed Taylor, Sept. 16, [1798], Creed Taylor Papers, UVA; Lemuel Sawyer, *A Biography of John Randolph of Roanoke* (New York, 1844), 12; Stokes, "Randolph of Roanoke: A Virginia Portrait," 141–46.

[5]Notable descendants of William Randolph of Turkey Island are listed in Bruce, *Randolph*, 1:13–16.

[6]Ibid., 1:19, 21.

[7]JR to Harmanus Bleecker, April 22, 1813, Randolph-Bleecker Letter Book, UVA.

[8]JR to Tudor Randolph, Dec. 13, 1813, copy, Grinnan Papers, UVA; JR to Francis Walker Gilmer, July 2, 1825, Davis, *Gilmer*, 185. See also Robert Dawidoff, *The Education of John Randolph* (New York, 1979).

[9]JR to Theodore Bland Dudley, Feb. 16, 1817, John Randolph, *Letters of John Randolph, to a Young Relative*, ed. Theodore Bland Dudley (Philadelphia, 1834), 191; JR to Tudor Randolph, Dec. 13, 1813, copy, Grinnan Papers, UVA.

[10]JR to Tudor Randolph, Dec. 13, 1813, copy, Grinnan Papers, UVA; Stokes, "Randolph of Roanoke: A Virginia Portrait," 69–72, 76, 82; JR to St. George Tucker, July 30, 1788, copy, Bruce-Randolph Collection, VSL; same to same, Jan. 26, Mar. 1, 1794, John Randolph Papers, Huntington Library, San Marino, Calif., microfilm, UVA.

[11]JR to Tudor Randolph, Dec. 13, 1813, copy, Grinnan Papers, UVA; Stokes, "Randolph of Roanoke: A Virginia Portrait," 93–104, 128–33. On the relationship between Randolph and Maria Ward, see Robert D. Meade, "John Randolph of Roanoke: Some New Information," *WMQ*, 2d ser., 13 (Oct. 1933): 256–64.

[12]JR to Littleton Waller Tazewell, Feb. 27, 1826, typescript, Bruce-Randolph Collection, VSL; Stokes, "Randolph of Roanoke: A Virginia Portrait," 141–42. In 1799 Randolph's estate in Charlotte County consisted of 39 slaves, 16 horses, and 4,657 acres (Land and Personal Property Records, Charlotte, 1799, VSL); the Cumberland County records for 1798–1800 have no entry for him.

[13]JR to Josiah Quincy, Oct. 18, 1813, Quincy, *Quincy*, 337; Bruce, *Randolph*, 1:98–100; Gerald W. Johnson, *Randolph of Roanoke: A Political Fantastic* (New

York, 1929), 96–98; Stokes, "Randolph of Roanoke: A Virginia Portrait," 50–51, 111–14, 134–36.

¹⁴JR to Citizen Creed Taylor, Sept. 16, [1798], Creed Taylor Papers, UVA.

¹⁵Mason G. Daly, "The Political Oratory of John Randolph of Roanoke" (Ph.D. diss., Northwestern University, 1951); Ralph H. Rives, "History of Oratory," 126–140; Bruce, *Randolph*, 1:141–42; Stokes, "Randolph of Roanoke: A Virginia Portrait," 142; Bouldin, *Home Reminiscences*, 55. For negative views, see Evert A. Duyckinck, *National Portrait Gallery of Eminent Americans* (New York, 1862), 2:93; Foster, *Jeffersonian America*, 165–66.

¹⁶Frederick W. Thomas, *John Randolph, of Roanoke* (Philadelphia, 1853), 14; Bouldin, *Home Reminiscences*, 11, 62, 66–67; Bruce, *Randolph*, 2:191–92, 200; Richard Heath Dabney, *John Randolph: A Character Sketch* (Danville, Va., 1898), 81; Garland, *Randolph*, 1:129; Hugh Blair Grigsby, "Sketches of Members of the Constitutional Convention of 1829–1830," *VMHB* 61 (1953): 330; William H. Sparks, *Memories of Fifty Years* (Philadelphia, 1872), 236; William E. Stokes, Jr., "Randolph of Roanoke," *American Heritage* 3 (Spring 1952): 49–51 (with color portrait); Thomas, *Randolph*, 14–16.

¹⁷Joseph Glover Baldwin, *Party Leaders: Sketches of Thomas Jefferson, Alex'r Hamilton, Andrew Jackson, Henry Clay, John Randolph, of Roanoke* (New York, 1855), 210; Bruce, *Randolph*, 2:190–91, 196; Sparks, *Memories of Fifty Years*, 237; Thomas, *Randolph*, 24.

¹⁸For his knowledge of district affairs and personalities, see JR to Dr. Brockenbrough, Dec. 26, 1827, Garland, *Randolph*, 2:297, and JR to Richard Kidder Randolph, Sept. 17, 1812, copy, Bruce-Randolph Collection, VSL.

¹⁹"John Randolph of Roanoke," *Harper's* 5 (Sept. 1852): 536. See also Baldwin, *Party Leaders*, 210–11, 267; Bouldin, *Home Reminiscences*, 53; Bruce, *Randolph*, 2:178, 203, 206, 211, 767; Foster, *Jeffersonian America*, 165–66; William P. Trent, *Southern Statesmen of the Old Regime* (Boston, 1897), 148.

²⁰Bruce, *Randolph*, 2:762; see also "Benjamin Ogle Tayloe Anecdotes and Reminiscences," 29, 48–49, typescript, Elizabeth Blanchard Papers, UNC.

²¹Bruce, *Randolph*, 1:597; JR Diary, Oct. 5, 1812, copy, Bruce-Randolph Collection, VSL.

²²Baldwin, *Party Leaders*, 269; Bruce, *Randolph*, 2:210, 213–15; [Francis Walker Gilmer], *Sketches of American Orators* (Baltimore, 1816), 11; Russell Kirk, *John Randolph of Roanoke: A Study in American Politics* (Chicago, 1964), 243.

²³Rev. John S. Kirkpatrick, in Bruce, *Randolph*, 2:193.

²⁴Baldwin, *Party Leaders*, 215, paraphrasing the Reverend Dr. Conrad Speece. See also Bruce, *Randolph*, 2:206.

²⁵See, for example, Bouldin, *Home Reminiscences*, 47, 55, 58, 64; Bruce, *Randolph*, 2:102; Garland, *Randolph*, 2:233–34.

²⁶William H. Elliott, in Bouldin, *Home Reminiscences*, 55; see also JR to Richard Kidder Randolph, April 24, 1830, typescript, Bruce-Randolph Collection, VSL.

²⁷Bouldin, *Home Reminiscences*, 48, 51, 53; Bruce, *Randolph*, 2:190–91, 196; Garland, *Randolph*, 1:311.

[28] Bruce, *Randolph*, 2:216.

[29] JR to Dr. John Brockenbrough, May 22, 1829, Garland, *Randolph*, 2:324.

[30] Bouldin, *Home Reminiscences*, 41. See also ibid., 42; Bruce, *Randolph*, 2:619; Kirk, *Randolph*, 183.

[31] Bouldin, *Home Reminiscences*, 50. For other aspects of Randolph's canvassing, see ibid., 28, 49–50, 64–66; JR's Diary, April 1811 and Sept.-Oct. 1812, copy, Bruce-Randolph Collection, VSL; JR's Diary, early months of 1817 and 1819, VHS. For examples concerning uncontested races, see the *Richmond Enquirer*, April 18, 1823, and April 15, 1825.

[32] Bouldin, *Home Reminiscences*, 37; Sawyer, *A Biography of John Randolph*, 41.

[33] Bouldin, *Home Reminiscences*, 49.

[34] Garland, *Randolph*, 2:171, 218; "Early Recollections of John Randolph," *Southern Literary Messenger* 28 (June 1859): 465; Randolph, *Letters to a Young Relative*, 139; *Mr. John Randolph's Motion, Feb. 7, 1806* (Washington, D.C., 1806), circular, UVA; *Richmond Enquirer*, April 1, 1815; JR to Edward Booker, April 2, 1817, Randolph Papers, UVA; Francis W. Gilmer to JR, April 29, 1824, Randolph-Gilmer Papers, VSL.

[35] Bouldin, *Home Reminiscences*, 95, 119–20, 124, 167. Henry Adams wrote that Randolph "at first adopted by instinct" the use of intimidation for political gain and then "by long experience developed [it] into a science" (*Randolph*, 257, 261).

[36] Adams, *Randolph*, 205; Bouldin, *Home Reminiscences*, 94–95, 122–23, 265; Bruce, *Randolph*, 2:100, 253, 410; Stokes, "Randolph of Roanoke: A Virginia Portrait," 158.

[37] JR to Joseph H. Nicholson, Aug. 25, 1805, Nicholson Papers, LC; JR to Richard Kidder Randolph, Mar. 25, 1811, William A. Whitaker Papers, UNC: James Mercer Garnett to JR, Mar. 29, 1811, JR to Garnett, April 11, 1811, JR to Theodore Bland Dudley, April 11, 1811, Randolph-Garnett Transcripts, LC; JR to Harmanus Bleecker, April 22, 1813, Randolph-Bleecker Letter Book, UVA; and numerous issues of the *Richmond Enquirer*.

[38] JR to James Mercer Garnett, Mar. 18, 1809, April 15, April 20, 1811, Sept. 14, 1812, Randolph-Garnett Transcripts, LC; JR to Harmanus Bleecker, April 22, 1813, Randolph-Bleecker Letter Book, UVA; *Richmond Enquirer*, Mar. 25, April 1, 5, 8, 1815.

[39] Richmond *Virginia Gazette and General Advertiser*, April 5, 23, 1799, microfilm, VHS.

[40] See JR to James Mercer Garnett, Mar. 18, 1809, April 16, 1811, Sept. 14, 1812, Randolph-Garnett Transcripts, LC; JR to Joseph H. Nicholson, May 27, 1808, Nicholson Papers, LC.

[41] Bruce, *Randolph*, 1:592.

[42] Ambler, *Ritchie*, 56; Anderson, *Giles*, 102; Bradshaw, *Prince Edward County*, 178; JR to James Mercer Garnett, June 4, 1806, Randolph-Garnett Transcripts, LC; Bruce, *Randolph*, 1:590–92, 599.

[43] JR to Harmanus Bleecker, April 22, 1813, Randolph-Bleecker Letter Book,

Notes

UVA; JR to Francis Scott Key, May 22, 1813, Garland, *Randolph*, 2:14; JR to Josiah Quincy, April 19, 1813, Quincy, *Quincy*, 329–30.

[44] JR to Tudor Randolph, Dec. 13, 1813, Grinnan Papers, UVA; Bruce, *Randolph*, 2:302–18; Stokes, "Randolph of Roanoke: A Virginia Portrait," 295–98; Curtis Carroll Davis, "The Devil and John Randolph," *American Heritage* 7 (Aug. 1956): 10–11.

[45] Bruce, *Randolph*, 2:252, 405; Johnson, *Randolph*, 175.

[46] JR to Harmanus Bleecker, July 20, 1817, Randolph-Bleecker Letter Book, UVA; Randolph, *Letters to a Young Relative*, 224; Bruce, *Randolph*, 2:344; Meade, "John Randolph."

[47] Bouldin, *Home Reminiscences*, 11, 24, 74; Bruce, *Randolph*, 1:672, 2:404–8, 414–15, 419–34, 436; Sparks, *Memories of Fifty Years*, 227; "Tayloe Anecdotes and Reminiscences," 40, 49. Randolph once estimated that he had written at least four letters "every morning of my life" (Daly, "Political Oratory of John Randolph," 9); the admittedly incomplete preliminary checklist, *The Papers of Randolph of Roanoke: A Preliminary Checklist*, comp. William E. Stokes, Jr., and Francis L. Berkeley, Jr. (Charlottesville, Va., 1950) includes 2,762 items, the vast majority being private correspondence.

[48] Coleman, *St. George Tucker*, 112.

[49] JR to Joseph H. Nicholson, Feb. 15, 1800, Nicholson Papers, LC; Bouldin, *Home Reminiscences*, 75; Bruce, *Randolph*, 2:456, 459–71, 493–94; "Early Recollections of John Randolph," 461–62; the recollections of Rev. John T. Clark, Bruce-Randolph Collection, VSL; the recollections of John Randolph Bryan, John Randolph Papers, UNC; "Letters of John Randolph, of Roanoke, to General Thomas Marsh Forman," *VMHB* 49 (1941): 201–16.

[50] Bouldin, *Home Reminiscences*, 73, 81, 229–30; Dabney, *Randolph*, 86; JR to Post Master [of Fayetteville, N.C.], John Randolph Papers, Duke.

[51] Dabney, *Randolph*, 59. Randolph exhorted a young kinsman: "Of all the virtues none is so important as Truth" (JR to Master John S. G. Randolph, Sept. 6, 1806, John Randolph Papers, Duke).

[52] Bouldin, *Home Reminiscences*, 116.

[53] Ibid., 28; Bruce, *Randolph*, 2:380; Garland, *Randolph*, 1:310; JR to Richard Kidder Randolph, Aug. 12, 1811, Bruce-Randolph Collection, VSL.

[54] Bruce, *Randolph*, 1:648, 2:357–59, 690–91, 702. See also Mathias, "John Randolph's Freedmen," 263–72.

[55] JR to Dr. John Brockenbrough, Sept. 25, 1818, Kirk, *Randolph*, 222; Bruce, *Randolph*, 2:515, 650; Meade, *Old Churches*, 1:33; "Tayloe Anecdotes and Reminiscences," 43.

[56] Thomas, *Randolph*, 22; JR to Francis Walker Gilmer, July 2, 1825, Davis, *Gilmer*, 185; Adams, *Randolph*, 205; Garland, *Randolph*, 2:104. Richard Beale Davis writes, "Argumentatively pugnacious, Randolph . . . made enemies among those who should have been his best friends" (*Gilmer*, 164), and a contemporary noted, "His proclivity . . . to antipathy was the great distinguishing characteristic of his private and public life" (John R. Cooke to Jno. G. Mosby, May 15, 1836, typescript, Bruce-Randolph Collection, VSL).

268

Notes

[57] Adams, *Randolph*, 251, 259; Bruce, *Randolph*, 2:112, 302, 331, 384; Bouldin, *Home Reminiscences*, 87; Dabney, *Randolph*, 80; Garland, *Randolph*, 2:104; Sawyer, *Randolph*, 115. The British diplomat Foster wrote, "John Randolph was as great a genealogist as could be found in the mother country and like others of his countrymen, fond of claiming kindred with our old families" (*Jeffersonian America*, 164).

[58] JR to Theodore Bland Dudley, July 24, 1821, Randolph, *Letters to a Young Relative*, 225. See also William Thompson, "Character of John Randolph," *Wheeling Repository*, Jan. 28, 1808.

[59] Sawyer, *Randolph*, 12; Grigsby, "Sketches," 325.

[60] Bruce, *Randolph*, 2:104, 111, 150–59, 710; Daly, "Political Oratory of John Randolph," 173–84; Kirk, *Randolph*, 60; Sparks, *Memories of Fifty Years*, 236. Powhatan County was in Randolph's district from 1799 to 1803 (Hening, 13:331).

[61] Trent, *Southern Statesmen of the Old Regime*, 91.

[62] Kirk, *Randolph*, 7; Quincy, *Quincy*, 339; Risjord, *Old Republicans*, 25; Stokes, "Randolph of Roanoke: A Virginia Portrait," 51–52.

[63] Stokes, "Randolph of Roanoke: A Virginia Portrait," 180; Stokes and Berkeley, *Papers of Randolph of Roanoke*, 12.

[64] The district winner, however, was Archibald Austin (*Richmond Enquirer*, April 15, 18, May 6, 1817).

[65] JR to Dr. John Brockenbrough (?), Jan. 19, 1822, Garland, *Randolph*, 2:159; Bruce, *Randolph*, 2:100, 103, 190; Risjord, *Old Republicans*, 226; *Richmond Enquirer*, May 13, 1823, April 15, 1825, April 27, 1827, April 23, 1833.

[66] Bouldin, *Home Reminiscences*, 53, 61; Bruce, *Randolph*, 2:189; Garland, *Randolph*, 2:171, 218.

[67] JR to Dr. John Brockenbrough, Dec. 26, 1827, Garland, *Randolph*, 2:297. See also Bouldin, *Home Reminiscences*, 122; Garland, *Randolph*, 2: 237; JR to Richard Kidder Randolph, Sept. 17, 1812, typescript, Bruce-Randolph Collection, VSL.

[68] JR to James Mercer Garnett, Feb. 5, 1812, Randolph-Garnett Transcripts, LC; Garland, *Randolph*, 2:132, 139, 155, 192, 284, 293, 308, 315–16.

[69] *Richmond Enquirer*, May 13, 1823, April 15, 1825; Nathaniel Macon Pawlett, "John Randolph of Roanoke: Virginia Senator, 1825–1827" (M.A. thesis, University of Virginia, 1973); Bruce, *Randolph*, 1:541–42; Garland, *Randolph*, 2:289–90; JR note, Jan. 31, 1827, Randolph Papers, VHS.

[70] Anderson, *Giles*, 231; Bruce, *Randolph*, 1:601; Garland, *Randolph*, 2:322.

[71] Eckenrode, *The Randolphs*, 221–22; *Richmond Enquirer*, April 23, 26, 1833.

[72] Bouldin, *Home Reminiscences*, 3:12–13, 84, 214; Bruce, *Randolph*, 2:98–101.

Chapter IX

[1] Thomas Jefferson to William Wirt, Jan. 10, 1808, Kennedy, *Wirt*, 1:208.

[2] Edmund Pendleton, "The Danger Not Over," Caroline County, Va., Oct. 5, 1801, Pendleton, *Letters*, 2:697.

Notes

³*CVSP*, 10:79; Fischer, *Revolution*, 384–85; Trumbo, "Mercer," 20, 37.

⁴William A. Burwell to [Major William Dickerson, of Bedford?] Nov. 20, 1808, Burwell Papers, LC. At his death Caperton's estate was valued at $600,000 (Johnston, *New River*, 389); for his will, see [William Alexander Gordon], *The Killing of Adam Caperton* (Louisville, Ky., [ca. 1918]), 33–42.

⁵Brown, "Congressman John George Jackson," 121; A. D. Kenamond, *Prominent Men of Shepherdstown* (n.p., 1963), 23.

⁶White, *Jeffersonians*, 303.

⁷Thomas J. Page to Col. Leven Powell, Feb. 5, 1801, "Correspondence of Leven Powell," 57–61; Spencer Roane to Wilson Cary Nicholas, Jan. 5, 1809, Wilson Cary Nicholas Papers, LC.

⁸William Pannill to John Dawson, April 20, 1798, Trist Woods Papers, UNC; Burwell–William Dickerson Correspondence, 1808–9, Burwell Papers, LC; "Missouri Compromise, Letters to James Barbour . . . ," *WMQ*, 1st ser., 10 (July 1901): 5–24; Wayland, *Stevenson*, 63.

⁹Van Rutherford to the Governor, Nov. 25, 1812, Richard Brent to the Governor, Feb. 11, 1814, *CVSP*, 10:173, 300.

¹⁰Collections of letters replete with favors asked or given are those of John Clopton, Duke; Thomas Newton, ed. James A. Padgett, *WMQ*, 2d ser., 16 (1936): 38–70, 192–205; and William C. Rives, 1823–29, *Tyler's Quarterly* 5 (1924): 223–37, 6 (1925): 6–15, 97–106.

¹¹John Clopton to John B. Clopton, Nov. 24, Dec. 7, 1814, Clopton Papers, Duke.

¹²Davis, *Jackson*, 97–98; Spencer Roane to Wilson Cary Nicholas, Feb. 11, 1809, Wilson Cary Nicholas Papers, LC (microfilm, UVA).

¹³William Naylor to John Baker, Feb. 2, 1812, VSL; Brown, "Congressman John George Jackson," 119; Edward Graham to James Breckinridge, June 10, 1809, Breckinridge Family Papers, VHS.

¹⁴The related custom of legislative "instructions" is discussed in chap. 10 below. See also Raymond C. Bailey, *Popular Influence upon Public Policy: Petitioning in Eighteenth Century Virginia* (Westport, Conn., 1979).

¹⁵See Harry Ammon, "The Genet Mission and the Development of American Political Parties," *Journal of American History* 52 (Mar. 1966): 730–37; Cunningham, *Republicans: Formation*, 59, 63, 65; *CVSP*, 10: 24–27; Woodfin, "Contemporary Opinion of Jefferson," 54–57. For examples of the memorials, see "Meeting . . . at Allen's Ordinary [April 26, 1798]," Clopton Papers, Duke; Pendleton, *Letters*, 2:608–13, 635–37; Virginia Broadsides: Staunton, Sept. 3, 1793, and Albemarle County, 1798, Rare Book Division, LC. The results of numerous political meetings in 1807–9 are analyzed in Jordan, "Virginia and Jefferson's Embargo."

¹⁶See Aler, *Aler's History*, 189; Ambler, *Sectionalism*, 104, 106, 118–21; Christian, *Richmond*, 98–99; Tyler, *Letters and Times*, 1:220–21, 333; Wayland, *Stevenson*, 63–64; Wertenbaker, *Norfolk*, 161–62, 166.

¹⁷Ammon, "Genet Mission," 730–37; Cunningham, *Republicans: Formation*,

59; Pendleton, *Letters*, 2:610–13; Quinn, *Fredericksburg*, 230–34; Woodfin, "Contemporary Opinion of Jefferson," 54–57.

[18] John Clopton to John Dawson, May 8, 1796, Clopton Papers, Duke.

[19] Summers, *Southwest Virginia*, 454–57. See also Washington *National Intelligencer*, April 6, 1803; *Petersburg Intelligencer*, Mar. 8, 1803; Wertenbaker, *Norfolk*, 98.

[20] A good example is the celebration of July 4, 1808, during the Embargo crisis (see the state's press for July; Jordan, "Virginia and Jefferson's Embargo").

[21] Andrew Stevenson to John Rutherford, *Richmond Enquirer*, May 27, 1834, in Wayland, *Stevenson*, 101.

[22] John Clopton to [?], Jan. 9, 1798, Clopton Papers, Duke; Bouldin, *Home Reminiscences*, 61.

[23] John Clopton, *To the People of the Congressional District . . .* , June 20, 1812, circular letter, VSL.

[24] Francis Preston, Circular, Philadelphia, Mar. 24, 1794, Cunningham, *Circular Letters*, 1:20.

[25] John Randolph to Joseph H. Nicholson, May 27, 1808, Nicholson Papers, LC.

[26] Richard Bland Lee to Leven Powell, June 12, 1789, "Leven Powell Correspondence," 223.

[27] Federalist Joseph Lewis, Jr., for instance, complained of "the Curiosity of the Democratic postmasters" in a letter to James McHenry, Dec. 26, 1809, UVA.

[28] Joseph C. Cabell to Isaac Coles, Mar. 29, 1808, Cabell Family Papers, UVA.

[29] For examples see John Stuart to James Breckinridge, Nov. 27, Dec. 20, 1811, Breckinridge Papers, UVA; Josiah Parker to "The Representatives of Accomack County," May 29, 1790, and John Stratton to John Cropper, Jan. 21, 1802, Jan. 10, 1803, John Cropper Papers, VHS; and John Marshall to Col. Charles Dabney, April 20, 1800, Charles William Dabney Papers, UNC. Jabez Leftwich wrote his brother Joel on Dec. 7, 1821, "By resolution of the House the members are to be furnished newspapers equal to three daily papers" (Joel B. Leftwich Papers, UNC).

[30] Burwell Bassett, circular, Washington, D.C., Feb. 26, 1809, Rare Book Room, LC.

[31] Abram Trigg to Col. John Preston, April 13, 1798, VSL.

[32] John W. Campbell to James Breckinridge, Feb. 3, 1810, Breckinridge Papers, UVA.

[33] Thomas M. Nelson, *To the Freeholders . . .* , Mecklenburg, Aug, 1, 1816, UNC. These circulars are now conveniently available in Cunningham's *Circular Letters*. Of 269 circulars printed by Cunningham, 76 originated with 35 different Virginia congressmen, making the Old Dominion the largest single source of the documents, with John Clopton as "the most consistent writer . . . over the longest period of time" (1:xxv). Cunningham concludes: "They did not always report fully or accurately, and they reflected personal, sectional, and partisan positions;

but, in general, they represented responsible reports directed to an informed electorate" (1:xl).

³⁴ William McCoy's eighteen-page pamphlet included a wish to cover other subjects, "but little can be added, without producing a weight, which will exceed my franking privilege; and moreover, as related to the finances and the proceedings of the executive department generally, I have distributed messages, reports, and other documents so generally, that the people in every neighborhood, have an opportunity of getting information more in detail than I could give it" (McCoy, *To the Citizens* . . . , [1829?], VHS). An incumbent's franking allowance could be a considerable campaign advantage over a challenger who had to pay regular rates, such as those enumerated in Couper, *Shenandoah Valley*, 1:686.

³⁵ Thomas Gholson, Jr., *To the freeholders of the Congressional District Composed of the Counties of Mecklenburg, Lunenburg and Brunswick*, Washington City, July 4, 1812, circular, UVA.

³⁶ Alexander Smyth, circular, Washington, D.C., April 13, 1818, Broadside Collection, Rare Book Room, Duke; John Claiborne, circular, Washington City, April 18, 1806, Duke.

³⁷ McCoy, *To the Citizens* . . . , [1829?], Duke; William J. Lewis, circular, 1819, Broadside Collection, Rare Book Room, Duke.

³⁸ Anthony New, circular, City of Washington, Feb. 18, 1803, UVA; John Stratton, *A Letter from John Stratton, Addressed to the Freeholders* . . . , Elkington, Mar. 3, 1803, WM; John Tyler, *To the Freeholders* . . . , Washington, D.C., Jan. 15, 1821, circular, Tyler, *Letters and Times*, 1:337; and Thomas Evans to John Rutledge, Accomack County, Dec. 8, 1801, John Rutledge Papers, UNC.

³⁹ John Page of Rosewell, *To the Citizens* . . . , Nov. 16, 1798, Virginia Broadsides, Rare Book Room, LC.

⁴⁰ Cunningham, *Circular Letters*, 1:xx.

⁴¹ Critic-editor Thomas Ritchie, ibid., 1:xxi.

⁴² John Clopton, circular, Jan. 24, 1797, Clopton Papers, Duke.

⁴³ See John Clopton to Thomas Ritchie, Feb. 4, 1815, Clopton Papers, Duke; Joseph Lewis, Jr., to James McHenry, Dec. 26, 1809, UVA. One of the many circular letters that appeared in newspapers is Thomas Claiborne's of Feb. 26, 1803, in the *Alexandria Advertiser and Commercial Intelligencer*, April 27, 1803, which also carried notice of one by Matthew Clay to his "late constituents," dated Feb. 22, 1803.

⁴⁴ John Clopton to Johnny, April 23, 1808, Clopton Papers, Duke. See also Philip Norborne Nicholas to Wilson Cary Nicholas, Mar. 13, 1809, Wilson Cary Nicholas Papers, LC (microfilm, UVA).

⁴⁵ Cunningham, *Republicans: Formation*, 121; John Clopton, circular, Philadelphia, June 19, 1797, Clopton Papers, Duke; Thomas Jefferson to Col. James Monroe, Sept. 7, 1797, Jefferson, *The Writings of Thomas Jefferson*, ed. A. A. Lipscomb and A. E. Bergh, 20 vols. (Washington, D.C., 1903–4), 9:423–24.

⁴⁶ Francis Adams to Leven Powell, Feb. 6, 1801, "Leven Powell Correspondence," 247.

⁴⁷ Tucker, "Autobiography," 60.

Notes

[48] Ambler, *Sectionalism*; Risjord, *Old Republicans* and "Virginia Federalists." Voting patterns are given by national regions rather than by states in Albert Castel and Scott L. Gibson, *The Yeas and the Nays: Key Congressional Decisions, 1774–1945* (Kalamazoo, Mich., 1975).

[49] Risjord, "Virginia Federalists," 507. Broussard, *Southern Federalists*, 183–84, argues historians have overestimated the nationalism of southern (including Virginia) Federalists after the War of 1812 but concedes the Old Dominion had a fairly cohesive sectional bloc favoring internal improvements.

[50] Risjord, *Old Republicans*, 182; see also Anderson, *Giles*, 162–63, 177–78.

[51] Lester, "Tucker," 64, 88, 98, 100–101; McLean, *Tucker*, 20, 23–24.

[52] Tyler, *Letters and Times*, 1:293.

[53] William Wirt to William Pope, Aug. 5, 1803, Kennedy, *Wirt*, 1:99–100.

[54] William Thompson, "Character of John Randolph," *Wheeling Repository*, Jan. 28, 1808,

[55] John George Jackson could at least joke about his own long windedness, observing that a colleague in 1809 had sent a Jackson speech to a constituent who was still reading through it in 1814 (Davis, *Jackson*, 70).

[56] Robert Allen to Charles Lanman, May 19, 1858, Charles Lanman Letters, VHS.

[57] Tucker, "Autobiography," 61–62.

[58] S. L. Campbell to James Breckinridge, Feb. 15, 1810, Breckinridge Papers, UVA; McNulty, "Breckinridge," 63.

[59] Fischer used this phrase to describe Virginia Federalists Breckinridge, Stephenson, and Stratton (*Revolution*, 383, 386).

[60] John Tyler to Dr. Henry Curtis, Jan. 19, 1818, Tyler, *Letters and Times*, 1:299.

[61] Thomas Jefferson to John W. Eppes, Jan. 17, 1810, typescript, Govan Papers, UNC.

[62] Gov. John Tyler to Thomas Jefferson, May 12, 1810, Tyler, *Letters and Times*, 1:247.

Chapter X

[1] Clement Eaton, "Southern Senators and the Right of Instruction, 1789–1860," *Journal of Southern History* 18 (1952): esp. 304–5.

[2] Hamilton J. Eckenrode, *A Calendar of Legislative Petitions Arranged by Counties: Accomac-Bedford* (Richmond, 1908), 5.

[3] *CVSP*, 10:98–99.

[4] Dodd, "John Taylor," 220; Merryman, "Page," 83; Ambler, *Sectionalism*, 98, 104; Gardner, "Stevenson," 278–79; Wayland, *Stevenson*, 49; Dingledine, "Rives," 48–49.

[5] Anderson, *Giles*, 160–67.

[6] Ibid., 160–67, 192–94; Tyler, *Letters and Times*, 1:274–75; Gardner, "Ste-

venson," 264–65; Wayland, *Stevenson*, 18; Edwin J. Smith, "Benjamin Watkins Leigh," *Branch Historical Papers* 4 (June 1904): 287; Joseph Lewis to the Governor, Feb. 29, 1808, *CVSP*, 10:8.

[7] Dingledine, "Rives," 48–49, which also touches on the distinction between *instructing* and *requesting*.

[8] Russell S. Wingfield, "William Cabell Rives, a Biography," *Richmond College Historical Papers* 1 (June 1915): 61; see also Eaton, "Southern Senators and the Right of Instruction," 305–6.

[9] Andrew Stevenson to the Governor, Feb. 24, 1834, *CVSP*, 10:618–19.

[10] See the letters of various Virginia congressmen to the Governor, Feb. and Mar. 1834, ibid., 10:618–21.

[11] Smith, "Leigh," 294–96.

[12] Hugh Nelson and Thomas Gholson to the Governor, Feb. 5, 1812, *CVSP*, 10:119; see also ibid., 10:288–90, 313–16, 420, 564–65; Merryman, "Page," 57; Wayland, *Stevenson*, 62–63.

[13] Weston Bristow, "William Grayson . . . ," *Richmond College Historical Papers* 2 (June 1917): 116; *CVSP*, 9:3, 10:58–60, 261, 295–96, 519, 545; Thomas Newton to Gov. William H. Cabell, Dec. 18, 1807, Executive Papers, VSL.

[14] John Tyler and Thomas Nelson to the Governor, Jan. 27, 1821, and letters to the Governor, Feb. 21 and 22, 1825, *CVSP*, 10:497, 518–19.

[15] Former state legislators among Virginia congressmen numbered forty-five of fifty-two from 1789 to 1801 (Jordan, "Virginia Congressmen, 1789–1801," 4); eighty-seven of ninety-eight from 1801 to 1825 (table 10 above); and fifty-five of sixty-six from 1831 to 1841 (Sydnor, *Southern Sectionalism*, 45).

[16] Harry Ammon, "The Richmond Junto, 1800–1824," *VMHB* 61 (1953): 399–401; Harrison, "Oligarchs and Democrats," 184, 186, 190, 192; Risjord, *Old Republicans*, 180.

[17] Virginia's presidential electors from 1789 forward are listed in Charles Lanman, *Biographical Annals of the Civil Government of the United States, during Its First Century* (Washington, D.C., 1876), 513–40. See also Cunningham, *Republicans: Formation*, 72–73, 257.

[18] "My great object," wrote Wilson Cary Nicholas to James Madison, "is to justify the embargo" (April 11, 1808, Madison Papers, LC, microfilm, VHS). See also Jordan, "Virginia and Jefferson's Embargo."

[19] Ammon, "Monroe and the Election of 1808 in Virginia," esp. pp. 43–47.

[20] See, for example, Leven Powell's recommendations, noted in Donald O. Dewey, *Marshall versus Jefferson: The Political Background of Marbury v. Madison* (New York, 1970), 77–78; and Thomas Newton to James Madison, Dec. 29, 1813, Newton, "Letters," 201–2.

[21] See Sen. Stevens Thomson Mason to James Monroe, July 5, 1801, Cunningham, *Republicans in Power*, 8. Cunningham states categorically that "The most pervasive influence in the Jeffersonian Congresses was that of party" (*Process of Government under Jefferson*, 293), and he regards Jefferson as an exceptionally able party leader (ibid., 188, 320).

[22] For praise of Jefferson's legislative leadership, see Cunningham, *Process of Government under Jefferson*, esp. chap. 9; and Dumas Malone, "Presidential Leadership and National Unity: The Jefferson Example," *Journal of Southern History* 35 (1979): 3–7.

[23] See James S. Chase, *Emergence of the Presidential Nominating Convention, 1789–1832* (Urbana, Ill., 1973), 18–28; George B. Galloway, *History of the House of Representatives*, 2d ed., rev. Sidney Wise (New York, 1976), chaps. 6–7.

[24] See Ketcham, *Madison*, chaps. 19–21.

[25] Ammon, *Monroe*, 380; see also Ammon, "Executive Leadership in the Monroe Administration," in Boles, ed., *America, the Middle Period*.

[26] White, *Jeffersonians*, 55; William G. Morgan, "The Congressional Nominating Caucus of 1816: The Struggle against the Virginia Dynasty," *VMHB* 80 (1972): 461–75; Ammon, "Executive Leadership," 115–16; Nielsen, "Indispensable Institution."

[27] Thomas Jefferson to John Randolph, Dec. 1, 1803, Jefferson, *Writings* (Ford ed.), 3:281; Bailey, "Eppes," 56, 59, 99; Quincy, *Quincy*, 172–73; Gaines, *Randolph*, 53–69 passim, 187.

[28] Ketcham, *Madison*, 430, 498–99, 551, 559, 660.

[29] Ammon, "Richmond Junto," 400–401; Dingledine, "Rives," 37n.

[30] Ammon, *Monroe*, 172; Merryman, "Page," 17; Thomas Jefferson to Wilson Cary Nicholas, Feb. 28, 1807, Jefferson, *Writings* (Lipscomb and Bergh ed.), 11:162–63; Jefferson to William Wirt, Jan. 10, 1808, Kennedy, *Wirt*, 1:209–10.

[31] Thomas Jefferson to Wilson Cary Nicholas, Feb. 28, 1807, Jefferson, *Writings* (Lipscomb and Bergh ed.), 11:163.

[32] Lacy, "Jefferson and Congress," 307. Cunningham deemphasizes the post in favor of other modes of leadership in his *Process of Government under Jefferson*, chap. 9.

[33] Anderson, *Giles*, 82, 85, 90, 93, 95; Cunningham, *Republicans in Power*, esp. chap. 4; Lacy, "Jefferson and Congress," esp. pp. 121–201; Weeder, "Nicholas," i, chap. 4; White, *Jeffersonians*, 30–35, 47–53, 73.

[34] See Noble E. Cunningham, Jr., "John Beckley: An Early American Party Manager," *WMQ*, 3d ser., 13 (1956): 40–52; Edmund and Dorothy S. Berkeley, *John Beckley: Zealous Partisan in a Divided Nation* (Philadelphia, 1973).

[35] Based on my tabulations of the standing committees posted at the outset of each session, 1801–25, as given in the *Annals of the Congress of the United States: The Debates and Proceedings . . . , 1798–1824*, 42 vols. (Washington, D.C., 1834–56).

[36] Cunningham, *Process of Government under Jefferson*, 218.

[37] *Annals . . . Tenth Congress*, 1st sess., 793–94; Washington *National Intelligencer*, May 26, 1809. At the outset of the second session of the Tenth Congress, new standing committees were added for the District of Columbia (chaired by John Love of Virginia) and for Post Offices and Post Roads (*Annals . . . Tenth Congress*, 2d session, 472–73).

[38] A handy list of persons holding influential congressional offices, 1789–1860, is in Lanman, *Biographical Annals*, 503–5.

[39] William A. Burwell, Diary, p. 35, Burwell Papers, LC.

[40] Cunningham, *Republicans in Power*, 257–58.

[41] Thomas Jefferson to Nicholas, Mar. 20, 1808, Jefferson, *Writings* (Lipscomb and Bergh ed.), 12:14. Jefferson also kept Nicholas posted; see Cunningham, *Process of Government under Jefferson*, 190.

[42] Thomas Jefferson to Dawson, Dec. 19, 1806, Cunningham, *Process of Government under Jefferson*, 192; Jefferson to Thomas Mann Randolph, Oct. 26, 1807, Gaines, *Randolph*, 69.

[43] Gaines, *Randolph*, 63; Bailey, "Eppes," 60; Anderson, *Giles*, 130–35; Weeder, "Nicholas," 93–95, which also shows Nicholas had private doubts while offering public support of the measure. Also among the Embargo supporters were the Virginia congressmen representing the port districts of Norfolk (Thomas Newton, Jr.) and Alexandria (John Love). See also Jordan, "Virginia and Jefferson's Embargo."

[44] Jefferson to Gallatin, Mar. 30, 1808, Jefferson, *Writings* (Ford ed.), 9:190; Anderson, *Giles*, 95; Brown, "Congressman John George Jackson"; Davis, *Jackson*, 155; Bailey, "Eppes"; John S. Pancake, "'The Invisibles': A Chapter in the Opposition to President Madison," *Journal of Southern History* 21 (1955); 17–37; Risjord, *Old Republicans*, chaps. 5–6; Ammon, "Executive Leadership," 127–28. On Monroe's use of another Virginia senator on a separate issue, see Ammon, *Monroe*, 526.

[45] Washington *Universal Gazette*, Mar. 19, 1801; Foster, *Jeffersonian America*, 53; Risjord, *Old Republicans*, 118; White, *Jeffersonians*, 63.

[46] Cunningham, *Republicans: Formation*, 67; see also pp. 31, 257.

[47] Ambler, *Sectionalism*, chap. 3; Ammon, "Republican Party," chaps. 3–4; Anderson, *Giles*, chaps. 2–4.

[48] Cunningham, *Republicans in Power*, 101; see also his chap. 5.

[49] Ibid., 110–11, 180–87, 230–35; William A. Burwell, Diary, p. 48, Burwell Papers, LC. See also Ammon, "Monroe and the Election of 1808 in Virginia."

[50] Ammon, *Monroe*, 354; Ammon, "Richmond Junto," 415n, which also notes that fourteen (of twenty-two) Virginia congressmen attended the 1824 caucus.

[51] Ammon, "Richmond Junto," shows influential Virginia opposition to Madison's nomination in 1808 (pp. 403–4), to Monroe's in 1816, including that of Senators Barbour and Giles, and to Monroe again in 1820 (pp. 412–13). For defenders of the caucus as late as 1824, see Ambler, *Sectionalism*, 131; Lester, "Tucker," 102–3; Wayland, *Stevenson*, 66.

[52] Edwin Gray to Sen. S. R. Bradley, Jan. 21, 1808, Edwin Gray Papers, Duke.

[53] Charles Fenton Mercer to Major Burr Powell, Feb. 11, 1824, Tucker Family Papers, UNC. Randolph had defended the caucus before his break with the party but became a critic of it afterward (Cunningham, *Republicans in Power*, 106–8, 115–16); he was dexterous enough, however, to criticize the procedure while supporting its nominee in 1824 (Tyler, *Letters and Times*, 1:357).

[54] Ammon, "Junto," 397, 399–400n.

[55] Anderson, *Giles*, 102; John Randolph to James Mercer Garnett, June 4, 1806, Randolph–Garnett Transcripts, LC; and chap. 8 above.

[56] Dodd, "Taylor," 22. Taylor opposed Madison in 1808 (Risjord, *Old Republicans*, 90).

[57] See especially Allan G. Bogue et al., "Members of the House of Representatives and the Process of Modernization, 1789–1960," *Journal of American History* 43 (Sept. 1976): 275–302; and Young, *Washington Community*, various tables.

[58] Table 18; Young, *Washington Community*, 90, table 4. Virginia's stability is also apparent when its percentages are compared with those cited in Morris P. Fiorina, David W. Rohde, and Peter Wissel, "Historical Change in House Turnover," in Norman J. Ornstein, ed., *Congress in Change* (New York, 1975), 29, table 1; and Samuel Kernell, "Toward Understanding 19th Century Congressional Careers: Ambition, Competition, and Rotation," *American Journal of Political Science* 21 (1977): 673.

[59] Table 10 above; Bogue et al., "Members of the House," 291, table 6.

[60] May 24, 1823.

[61] Table 4 above; Bogue et al., "Members of the House," 282, table 1; Sydnor, *Southern Sectionalism*, 65.

[62] Table 6 above; Bogue et al., "Members of the House," 286, table 3.

[63] Table 7 above; Bogue et al., "Members of the House," 284, table 2; Young, *Washington Community*, 92, table 6.

[64] Tables 2 and 10 above; Bogue et al., 287, 289, tables 4 and 5; Young, *Washington Community*, 88, table 3.

[65] Table 10 above; Bogue et al., "Members of the House," 291, table 6. Bogue and his associates have a table entitled "Reason for Termination of House Service . . . ," but the large number of unknowns (42 to 47 percent) limits its usefulness.

[66] White, *The Federalists*, 256, table II, which also shows Massachusetts having more (529 to 376) such officials than Virginia. White also states that of "departmental clerks . . . near-by Maryland and Virginia tended to produce the largest numbers" (*Jeffersonians*, 360–61).

[67] Davis, "Jeffersonian Virginia Expatriate," 51, 53–58. According to Sydnor, "over half of all Southern Representatives in Congress in 1820 had come from Virginia, North Carolina, and South Carolina" (*Southern Sectionalism*, 47). See also Fischer, *Revolution*, 219.

[68] Typical was Marshall's reaction to the Embargo, about which he wrote C. C. Pinckney, Dec. 21, 1808, "I . . . can only look on with silent and anxious concern. I can render no service" (Fischer, *Revolution*, 381). George Washington's nephew Bushrod was on the bench from 1798 until his death in 1829. On him, see Lewis F. Powell, Jr., "Supreme Court Justices from Virginia," *VMHB* 84 (1976): 131–41.

[69] See, for instance, Dodd, "Taylor," 219; John Randolph to James Mercer Garnett, April 18, 1809, Randolph-Garnett Transcripts, LC.

[70] See, for example, the figures given in White, *Federalists*, table II, 256.

[71] Jordan, "Virginia and Jefferson's Embargo."

Notes

Epilogue

[1] James Barbour to John J. Crittenden, May 31, 1820, Lowery, "Barbour," 247.

[2] Sutton, "Nostalgia, Pessimism and Malaise."

[3] Risjord, "Virginia Federalists," 516.

[4] Dabney, *Virginia, the New Dominion* (Garden City, N.Y., 1971), chaps. 23, 25; Sydnor, *Southern Sectionalism*, 61, 83–84.

[5] The contributions of these Virginians are described in detail in Lowery, "Barbour"; McNulty, "Breckinridge"; Tanner, "Cabell"; Davis, *Jackson*; Trumbo, "Mercer"; Gaines, *Randolph*; and Craven, "Taylor."

[6] *BDAC*, 101–71; Powell, "Supreme Court Justices from Virginia," 139–40; Robert Sobel, ed., *Biographical Directory of the United States Executive Branch, 1774–1971* (Westport, Conn., 1971), 365–69.

[7] See pp. 32–33 above; see also Sutton, "Nostalgia, Pessimism, and Malaise."

[8] Tyler, the only resident of Virginia to hold the office later, ran for and won the vice-presidency and ascended to the presidency upon Harrison's death. Since 1861, furthermore, only two Virginia politicians (Carter Glass and Claude Swanson) have served in presidential cabinets, and only one Virginia native (Lewis Powell) has been appointed to the Supreme Court.

[9] General explanations for the decline are found in Dabney, *Virginia, the New Dominion*, chap. 25; Parke Rouse, Jr., *Virginia: The English Heritage in America* (New York, 1966), chap. 9; and Louis D. Rubin, Jr., *Virginia, a Bicentennial History* (New York, 1977), chap. 6.

[10] Howison, *History of Virginia*, 2:511–20. Howison concluded "the fault is in her *people*, and not in her physical condition" (p. 510).

[11] Dumas Malone, "The Great Generation," *Virginia Quarterly Review* 23 (Winter 1947): 108.

. [12] See, for example, Goodman, "First American Party System," 81–84; and McCormick, *Second Party System*, 178–79.

[13] Rives, "History of Oratory," 303; see also p. 307.

[14] David R. Goldfield, "Men of Power: Virginia, 1789–1861" (M.A. thesis, University of Maryland, 1968), 78, table 3.

[15] Meade, *Old Churches*, 1:17; see also Risjord, *Chesapeake Politics*, 51–52, 203–10.

[16] Mrs. Edward Carrington, in Meade, *Old Churches*, 1:142; Foster, *Jeffersonian America*, 135–36.

[17] Davis, *Intellectual Life*, 130. See also Brydon, *Virginia's Mother Church*, 2:478, 482.

[18] Boles, *Great Revival*, 7–8, and passim; and Edwin S. Gaustad, *Historical Atlas of Religion in America* (New York, 1962), apps. B and C, which offer startling comparisons, 1750–1850, of Virginia church statistics by denominations.

[19] Tucker, *Letters from Virginia*, 122.

[20] Tyler, *Letters and Times*, 344–45.

[21] See especially Novak, *Rights of Youth*, 96–106.

[22] Bogue et al., "Members of the House of Representatives," 286, table 3. The percentage of congressmen with military experience declined from 40 in 1801–10 to 22 in 1841–50. One might also surmise that the militia experience in Virginia was less significant with the passing of time from earlier periods of war and Indian alarms, though slave disorders, particularly those associated with Gabriel Prosser (1800) and Nat Turner (1831), momentarily rejuvenated that ancient institution, as did the War of 1812.

[23] See Kuroda, "County Court System," and Roeber, *Faithful Magistrates*.

[24] Goldfield, "Men of Power," 26–27. A majority of state legislators in the Upper South in the 1850s had no prior experience, as noted in Wooster, *Politicians, Planters, and Plain Folk*, 42–43.

[25] Donald B. Dodd and Wynelle S. Dodd, *Historical Statistics of the South, 1790–1970* (University, Ala., 1973), 58.

[26] Goldfield, "Men of Power," 39–43, 57–60, 71–72, 78, table 3. In his study of the Virginia House of Delegates, 1800–1815, Charles D. Lowery notes the political emergence of lawyers and other professional men whose "wealth placed them below the highest stratum of Virginia society" ("Political Leadership in Jeffersonian Virginia: The Decline of the Old Aristocracy," paper presented at the annual meeting of the Society for Historians of the Early American Republic, Siena College, Loudonville, New York, July 1981).

[27] Goldfield, "Men of Power," 71–72. On the persistence of antislavery sentiment, see Patricia P. Hickin, "Antislavery in Virginia, 1831–1861," 3 vols. (Ph.D. diss., University of Virginia, 1968). Nonslaveholders numbered about a third of the members of the Virginia General Assembly in the 1850s (Wooster, *Politicians, Planters, and Plain Folk*, 163, table 7g).

[28] William C. Rives, "Virginia Historical Society [Presidential Address]," *Southern Literary Messenger* 14 (1848): 53. Though uttered on Dec. 16, 1847, Rives's remarks fit the late Dynasty era, as noted throughout this study and in Sutton, "Nostalgia, Pessimism, and Malaise."

[29] See Bogue et al., "Members of the House of Representatives."

[30] Kuroda, "County Court System," 164, 185–88.

[31] Alonzo T. Dill, "Sectional Conflict in Colonial Virginia," *VMHB* 87 (1979): 300–15.

[32] Paulding, *Letters from the South*, 1:49.

[33] Avery O. Craven, *Edmund Ruffin, Southerner: A Study in Secession* (New York, 1932), 41.

[34] April 4, 1809.

[35] See Brown, *Cabells and Their Kin*, 286–90; Tanner, "Cabell"; Edward A. Wyatt IV, "George Keith Taylor, 1769–1815, Virginia Federalist and Humanitarian," *WMQ*, 2d ser., 16 (1936); 1–18; Kennedy, *Wirt*; Robert, "Wirt."

[36] Diary of Washington notable Margaret B. Smith, quoted by Richard Beale Davis, "The Early American Lawyer and the Profession of Letters," in his *Liter-*

ature and Society in Early Virginia, 1608–1840 (Baton Rouge, 1973), 302n; Elizabeth Langhorne, "Edward Coles, Thomas Jefferson, and the Rights of Man," *Virginia Cavalcade* 23 (Summer 1973): 30–37.

[37]*DAB*; Douglas S. Freeman, *R. E. Lee, a Biography*, 4 vols. (New York, 1934–35), 1:638–43.

[38]Littleton Waller Tazewell, "Sketches of his own family . . . 1823," copy, VSL, and conveniently available in typescript in Heaton, "Tazewell's Sketch," with the Wythe story on pp. 98–103.

[39]Grigsby, *Tazewell*, 120.

[40]Rives, "Virginia Historical Society [Presidential Address]," 54.

[41]John George Jackson to James Monroe, Mar. 11, 1819, Brown, "John George Jackson," 33.

[42]Wayland, *Stevenson*, 8.

[43]Obituary of A., *Richmond Enquirer*, Oct. 6, 1837.

[44]Schouler, *History of the United States*, 3:234.

Index